THE PAPERS OF WILLIAM F. "BUFFALO BILL" CODY

SERIES EDITORS
Jeremy M. Johnston, Frank Christianson, and Douglas Seefeldt

Memories of Buffalo Bill

LOUISA FREDERICI CODY
IN COLLABORATION WITH
COURTNEY RYLEY COOPER

With an introduction by Sherry L. Smith

University of Nebraska Press
Lincoln

© 2025 by the Board of Regents of the University of Nebraska

All rights reserved

Support for this volume was provided by the State of Wyoming

The University of Nebraska Press is part of a land-grant institution with campuses and programs on the past, present, and future homelands of the Pawnee, Ponca, Otoe-Missouria, Omaha, Dakota, Lakota, Kaw, Cheyenne, and Arapaho Peoples, as well as those of the relocated Ho-Chunk, Sac and Fox, and Iowa Peoples.

Library of Congress Control Number: 2024051538

Set in ITC New Baskerville by A. Shahan.

CONTENTS

Series Editors' Preface	vii
Introduction by Sherry L. Smith	ix
Memories of Buffalo Bill	1
Appendix 1	187
Appendix 2	197
Appendix 3	297
Notes	303
Index	311

SERIES EDITORS' PREFACE

The name "Buffalo Bill" conjures a variety of iconic images of people and events we identify with the Old West: cowboys vs. Indians, the attack of the Deadwood Stagecoach, Custer's Last Stand, Annie Oakley, Sitting Bull, Buck Taylor, and more. In his 1970 study of Wild West shows, Buffalo Bill biographer Don Russell identified 116 different western-themed traveling shows, yet William F. "Buffalo Bill" Cody's enterprise is the only one most people recognize today. Often the celebrity status of William F. Cody masked his other contributions to the historical evolution of the American West, including his roles as irrigation developer, town founder, and promoter of tourism, activities that do not often come to mind when thinking of Buffalo Bill. George Beck's account, previously only available in fragments at various archives, offers readers a firsthand version of this often-overlooked aspect of Buffalo Bill's legacy. This work also offers readers an inside view of western economic development, one that succeeded through collaboration as opposed to individualism, where companies and agreements superseded violence and threats.

The Papers of William F. "Buffalo Bill" Cody series is the result of a partnership between the University of Nebraska Press and The Papers of William F. Cody at the Buffalo Bill Center of the West in Cody, Wyoming. This series is dedicated to publishing scholarly editions of autobiographies, histories, and unpublished memoirs that provide more in-depth insight into this renowned, yet often misunderstood, western figure. While promoting editions of memoirs written by Buffalo Bill and his contemporaries, this series also strives to provide scholarly insight into how these historical works reflect broader themes related to the history of the American West and the global fascination with the region's landscape, history, and cultures.

One of the primary missions of The Papers of William F. "Buffalo Bill" Cody is to preserve and interpret the published and unpublished historical works of Buffalo Bill and his companions, offering readers primary resources to better understand the complex historical development of the American West and its mythic representatives. In addition to this series, readers can view historical documents on the project's digital archive: CodyArchive.org, and its digital interpretive site: CodyStudies.org. This project began with a generous appropriation from the State of Wyoming and the Geraldine W. and Robert J. Dellenback Foundation, with further funding provided by Adrienne and John Mars, Naoma Tate and the Family of Hal Tate, the National Endowment for the Humanities, the McMurry Library Endowment Fund, W. Richard and Margaret Webster Scarlett III, Deborah and Rusty Rokita, and many more private contributors. This volume and subsequent material available on CodyArchive.org resulted from a partnership with the American Heritage Center at the University of Wyoming and was partially funded by a grant from the Wyoming Cultural Trust Fund. Our sincerest thanks to these individuals, whose contributions brought this volume, and many more, to fruition.

INTRODUCTION

Sherry L. Smith

Louisa Frederici Cody is not a well-known figure. She married, however, a man who became world famous, and so she occupied a literal ringside seat to an international celebrity. Eventually, she shared her unique perspective through this book *Memories of Buffalo Bill.*

Publicity for the book emphasized its "picturesque characters" and the "pulsating . . . excitement" of its Old West anecdotes. Louisa was there through it all—from the moment she slapped William F. Cody's face upon first meeting him until his death. Their whirlwind courtship, Buffalo Bill's daring fights with Indians, his part in avenging George Armstrong Custer's death, and amusing anecdotes from his stage career all add up to a "thrilling story." Louisa's authorial vantage point is that of a loyal wife and great admirer.[1] What the promotion and the book leave out is the more complicated story of the Codys' life together. *That* tale is equally interesting.

Little in Louisa's background would have predicted such a literary venture or the life that inspired it. The daughter of French-speaking immigrant John Frederici, a man of Austro-Italian ethnicity from Alsace, Louisa grew up in St. Louis, Missouri. Her father was a merchant; her mother, a native-born American of German ancestry. After her birth in 1844, Louisa lived a conventional, sheltered life in a middle-class family. She attended a convent school, where her training prepared her for a quiet, respectable, domestic, middle-class existence.[2]

And then William F. Cody strode back into town. He and Louisa had met in 1864 and Cody returned to renew the acquaintance while a teenage Civil War soldier. After his military service ended, he cast about, taking odd jobs such as stagecoach driving, but he had yet to settle down in a business that would provide the stability and respectability Louisa, and probably her parents, had in mind for a husband. That apparently did not dissuade her from encouraging his attention, however. As she later recalled, "He was tall and straight and strong. . . . His hair was jet black, his features finely molded, and his eyes clear and sharp." In short, he was handsome, "about the most handsome man [she] ever had seen." He was "the most wonderful man" she had ever known, though she "almost bit [her] tongue to keep from telling him so."[3]

Sparks flew in both directions. The couple married at the Frederici home on March 6, 1866. The groom had just turned twenty. The bride was a bit older. Given their relative youth and infrequent opportunities to get to know each other, one might wonder why they rushed to wed. It is probably not irrelevant that their first child was born exactly nine months after the wedding. Or, as historian Joy Kassen speculated, "Cody's sexual magnetism may have hurried him into an early and ill-considered marriage." Sadly, that last assessment of the relationship is accurate. The marriage was often, though not always, unhappy, although only hints of that discord appear in Louisa's memoir.[4]

Tensions, nevertheless, emerged early as Cody pinballed around the central plains of Kansas: attempting and failing as a hotelier, laboring for the Kansas Pacific Railroad, selling whiskey, and hunting and supplying buffalo meat to railroad and army contractors. In 1867, demonstrating a potentially troublesome combination of ambition and recklessness, Cody tried something daring. He invested all his money in an effort to found a town—dubbed Rome—along the railroad near Fort Hays. It was a hugely speculative venture that fell to pieces when the railroad laid its tracks elsewhere. Town founding was a respectable venture, in Louisa's mind; buffalo hunting was not. In the wake of this financial disaster, she had had enough and left for St. Louis with their young daughter, Arta.[5]

Cody retreated to buffalo hunting—the occupation that earned him his sobriquet "Buffalo Bill"—but his enterprises eventually expanded beyond feeding soldiers to hunting down those who deserted from service. Later, he began guiding and scouting expeditions for the army. He participated, for example, in General Eugene Carr's 1868–69 winter expedition during the 1868–69 campaigns against Native people on the plains. Although he engaged in no battles, he helped rescue Third Cavalry troops who came near to starving. This was respectable, even heroic, duty.

When Cody encouraged Louisa to join him at Fort Leavenworth in June 1868, she complied—but only to quarrel and separate once again. Not until Cody obtained a secure position with the U.S. Army at Fort McPherson, Nebraska, did the couple reunite. This time, Cody enticed her with a small cabin complete with a picket fence, framed windows, and a carpet. Their social life also improved. Although the Codys were not exactly social equals to the officers and their wives, they mixed with and found friends among them. In sum, Fort McPherson provided a more stable life for the family. If tensions did not completely disappear between Will and Louisa, they had dissipated, and in November 1870, Louisa gave birth to their second child, Kit Carson Cody.[6]

By the early 1870s, Cody pivoted away from hunting and scouting and toward show business. Dime novelist Ned Buntline found the dashing man's story perfect material for a piece in *Harper's Monthly*, and not long after followed it with a theatrical adaptation starring Buffalo Bill himself. In the fall of 1872, Cody debuted on stage in Chicago in a melodrama wherein he rescued a virtuous woman from "savage" Indians and restored her to home and family. This proved to be Cody's ticket to fame and fortune. Over the years that followed, he built upon the enormous popularity and profitability of such fare to create a Buffalo Bill theatrical touring company and, eventually, Buffalo Bill's Wild West Show.[7]

Initially, Louisa and their offspring, to which a third child had been added, joined Will on tour. Then they settled down, first in West Chester, Pennsylvania, and then in Rochester, New York, to be near the theater circuit. Touring did not cohere well with child-raising, nor did living apart for long periods strengthen the marriage. Stresses and strains escalated. The death of their only son, Kit, in 1876 was one of the biggest blows. However, Buffalo Bill was becoming a wealthy man—he purchased a house in North Platte, Nebraska, not far from Fort McPherson, that became Louisa's and the children's permanent domicile. He also purchased and further developed a ranch outside North Platte that he named Scout's Rest Ranch. Louisa preferred the home in town, however. Nebraska became Cody's base, too, although a place from which he mostly came and went. These frequent and lengthier separations (especially once the Wild West Show went international); Cody's growing celebrity; his attractiveness to women and inclination to womanize; and the life of the theater, with its more liberal attitudes toward liquor consumption and sexual relations, all further undermined Will and Louisa's bond.

Still, they remained married, had one more child, and settled into a period of détente, though mutual suspicion, tension, and unhappiness rested at its core. Finally, conflicts over money and property provoked Cody into initiating divorce proceedings in 1883. However, the sudden death of their daughter Orra, just a few years after their son died, led him to drop the suit.[8] Not surprisingly, their problems did not go away. In fact, the gulf between them only grew. Living apart most of the time and suffering the tragic losses of two children would undermine most marriages. Cody's affairs and the couple's continued conflicts over money only exacerbated the friction. Finally, in 1904, nearly forty years after their wedding, Will revived his plan to end the marriage. Louisa refused to consider divorce, and so the case went to court. The depositions and court testimony, being public documents, became fodder for newspapers. It was a disaster for both, but especially for Will. The divorce proceedings revealed the stark difference between Buffalo Bill's show-business persona as a family man and the reality of his marriage. Not only did he damage his reputation, as well as Louisa's, he failed in the suit. The court would not grant him his divorce.[9]

Remarkably, in the years that followed, Will and Louisa reconciled ... to a degree. As his celebrity dimmed and his financial failures stripped him of much of his wealth, Louisa sometimes visited and even traveled with her husband. Upon Buffalo Bill's death in 1917, Louisa joined forces with a Denver, Colorado, business- and newspaperman who fought to bury the showman's remains on Lookout Mountain, outside Denver, to create a "perpetual tourist attraction."[10] However, Cody had expressed his wish to be buried near Cody, Wyoming, a town he had founded years before. That was not to be. Not only did the widow prevail regarding the Colorado site, but Louisa requested that her casket be placed, interestingly, directly above Cody's upon her death. If anyone tried to exhume Cody, they would have to do it over her dead body. Lookout Mountain is where the two rest today.

Two years after Cody's death, Louisa published this memoir with the help of Courtney Ryley Cooper, a former circus clown, press agent, and writer. Unlike her husband, Louisa had always shunned the spotlight. Yet, publishing a memoir of her marriage to one of the most famous Americans of his era seemed likely to swing that unwelcome light squarely in her direction. She had already lived through a most searing public humiliation when Buffalo Bill filed for divorce—newspapers had published Cody's most damaging complaints about her for all the world to see. Why risk renewing the scrutiny of that sordid chapter of their lives?

A closer look at the divorce depositions provides some answers, offering a sharp contrast to the image Louisa eventually presented in this memoir. Most of the details of the marriage gone wrong we know only from Will's divorce testimony. Louisa's courtroom responses consisted of short, simple denials of her husband's complaints. It seems reasonable to assume that at least part of Louisa's motivation in writing the book was to reply to those charges in *this* way, in *her* time, and outside the courthouse—where she could shape the narrative as she preferred *and* have the final say, to boot. While Will's testimony received widespread attention and newspaper coverage, such sources can be ephemeral and largely forgotten. A book, however, is more weighty, more expansive, and more likely to stand the test of time. That we are reading it more than a century after Louisa published it underscores the long life a published work can have. It is fair to say that Louisa won the divorce case and the battle of their dueling narratives. This was one fight Buffalo Bill lost . . . although not altogether.

Although Cody's lawyer had warned in 1883 that his grounds for divorce—claims of incompatibility—were weak, Buffalo Bill never stopped longing for his freedom. So, nearly twenty years later, he revived the prospect. In 1904 the stigma of divorce remained strong in America, even though western states and territories led the nation in easing barriers to it, eventually, granting divorces at twice the rate of the North Atlantic states and seven times that of the South. Some states, such as Utah and Nevada, turned themselves into divorce mills by reducing the residency requirements for those seeking divorce and increasing the number of acceptable grounds for separation. However, neither Nebraska nor Wyoming, where the Codys lived and owned property, followed that route. Nationally, successful suits based their case on desertion (50 percent), adultery (28.7 percent), and cruelty (10.5 percent). Only 1.1 percent of divorces between 1887 and 1906 cited drunkenness as cause.[11]

Had Louisa initiated the suit, she may have been successful on several of these grounds. Will, however, could not charge his wife with desertion, adultery, cruelty, or drunkenness. The bedrock of his complaint? They did not get along, or, as he put it in his deposition, their "dispositions were not such as to get along well together," something he had realized early in the marriage.[12] Knowing that incompatibility was not an acceptable option in any American courts at this time, he tried it anyway, understanding he would be fighting an uphill battle.

Perhaps he believed his celebrity and his spellbinding storytelling would sway the judge in his favor. Folksy, loquacious, and detailed in his testimony, Cody attempted to build a case with complaints about his wife that ranged from the petty to the slanderous. Of course, every element of his testimony came filtered through his purpose: to end the marriage. It was not an objective assessment of the relationship but one designed to paint a dreadful picture of it, stoke sympathy for himself, and set him free. The memories evoked, in other words, were highly selective and purpose driven.

According to his testimony, Cody's wife was primarily to blame for the troubles that quickly emerged and became more frequent (and dangerous) over time. Soon after their wedding, Louisa tagged him as a failure as a husband and provider. She nagged him about his setbacks, and she fought with his family members, with whom she often stayed when Will was away from home in the early years. Louisa's constant fault-finding of him and his kin "kind o' grated on [his] nerves."

When it became too much to bear, "[he] pulled out to the plains again." Cody continued to support her financially, however. After his Rome, Kansas, town development investment failed, he provided her with funds to return to St. Louis "so that [he] could get free-handed and try something else." Eventually, at Fort McPherson, he achieved more economic stability and the family reconciled. Nevertheless, Cody insisted, while they did not have as much trouble during those years, it was mostly because he "was at home so little of the time."[13]

The relationship's fissures deepened after 1872, Cody noted, when he began his show-business career, and earlier sources of tension multiplied. Louisa, he claimed, was jealous of the actresses in the theatrical company and, later, the Wild West Show. When she saw some of the women kissing Will goodbye at the end of the touring season, for example, she became irrationally infuriated. She complained of his extravagances with money, not understanding the economics of theatrical companies and the huge expenses required, and resented his gifts to staff members, family, and friends. After the Codys moved to North Platte, Nebraska, Will was absent most of the year, but when he did come home and invited guests to their house, Louisa, he insisted, could be rude, insulting, and angry with them. At best, she made them feel uneasy until they departed; at worst, she threatened to pour boiling water on them. The situation "was utterly unbearable" and humiliating.

Most important, he claimed, conflicts over money and property fueled the animosity. Cody conceptualized all their money as his—earned by him and "given" to Louisa. When her lawyer noted that she worked too, keeping their home and raising their children while Will was on the road, he admitted the truth of that. Still, he saw placing her name on some of the properties as a gift and deeply resented her refusal, on occasion, to agree to mortgage some of that real estate for other ventures. Further, he complained, Louisa bought other properties with the money he provided her and put those properties solely in her name.

All of this came to a head in 1901. While visiting Scout's Rest Ranch with his wife, Will listened as Louisa informed the ranch foreman that she was "the boss of this ranch" and he should take orders from her, not Will. True, her name was on some of that property, but it "was a staggerer [*sic*] to [him] to realize that that beautiful ranch that [he] had built, these cattle and horses which [he] had bought and paid for, were no longer [his]."[14] Louisa was, he told the court, overbearing in her insistence that she now ran the place. It was one humiliation too many. Not wishing to contradict his wife in front of the foreman, though, Cody said nothing. Instead, when they returned to their home in town, he testified that he packed his trunk, taking only a few personal items, and "left her and that house forever and I haven't been back since."[15]

There was one more thing, shocking in its implications: he alleged that Louisa attempted to murder him. First, Cody claimed, she poisoned some of his dogs—valuable greyhounds he brought home from England, "beautiful, lovable creatures." He returned home to the ranch, one day, to learn several of them had already died and another was sick from strychnine. Will rushed to treat the poor animal and then demanded an explanation from the foreman, who, in turn, asked the stableman to explain "the truth about the poisoning of these dogs." Mrs. Cody, he explained, scattered the poison around the barn, ostensibly to kill rats. Although the hired man warned her the dogs were likely to be poisoned, too, she ignored him and proceeded to spread it outside and in the barn anyway. When Will confronted her with "how cruel and inhuman it was for her to poison [his] beautiful dogs," she angrily walked away.[16]

His concerns about Louisa's murderous intentions did not stop there. Cody testified he feared for his own life, too. Servants, friends, and family members warned him to be careful of anything she gave him to eat or drink. On at least one occasion, he claimed, Louisa did try to poison him. This was the most explosive and, to Louisa, the most hurtful charge of all.

Whereas Cody's testimony was fulsome, Louisa's deposition was spare, concise, and consistent. It is difficult to know how much her short, clipped responses reflected her personality and how much they reflected her lawyer's guidance. But to every charge her husband made against her, Mrs. Cody emphatically and curtly denied it.

They never quarreled during the early years of their marriage or in their later years in Nebraska. He never complained about her and was "very indulgent" and "tried to keep [her] as happy as possible." She always treated his guests "the best [she] knew how." She was never rude and never threatened to douse them with boiling water. Louisa insisted she never told the Scout's Rest Ranch foreman she was the boss. She never put poison out for the dogs (though she did admit she placed rat poison under the floors of the house). She never gave her husband drugs or tried to poison him. The only problem she acknowledged in their marriage was Cody's drinking.[17]

When her lawyer asked how she felt about Cody "now," Louisa somewhat evasively replied, "He is the father of my children and I love him; and I bore my troubles without complaint." The lawyer repeated the question, Did she love him at this time (the time of the divorce)? to which she said, "I do. He is the father of my children." Would she be willing to reconcile with him? Yes, she replied, on one condition: that he would rescind his false accusation that she tried to poison him. When Cody's lawyer asked her the same question about possible reconciliation, she gave the same answer with additional comments. She would agree to reconciliation on the condition that he clear her name as a "would-be murderer" in court documents and in a public statement to the press because, as she asserted, "he has disgraced me and I have a right to protect my character."[18] Of all the humiliating charges Cody flung at her in the legal proceedings, this was the one that caused the deepest wound.

Nevertheless, Cody would not retract it. So the trial proceeded, though only after another Cody daughter, Arta, died. In this moment of shared sorrow, Will suggested a temporary reconciliation with Louisa while they carried on the solemn duty of burying yet another of their children. Louisa refused such reconciliation, which would last for only a brief period—reconciliation had to be forever or not at all. Cody declined her counteroffer. One year after Will's initial petition for divorce, witnesses for both sides gathered in the Cheyenne, Wyoming, courthouse to offer depositions in open court. According to one newspaper account, an audience of three hundred "women, cowboys and officers from Fort Russell" attended. For them, the trial served as a form of entertainment.[19] But it would be a judge, not a jury or even the public, who would ultimately decide the outcome of Cody's suit.

Buffalo Bill biographer and historian Louis Warren described the trial as "a battle of narratives." One fascinating aspect of Cody's version is the link between his sensational allegation that Louisa tried to poison him and the popular nineteenth-century melodrama *Lucretia Borgia*, the story of an unscrupulous, deceptive woman who attacked a man in his own home, the place where he should have been safest. Cody knew the story and liked it so much that he named one of his buffalo rifles after the evil female character. In accusing Louisa of poisoning him in their home, he may have hoped, consciously or unconsciously, to connect in the audience's and judge's minds this "mythic trope," which revealed a darker side to home and domesticity —a woman willing to destroy the man who had created a home and wealth in order to gain complete control over both.[20]

He did not, however, rely solely on allegorical suggestion. Cody and his lawyers marshaled a parade of witnesses—servants, seamstresses, other working-class folks, and a foreman's wife—to support his contention about her poisonous personality and nefarious intentions. Some claimed to see her slip potions into his glass. Others testified she drank too much herself and used coarse language.

Louisa's lawyers responded with their own parade of witnesses. Her supporters represented the respectable middle-class people of North Platte: lawyers, doctors, and bankers. Louisa, they insisted, was always ladylike, loyal, and loving to her husband; courteous to guests; modest; and honest, as well as a good businesswoman. They emphasized Cody's faults, especially his heavy drinking. Of course, Will flatly and energetically denied these allegations as he did Louisa's lawyers' efforts to pin him down on charges of philandering. Though they were not able to prove absolutely that Cody engaged in extramarital affairs, their persistent questioning about particular women and details about those relationships (as provided by former employees) left a strong impression of likely infidelity. Certainly, the overall result of the testimony proved more detrimental to Will than to Louisa.[21]

If Cody hoped his charisma and storytelling skills would help him prevail in court, he had not considered the power of the pen. Louisa's lawyers effectively produced letters he had written to his wife over the years, expressing affection, appreciation, and even reliance upon her business abilities. Perhaps she did tell the Scout's Rest Ranch foreman that she was the boss in the 1901 incident. Earlier that year, however, he thanked her in a letter for relieving him of worry over ranch concerns through her management skills. She was "making no fuss about it, as though it was nothing to do." And, he added, she knew "more about it than [he] ever did."[22] In this case, words spoke louder than purported actions.

On March 8, 1905, Judge Richard H. Scott issued his ruling. Its first sentence made clear Cody had lost the case on its basic premise: "Under the laws of this state incompatibility is not grounds for divorce." The judge went on to declare the suit lacked evidence regarding the poisoning allegation. In fact, whatever Louisa had given him was an effort to "rescue" Will from intoxication at a public banquet. Scott rebuked Cody for making the charge in the first place, for in doing so he had "voluntarily inflicted an irreparable injury, not only upon the defendant, but upon their children and their offspring yet to follow." Exhibit A for this conclusion was a "most pitiful" letter their daughter Arta sent her mother, only days before Arta's death, lamenting her father's divorce suit: "Oh why did he do it. My heart is just broken over it. I cannot find words to express how dreadfully I feel about it."[23]

Cody also failed to convince the court that Louisa mistreated their guests or that she refused to sign deeds of conveyance. His complaint that his wife treated him with extreme cruelty in the events surrounding Arta's funeral was not backed with adequate or convincing testimony. Even if she had expressed anger with her husband in that moment and refused to reconcile temporarily, it was understandable, for she was undoubtedly "distracted with grief and broken-hearted." Otherwise, Judge Scott believed Louisa had demonstrated "years of devotion as a wife and mother," based on her testimony and that of others.

Her courtroom decorum was always appropriate. She kept her focus on the issues, offered direct and clear evidence, and slighted no one's reputation, apart from her husband's and one of his accused paramours, Bessie Isabel. Cody, on the other hand, cruelly "heaped indignities upon" his wife. Louisa's witnesses were neighbors—acquaintances of thirty years—"good men and good women," respectable people (the implication being in contrast to the show-business people, servants, hired hands, or working-class folks who took Will's side). They testified to her womanly virtues, dignity, cordiality, and wifely devotion.

In sum, Judge Scott believed Louisa's narrative and rejected Will's, finding "generally for the defendant" and pronouncing that Mrs. Cody would recover all costs of the suit.[24] Cody did not appeal. The ordeal ended with both Louisa's and Will's reputations in tatters.

Why risk reviving all this by publishing a book about the marriage? Even if Louisa ignored the divorce attempt, wouldn't many readers remember the humiliating publicity that the suit produced? Why *did* Louisa write the book? What was her aim or purpose? And, for that matter, how did she manage to write the book, given her limited education?

Many people assume writers produce books—especially celebrity memoirs—to make money. Although Mrs. Cody was not averse to income, she was not destitute when Buffalo Bill died. In fact, because she had wisely moved some of their jointly owned property into her own name (including several houses and 1,200 acres of land in Nebraska), Louisa had assured her economic security in old age, whereas Cody, famous for his generous—some would say profligate and reckless—spending had fallen on hard times by his death. For Louisa, financial need does not seem to have been the primary impetus to publish.

It is difficult to know if the memoir was Louisa's idea or that of her cowriter, Courtney Ryley Cooper. However the idea originated, it is clear that without Cooper's heavy involvement, Louisa would not have been able to create the book. Interestingly, Cooper had once worked as Will's press agent. And, if one can believe him, he deeply admired the showman. He explained, "[Buffalo Bill] was the man in whom my sun of work and endeavor rose and set. More, Buffalo Bill, bluff, goodhearted, roaring Buffalo Bill realized that had it not been for the first press stories which appeared in the guise of fiction and through which Buffalo Bill rode, shot, scalped Indians, saved fair maidens in distress and did everything else that a godlike hero should have done, his life might have been in vain as regarded public recognition."

In other words, Buffalo Bill's persona was birthed in fiction and burnished by his press agent. An entertainer such as Cody depended on the press, but the press could not always be depended upon to portray the man in positive terms. Newspapers thrived on controversy, gossip, and scandal. The press agent had "one duty, one desire—to outwit the newspaper." The best of them, among whom Cooper most likely considered himself, succeeded.[25]

That Cooper and Louisa joined forces after Cody's death to write the memoir suggests, then, that this press agent and his new client intended to renew that goal: outwit the newspapers and reclaim, this time, not only Will's but Louisa's reputation. Scarred by the divorce publicity, Louisa now had an opportunity to present to the world *her* version of the Cody marriage and, relying on the power of widowhood, fend off detractors. Forever moldering in his grave on Lookout Mountain, Buffalo Bill could not dispute Louisa's spin on their relationship. She would have the last and, she probably hoped, enduring word on the topic. Widowhood not only meant the dead partner could not object or debate but that the larger world would be inclined to accept quietly and respectfully what the widow had written. Victorian America's cultural precepts still carried weight, and publicly challenging a widow's word on the sanctity of her marriage or her deceased husband's character was simply out of bounds.

Louisa had several possible models in mind when it came to this project. Most notably, Elizabeth Custer wielded enormous power over the "memory" of her husband and the interpretation of the Battle of the Little Bighorn. She did so for decades. That military disaster of June 1876 led to the deaths of 274 American soldiers and scouts—it was an enormous catastrophe that shocked the nation. In its aftermath, it would be reasonable to assume that the man who had led those soldiers into battle—George Armstrong Custer—would come under intense scrutiny and criticism. But "Libby" Custer held her husband's critics at bay, publishing a series of widely read and lucrative memoirs that reified him as a dashing hero to the bitter end. She lived until 1933, nearly fifty years after her husband's demise. The power of widowhood mostly silenced Custer's critics during those decades, and only after Libby's death did reinterpretations and criticism of her gallant husband appear.[26]

It seems quite likely that Cooper and Louisa knew of Elizabeth Custer's books and possibly read them. The Codys took pride in Buffalo Bill's western U.S. Army service as hunter, scout, and occasional fighter, and Will knew Custer. To model Louisa's memoir on Mrs. Custer's would have been altogether reasonable and, perhaps they hoped, equally influential and profitable. One difference, however, is that the Custers never went through a divorce trial. There is not a whiff of marital tension in the Custer books, nor, as noted above, much in Louisa's book. In telling their story their way, Louisa and Libby could assert an image of their marriages that suited them.

Louisa did this in several ways, including stopping the story far short of the divorce trial. She kept the focus on the Codys' early years in the West. She gave short shrift to the show-business era—those years of separation and strain when Cody gallivanted across the globe and pursued relationships with other women while Louisa stayed home. By truncating the story chronologically, Louisa effectively erased the most dramatic episodes of discord and disagreement.

In the process, she restored respectability not only to the marriage but also to herself and, interestingly, to her husband. One article, published during the divorce trial and titled "What's the Matter with Buffalo Bill," concluded that "adulation corrupted his staunch manhood." The divorce episode revealed a different side to his character: "a newer but very much commoner mould. . . . It is unpleasant to see a national idol fall from its pedestal. But why worship at a shrine that has no illusion left or that has been desecrated by the idol itself."[27] Harsh words, indeed, for a heretofore unchallenged American hero.

In this moment of crisis, Cody could not sustain control over his public image. His celebrity, confidence, and bravado could not fend off the critics. The divorce proceedings revealed "dissonance" between his performance in the Wild West Show and the life he lived away from the spotlight. As historian Joy Kassen put it, Cody learned public acclaim could quickly disappear when personal behaviors that conflicted with that image emerged.[28]

And so it was Louisa Cody who rode to his rescue. Her memoir is a far cry from a "tell-all tale" of the twenty-first century—it is "tell some and leave much out." It is a nineteenth-century creation (albeit published early in the twentieth century) designed to erase the salacious publicity of the divorce and reinstate romance in the public's perception of Cody domesticity. Louisa's life was inevitably linked to Will's, and her appeal as a literary subject depended solely on the public's interest in her husband. His marital failures, if allowed to become the last word, would become her failures as well. To ignore the damaging testimony and replace it with a tale of true love and devotion would hopefully erase the stain of Will's allegations against her while restoring him to an unblemished position in the pantheon of American heroes. Thus, their reputations remained indisputably intertwined.

Notably, Cody's death—a dozen years after his failed suit—had already helped stanch the erosion of his standing. Twenty-five thousand people turned out to memorialize Cody as his body lay in state in the Colorado State Capitol, his faults seemingly forgotten. To destabilize that return to respectability would have undermined Louisa's capacity to benefit from it. Instead, Louisa's memoir became part and parcel of the rehabilitation of their reputations.

Courtney Ryley Cooper shared this goal. He had always admired Cody, insisting in his book *Under the Big Top* (published four years after *Memories of Buffalo Bill*) that Cody was "every inch the man Young America believed him to be. . . . As the years go by his place in the history of western civilization will grow bigger, constantly more important." Even some Native Americans considered him "little less than a god." Cooper wrote, "But of what use is all the traditional glory in the world from a monetary standpoint, if the public doesn't know it and the public isn't constantly reminded of the fact?"[29] Buffalo Bill's wife and his former press agent did their best to remind the public and sustain that glorious memory.

At least one book review suggests these efforts worked, concluding that while the book fell short of a "literary masterpiece," it presented

Buffalo Bill as "a real man and an admirable character." The writing was lively, entertaining, and "in good taste."[30] A more extensive review published in the *Mississippi Valley Historical Review* (precursor to the *Journal of American History*) explained that the book focused on Cody's domestic life and presented it as "romantic, if somewhat sentimental." Instead of focusing on Cody, the review concentrated on the book's depiction of frontier homemaking, particularly on how Louisa experienced the West's "primitive" conditions. That Louisa shot buffalo from horseback with her little daughter in tow; met and danced with Wild Bill Hickok; entertained the Earl of Dunraven and the Grand Duke Alexius of Russia in her humble home; and coped with the presence of the Sioux and Pawnee, "who swarmed about the country," was of greater interest than her husband's escapades. The book offered little new about Buffalo Bill even as it dispelled "the haze of the theatrical and the sensational which has surrounded" Cody for so long. Its greater value rested in Louisa's story, which served as a tribute to all the women who "played their important part in the winning of the west."[31] Surely Louisa found both reviews satisfying. In lifting Will, she found herself lifted, too.

The second review rightly pointed out there was more to the book than the Cody marriage. It offered a woman's perspective on the West and its conquest by the United States. It is noteworthy that *Memories of Buffalo Bill* appeared in bookstores the same year suffragists marshaled their final push to achieve an amendment to the United States Constitution that would enfranchise American women.[32] The early decades of the twentieth century witnessed women breaking boundaries beyond the ballot box, including access to higher education and professions formerly closed to women and greater equality within the home. Louisa Cody was not, however, one of these women.

Born in the mid-nineteenth century, she remained a nineteenth-century woman and wife. Neither a feminist nor a "New Woman," Louisa presented herself from the earliest pages of the memoir as demure, dependent, and devoted to her husband. On their honeymoon boat trip up the Missouri River, the sound of gunfire causes Louisa to swoon and faint in Will's arms. When she awakes, she trembles and clings to her strong, manly Will. He promises to protect her. He also promises to work hard, to be the husband she wants. On the spot, they supposedly repeat their wedding vows to remain together "until death do us part."[33]

Louisa is compliant, occasionally plucky, and adaptable—but mostly fearful, nerve-racked, and sometimes in such poor health that she has to return to St. Louis to recuperate. She always longs to be with Will, however, in their shared goal to "fight for civilization" in the West. It is noteworthy that the only mention of divorce appears in a scene in which Will, having been elected justice of the peace, presides over a divorce case. Concluding divorce isn't "natural," he takes the husband aside while Louisa takes the wife aside to listen to their respective complaints. Then Will presses the man to reconcile with the woman. The husband agrees to go halfway, the couple kisses, and the case is settled, husband and wife "agreeably hitched in the Cody brand of 'double harness.'"[34] Written in the wake of Louisa's much more unpleasant divorce experience, it is difficult to see this as anything other than Louisa's fantasy of how she wished her own case had been resolved.

In other ways as well, her nineteenth-century mentality is on full display. To point this out is not to chastise Louisa for not anticipating and sharing twenty-first-century attitudes and values but to demonstrate how perceptions and perspectives have changed over time. This is especially true regarding acknowledgment and understanding of the destructive consequences of unexamined racism and the wanton waste of wildlife and other western "resources."

Louisa's depictions of African American soldiers and Native Americans are demeaning and dehumanizing. She describes the former as quarrelsome and threatening, the latter as vicious at worst and as foolish, thieving nuisances at best. Native peoples' claims to land or even to life itself are nonexistent in this narrative. Instead, Natives stand as obstacles to "civilization" or threats to her husband. She was proud that Will sustained only one wound in all his fights with Indians. She noted, "In spite of the fact that never was there an Indian fight in which he participated that he was not in the hottest of it, never a brush with the savage that he did not return with a new notch to his gun." At one time she tried to keep a record of how many Indians "'bit the dust' as a result of [her] husband's fire" but she lost count. Killing Indians was just part of the day's work. She gave no thought to the men who died or the wives and children left behind. Louisa did not consider the motives of Indigenous people fighting to protect *their* homes. Instead, she concluded, her husband's days in the West were "happy, care-free . . . with just enough of the zest of danger in it to keep it interesting, just enough novelty to put an edge on the otherwise dreary life of the plains. And when novelty did not come naturally, Will made it."[35]

As for buffalo, Louisa related stories about the profligate hunting and consequent waste of the bison herds, to which her husband was clearly a party. On this issue, she (or perhaps Cooper) admitted attitudes about the slaughter had changed. While she admired her husband's hunting prowess, Louisa wrote, "I cannot help reflecting . . . how the waste of yesterday has given way before the enforced economy of today and how much might have been saved to this generation if the West had only known and understood that the glorious days of plenty would not last forever."[36]

Such sentiment, however, was more passing commentary than a major theme. Buffalo Bill's Wild West Show made murdering Indians, slaughtering buffalo, rescuing white women from "savages," and building white communities and homes in the West the heart and soul of its message. The hugely popular production became a powerful force in shaping Anglo-Americans' national memory regarding the nation's expansion into and "conquest" of the West. Louisa's book offered a domestic corollary to her husband's version of history—one where she wholeheartedly embraced "the life of the wife of a winner of the West."[37]

By the time Louisa Cody died in 1921, she had buried not only her husband but all four of her children. What an enormous amount of sorrow and trauma she experienced in her life. If she found solace and relief from some of that pain by crafting her life story in an affirming, positive way, one can sympathize with and even understand her compulsion to do so. We know the pages do not provide a complete or an accurate picture of Louisa and Will Cody's marriage or their lives in the West. She ignored the most painful parts while she reified and reinforced the myths—including the more destructive ones—promoted by her husband's show-business career.

Still, there is something heartfelt and authentic here, particularly regarding her family. In the last sentences of the book, Louisa revealed that her youngest daughter, Irma, had recently died in the 1919 flu epidemic. Louisa had endured the deaths of her husband and all of her children, one by one. Now, she wrote, she "face[d] the sunset . . . alone." It was "hard to say the last good-by [*sic*] and stay behind." Yet she felt "a sense of satisfaction" that it would not be long until she saw "the fading on the sunset of [her] own little world." When that time came, she assured her readers, she would be reunited "with the children [she] loved, and the man [she] loved on the Trail Beyond."[38] Not even death would part them. In fact, they would reunite for eternity.

Memories of Buffalo Bill

CHAPTER 1

It was more than a half century ago, May 1, 1865, to be exact. The twinge of early spring had not yet left the air, and I sat curled up in a big chair in front of the grate fire in our little home in Old Frenchtown, St. Louis.

There was a reason for the fact that we lived in Frenchtown; it carried a thought of home to my father, John Frederici, who saw in it an echo of Alsace-Lorraine, where he was born, and where he lived until the call of America brought his parents to this country.[1] And so, when it had become necessary for him to move into town from his farm on the Merrimack River, near St. Louis, he had naturally chosen Frenchtown, with its quaint old houses of Chateau Avenue, its rambling, ancient French market, and its people, reminiscent in customs and in language of the country from whence he came. My mother, plain American that she was, with the plainer name of Smith, nevertheless understood my father's yearnings and enjoyed with him the community in which he found pleasure. And so, in Frenchtown we lived and were happy.

For my part, on that evening, I was especially happy. My convent days were over, and my age had reached that point when my mother would only smile and nod her head at the thought of beaux. And tonight, I was to have two!

One I had seen many times before, Louis Reiber, who once or twice had told me that he liked me very much, and who, on more than one occasion, had shown that he could be fully as jealous as any young beau could be expected to appear. The other I did not know even his name. I was sure of only one thing, the fact that my cousin, William McDonald, had asked for the privilege of bringing him out and had explained that he was a young man who had fought well on the Union side in the Civil War, and that he believed I would like him.

So, comfortable in the knowledge of having two young men to talk to, I was even more comfortable in the fact that I was curled up in the big chair before the fire reading the exciting adventures of some persecuted duchess and a heinous duke, as they trailed in and out of the pages of the old *Family Fireside*. Upstairs, my sister, Elizabeth, preparing also for an engagement that evening, sang and hummed as she arranged her toilet. The fire crackled comfortably; the adventures of the duke and duchess through their sheer nonsensical melodrama began to have a bromidic effect upon me. I nodded—

Suddenly to scramble wildly, to scream, then to struggle to my feet as I felt the chair pulled suddenly from beneath me. I heard someone laugh; then I whirled angrily and my right hand sped through the air.

"Will McDonald!" I cried as I felt my hand strike flesh. "If you ever do that again, I'll—"

Then I stopped and blushed and stammered. For I had slapped, full in the mouth, a young man I never before had seen!

The young man rubbed his lips ruefully, eyed me for a second, then began to laugh. My cousin, doubled over with joy at the unexpected success of his joke, at last managed to choke out the words:

"Louisa, this is the young man I told you about. Allow me to present Private William Frederick Cody of the United States Army."

I stammered out some sort of an acknowledgment. My face was burning, and if I only could have had the chance, I would have given almost anything to have pulled out, separately and with the most exquisite torture, every hair on the head of that rollicking cousin. But Private Cody did not seem to notice. He rubbed his lips with his handkerchief, and then, his eyes twinkling, answered:

"I believe—I believe Miss Frederici and I have met before."

"Where?" I asked innocently.

"In battle," came the answer, and I flounced out of the room.

Nor would I return until my cousin had sought me out and apologized voluminously for his practical joke.

"I just couldn't resist the temptation," he begged. "I'll never do it again, honest. And listen, Louisa, if you'll forgive me, we'll have all our fun tonight at Lou Reiber's expense. You know how jealous he is. Well, you and Will Cody just pretend that you've known each other a long time and we'll have plenty to laugh about. Won't you—now like a good girl, if I buy you some flowers—won't you?"

"And a box of candy?"

"Yes, and a box of candy. But from the way Cody looks at you, I'm thinking that he'll be the one—"

"Will McDonald!"

"Well, it's the truth. He didn't take his eyes off you."

"How could he help it?" I asked acidly. "If I were a man and a girl jumped out of a chair and slapped me in the mouth, I would want to see what she looked like, too. Oh, Will," and my lips quivered, "he'll think I'm a regular vixen."

"No, he won't honestly, Louisa," and he petted me. "Come on now please, like a good girl. Lou Reiber will be here almost any moment."

So I returned, while Private Cody apologized very seriously, while I spent the time noticing that he was tall and straight and strong, that his hair was jet black, his features finely molded, and his eyes clear and sharp, determined and yet kindly, with a twinkle in them even while he most seriously told me how sorry he was that he had hurt my feelings.

And he was handsome, about the most handsome man I ever had seen! I never knew until that evening how wonderful the blue uniform of the common soldier could be. Clean shaven, the ruddiness of health glowing in his cheeks; graceful, lithe, smooth in his movements and in the modulations of his speech, he was quite the most wonderful man I had ever known, and I almost bit my tongue to keep from telling him so.

The apologies over and Will McDonald safely planted in a corner where he could do no more harm, we joked and chatted and planned for the arrival of Louis Reiber. When he came, we were to act as though we had known each other for years, and, in fact, appear mildly infatuated.

"And if he asks us where we knew each other, I'll think of some foolish thing to say that will make him wonder more than ever," said Private Cody. "We'll just make him guess about everything."

"But if I've known you so long," I countered, "certainly I wouldn't call you simply Private Cody or Mr. Cody. That is at least, if I'd known you as long as I'm supposed."

"Certainly not." He was chuckling at the predicament I'd gotten myself into. "You'd call me Willie, just like my mother used to do."

"But—" It was my first chance at repartee. "You don't look like the sort of a man to be called Willie. Do all men call you Willie?"

"Men call me 'Bill,'" came simply, and there was a light in his eyes that I had not seen before, a serious, almost somber glint. "Only one person has ever called me 'Willie.' That was my mother—I've always been just a little boy to her, and she liked the name. And because she liked it, I liked it. You are the only other person I ever have asked to call me by the name."

I held out my hand.

"Thank you, Willie," I said seriously. Then he chuckled again.

"All right, Louisa. Now, that's settled."

And so, when Louis Reiber arrived, I hurried to him with the information that I wanted him to meet a very old and dear friend of mine, Private Willie Cody of the United States Army. Mr. Reiber's black eyes flashed.

"I don't believe I've ever heard you mention him," he said somewhat ungraciously. Mr. Cody smiled.

"But that doesn't mean I haven't been in her thoughts, does it, Louisa?"

The mention of my Christian name caused Mr. Reiber to stare harder than ever.

"I thought you were joking at first," he began. "Now, I really believe you're in earnest. Tell me, how long have you known each other?"

"Oh, for a long time," I bantered. "Haven't we, Willie?"

"A very long time," he answered.

Then the conversation switched, only to be brought back by Mr. Reiber to the subject of our acquaintance. We played him between us, teased him and tormented him, and at last, in answer to one of his questions, Mr. Cody leaned forward in mock seriousness.

"If you want to know the truth," he said, "I'll tell it for the first time. Louisa and I are to be married."

"You're engaged?" Louis Reiber sat straight up in his chair.

"Of course," answered Mr. Cody. Then he turned to me. "Isn't that the truth?"

"The absolute truth," I answered.

Louis Reiber fidgeted.

"But where did you meet each other? Of course, I understand, I haven't any right to ask the question, but I'd really like to know. I—"

"If you'll promise never to tell?" Mr. Cody held up a hand in a mock oath.

"Why—why certainly."

"Well—" and the corners of Will Cody's lips curled in spite of his attempt to be serious. "When I went out of the penitentiary, she went in!"

"Willie Cody, how dare you!" I giggled.

"Well, he wanted information."

I remember that it was just about that time that Mr. Reiber ran a finger around his collar and rose.

"I—I'm sorry I can't stay any longer," he said at last. "I just dropped in for a moment. I rather promised Miss Lu Point that I'd come by this evening." He held out his hand. "I certainly congratulate you, Mr. Cody."

"Oh, I congratulate myself," Will agreed.

"And I feel very happy about it too," I added.

"So do I," chimed in Will McDonald, who had listened, grinning, all the while. "You see, I'm really the one who arranged it."

Mr. Reiber didn't say a word to him—he just looked, and that was enough. Then he bade us good night, and we laughed at what we thought was the great joke that we had played on him. I was especially struck by the humor and nonsense of it all. But the next morning, I realized that it wasn't as nonsensical as I had imagined, for bright and early, a messenger boy was waiting with a letter for me. I never had seen the writing before, but the moment I began to read, I knew. It was from the handsome young man of the night before, the man whose eyes always twinkled and whose lips were continually smiling, and I couldn't help wondering whether this was a continuance of the joke.

The letter long ago was lost, but I always will remember the sense of it. It ran something like this:

> My Dear Louisa:
>
> I know you will forgive me for calling you this because you will always be Louisa to me, just as I will be glad if I may always be Willie to you.
>
> We joked a great deal last night. I realize now, however, that it was not all joking. May I call again, tonight?
>
> Respectfully,
> Willie.

I left the messenger at the door and hurried, somewhat panic-stricken, to my sister, Elizabeth.[2]

"Certainly not," she said wisely. "If you let him come tonight, he'll begin to believe that you think something of him."

"Well." I hesitated. "He's—he's terribly handsome."

She looked at me sharply.

"That hasn't anything to do with it. If he thinks enough of you to really want to come, he'll ask again. Tell him that you're very sorry, but that you have an engagement for this evening and—"

"Then, suppose he should never ask again," I faltered.

"Just you see," she answered wisely. "A man never likes to get what he wants right away."

"But I'd—I'd like to see him a great deal."

"Then what did you ask my advice for?"

So, dutifully I sat down and wrote a very regretful note, telling him that it was impossible for him to come that evening, but that I hoped that he would not leave the city without making another effort. I gave it to the messenger with misgivings and watched him as he hurried down the street, wishing that a girl's life were not bound by so many conventions and that—well, that he'd come anyway.

But he didn't. The next day, it was necessary for me to go into the downtown district, and according to the fashion—for the weather had changed and the sun was blazing hot—I wore the several veils which were then believed so necessary to protect one's complexion against sunburn.

So heavy were they that I could hardly see, and like all other girls, I groped my way through the downtown district and back home again without recognizing anyone. But an hour or so after I had returned, I realized that while I had not seen anyone I knew, someone else had seen me. A messenger was at the door, and this time I knew the writing. It was poetry, and I'll never forget it:

> The blazing sun of brilliant day—
> May veil the light of stars above,
> But no amount of heavy veils
> Can e'er deceive the eyes of love.

Then at the bottom was written:

> I am not going to ask this time. I hope I may see you this evening.

And while the locusts sang in the old trees that lined the street that evening, he came, and I heard later that the children playing along the street—always an encyclopedia of information regarding my callers—announced among themselves that I had a new and very handsome beau. As for myself, I'm afraid that I was not very self-possessed. I had never met a man exactly like him before.

It was very warm that evening, and so we abandoned indoors for the coolness of the porch. For a while, we talked of nonentities, while the children played about the sidewalk and while the family came and went. At last, the lazy evening changed to night, the locust ceased its singing in the maples, and the lamplighter, his ladder slanted across his shoulder, made his trip along the old street. Will and I had seated ourselves on the steps of the porch, I leaning against one pillar, he against another, across the way. Suddenly he changed position and came nearer me.

"You're not angry?" he asked. We were alone now.

"About what?"

"That poetry?"

"Of course not. But you didn't make it up. You copied it from something."

"Honestly I made up every word of it," he protested. "I thought it was real good."

"So did I—only I couldn't see much sense to it." I wouldn't tell him, of course, that I had it with me at that moment. "I couldn't understand it at all."

"Well." And he laughed. "I guess I'm better at killing Indians."

"Sho' now." I looked toward him with interest. "Did you ever kill an Indian?"

"A good many," came quietly. "I killed my first one when I was eleven years old."

"Yes." I laughed. "Just like you and I were friends for years and engaged and all that sort of thing. Willie Cody, can't you ever be serious?"

But when he answered me, there was a different note in his voice, a note of sadness quite different from the jovial, rollicking tone that usually was there.

"I killed my first Indian when I was eleven years old," came the slow repetition. "Sometimes I think I've been fighting my way through life ever since the day I was born. Not that I'm sorry," he added quickly; "it was my own life and I chose it and I wouldn't give it up—but it hasn't been easy."

"And you've really killed Indians?" The thought was uppermost in my mind. St. Louis, it is true, was far West then, and we saw Indians now and then who came into the city from beyond the borders of civilization, but they, as a rule, were friendly scouts who had joined the Union forces and were acting as guides for the various contingents of the United States Army operating in Missouri. To us, the land of the buffalo, the war whoop and the tomahawk were far away, for Leavenworth, Denver, and cities that now are but a ride of a day or two from St. Louis were then, through the lack of transportation, far in the distance.

The real West began at Kansas City—Westport, it was called—then, and from there came many a harrowing story of bloodshed, of Indian attacks and outlawry. And to actually look on someone who had been through this, who could talk calmly of having killed Indians, and of having killed his first Indian when he was nothing more than a boy, was something I never before had experienced. To me, it was wonderful. But to Will Cody, sitting by my side, it was only a recital of a hard, grueling childhood and youth, spent in the midst of turmoil and danger.

"I can't remember much else but hard knocks," he said at last. "The first one came when I was seven years old. We'd moved to a place called Walnut Grove Farm, in Scott County, Iowa, near where I was born."

"When?" I asked.

"When was I born? In Scott County, February 26, 1845."

"Then you're only twenty years old?"

"That's right." He laughed a short hard laugh that I did not like. "But I've seen enough and done enough to make it seem longer. It all began when Samuel—he was my brother—was killed.[3] He was twelve. I was only about seven. We'd gone out on horseback together to bring in the cows. Sam's horse reared and fell on him. I dragged him forth, crying over him and trying to bring him back to consciousness, but I could not, and I had to jump to my horse again and ride to find my father and tell him about it—leaving my brother dying. There wasn't a chance for him—he died the next morning, and soon after that my father decided to emigrate. We were all glad. I was more glad than the others; I wanted to get away. It seemed to me that I could always see that horse just as it toppled and fell and hear Sam screaming beneath it."

He was silent a moment, then went on—as though he felt I should know the whole story of all that he had done, all that he had experienced before that night when I jumped from my chair and slapped him.

"Kansas wasn't even as well settled then as it is now," he began again, "but my father decided to go there, and bundled up my mother and all of the children, Martha and Julia and Nellie—Mary and Charles, my other sister and brother, were born later—and with an old carriage, three wagons, and some horses, we started out.[4]

"When we got to Weston, Missouri, my father decided to stay a while with his brother, Elijah, who ran a trading post there; then we went on to Fort Leavenworth.[5] The cholera was raging then. Every once in a while we would see some Mormon emigrant train stopped along the road to bury its dead, and as we would pass the place we would hold our breath to keep from catching the disease. At last father established a camp near Rively's trading post, on the Kickapoo agency, and I came to know men who carried guns and knives and who fought just for the love of killing.[6]

"While we were there an uncle who had been in California came to visit us. His name was Horace Billings, and he was an expert rider. I liked him, he liked me, and he taught me to ride. Then we went out to hunt wild horses together—he had taught me to use a lasso, and I could handle it pretty well."

"Wild horses?" I asked. My eyes were wide. "I didn't know—"

"A number of them had escaped a year or so before from the government reservation at Leavenworth," Will answered.

"But weren't you afraid?"

"A little—at first," he agreed.

"But your mother—didn't she object?"

Will Cody laid a hand on my arm.

"My mother always objected," came his answer.[7] "But she never said 'no' to me. The night I went away on my first hunt, she cried, but she did not let me know it. We were very poor—almost," and he laughed, "as poor as I am right now. And the government was paying ten dollars a head for every horse that was recovered."

"And you slept outdoors and everything like that?"

"Of course," he answered me. "And killed our own game and cooked it. So you see, I began getting my education early. My uncle had had some schooling, and in what time we had around the campfire at night, he taught me the things that my mother would have liked for me to have learned. But at the same time, I was learning more about how to ride and how to shoot and handle myself on the plains.

"We kept that up for a while, then my uncle decided to rove on again and I went back home. About that time, the Enabling Act for Kansas Territory had gone through and there was a rush into the country.[8] Every trail seemed to be loaded with emigrant wagons, and I saw more than one homestead staked out with whiskey bottles.

"It was a while after this that the slavery question came up and my father announced himself as an abolitionist. Nearly everyone was against him, and one night they all gathered at the trading post and forced him to make a speech. While he was telling them his views, the crowd started at him and one of them stabbed him. That's why I'm in this uniform."

I remember how tightly I clenched my hands.

"And they killed him!" I exclaimed. But in the half darkness, I could see Will Cody shake his head.

"No—worse. They only injured him so badly that he lay for weeks in danger of death. We got him away that night and hid him. After that, it was almost a constant thing for bands of pro-slavery men to come to the house hunting him. One night, a group of them on horseback surrounded the house, and, weak as he was, my father was forced to disguise himself in my mother's bonnet and dress and shawl and hide in a cornfield three days, until we could find the chance to get him to Fort Leavenworth.

"After that, we moved to Grasshopper Falls, Kansas, thinking to get away from the pro-slavery men, but it wasn't much use. My father was building a sawmill there, and one night a hired man came hurrying home to tell us of a plot to kill Father at the mill. Mother called me and put me on Prince, my horse, and started me to save my father.

"I rode about seven miles when I suddenly came on a group of men. One of them started for me.

"'There's that old abolitionist's son,' he shouted, and commanded me to halt, but I kept on. They started after me, but I was light on Prince's back and I outdistanced them. I warned father and we hurried to Lawrence, where he joined the Free State men, who protected him.[9]

"But there never was any peace after that. The pro-slavery men came to our house regularly; once mother only drove them away by pretending there was a large body of armed men in the house. At another time, they stole my horse, Prince. Often they would come and ransack the place, taking everything of value. My father could not stay at home, and money was scarce. I went to work for Russell and Majors, who owned a great many wagon trains and cattle, herding for them at twenty-five dollars a month.[10] And then I was only ten years old."

It all seemed inconceivable. And yet there was something about the quiet, modest seriousness of the tone that told me that every word he was speaking was the truth. There were no frills about Will Cody's story as he told it to me that night on the porch, no embellishments—it was only the natural story of a young man who had faced hardships and who, no doubt, was forgetting more than he told. After a moment, he went on again:

"Things kept up that way until 1857—with the exception of the fact that I went home for a while and went to school. Then, my father died, almost as a direct result of that stab wound, and I was left to be the provider for the family. I went back to the people I had worked for before, Russell and Majors, and was detailed to ride with a herd of beef cattle, under Frank and William McCarthy, for General Albert Sidney Johnson's army, which was being sent across the plains to fight the Mormons.[11]

"We got along all right until we got to Plum Creek on the South Platte River, west of old Fort Kearny.[12] Then, all of a sudden, shots began to sound, and we heard the war whoop of Indians. We had been camping and jumped to our feet. Already the cattle had been stampeded by the Indians, who had shot and killed the three men guarding them.

"I was only eleven years old then and I guess I was scared." He laughed at the recollection of it. "I don't remember much until I heard Frank McCarthy tell us to make a break for a little creek, and I was running as fast as I could. The bank gave us good protection, and we started to make our way back to Fort Kearny.

"Of course, I was the youngest of the party, and I fell behind. By and by night came and the moon came out, and I got more scared than ever. All of a sudden I heard a grunt from above and looked up on the creek bank to see an Indian staring about him. My gun went to my shoulder, and I had fired almost before I knew what I was doing. There was a whoop, and then an Indian tumbled over the bank—stone dead."

There on the porch, listening to the quiet recital, I felt a shiver run through me. I had always been romantic, dreaming of adventures and of weird happenings just like many another convent-bred girl—but I never had imagined that I ever would meet a man who had killed an Indian. I think my teeth must have chattered a bit, because I remember Will moving closer and saying to me:

"Am I scaring you?"

"No—not at all," I hastened to answer, "it's just a little chilly."

"Shall we go in the house?"

"No—let's stay out here. And tell me some more. What happened next?"

"Well, nothing much happened right then. The rest of the men came back, and I immediately got brave and told them how easily I had done the trick. And whether I was scared or not—it wasn't such very bad work, was it?"

I admitted that it wasn't and asked for more. For I had found someone who was infinitely more interesting than the *Family Fireside*. That was only so much paper. Here was a young man who had lived more adventures than the paper ever had printed. So he went on with his story:

"I guess that must have initiated me, because things moved pretty fast after that. The Indian must have been a lone scout, as we made our way to Fort Kearny safely, got the troops, started after the Indians, and went with them. But all we found was the place where the camp had been and the three bodies of the men who had been killed. The cattle were gone—as well as the Indians. So we buried our dead and went back to Leavenworth.

"After that, I got a job as an extra hand with the wagon trains that were going across the plains for Russell, Majors and Waddell—they'd taken in a new partner and had about six thousand wagons and seventy-five thousand oxen. Some of the men abused me, and one tried to beat me one night, when a plainsman named 'Wild Bill' Hickok stepped in and helped me.[13] He was about twenty years old then and had already killed three or four men, and when the rest of the train men saw he'd taken me for a friend, they were afraid to abuse me anymore. 'Wild Bill' and I are still friends. You'll meet him someday," he added with a queer inflection.

"Why will I meet him?" I asked quickly.

"You'll meet him, all right," Will answered. "Just wait and see."

"I'd like to see how a man with a name like that looks," I confessed. "But go on. Tell me some more."

"It's all about the same after that," he told me. "I became a bull whacker for a while, hunted buffalo, and then was a pony express rider.[14] For a while I did some trapping on Prairie Dog Creek."

"And did you kill any more Indians?"

"Six or eight, maybe more."

"Tell me about them."

Will laughed.

"You won't sleep a wink if I do. Anyway, there isn't so much to killing Indians. If you get the first shot, it isn't any trouble at all. Of course, if they surprise you, that's different. I've been in both fixes—but I got out all right. It was a lot worse up on Prairie Dog Creek. I broke my leg up there and had to lie in a dugout for twenty days while my partner hunted out oxen that had strayed away. But still, I got along all right; he'd laid my rations right beside me. Only, I got snowed in and it was pretty cold. So after that, I went back home and went to school for a while."

"Is it very hard riding pony express?" I remember asking. Will Cody laughed.

"Well, try it once," he answered. "I rode three hundred and twenty-two miles once, with rest of only a few hours at a stretch."

"When was that?"

"Just a little while after I broke my leg."

"Will Cody," I asked, "are you trying to fool me?"

"I'm only telling you what happened," was his answer. "And I'm not going to hide anything—even the fact that I've been an outlaw."

"You?"

"My mother called me that. I thought it was honest and just. After I went to school for a while, I turned back to the plains, rode pony express, and handled wagon trains. Then the war broke out, and I went back to Leavenworth and joined Chandler's gang."

"Chandler's gang—the horse thieves?"

"I guess you've got the same opinion of it that my mother had," came slowly. "I didn't look at it that way. We only fought the slavers. And didn't I have cause to fight them?" he asked bitterly. "Didn't one of them stab my father—and didn't he die from the wound? Didn't they hound us and harry us and keep us in misery every minute that my father was alive? I thought that I had a right to hound them too and drive off their horses and cattle and make life miserable for them. That's why I joined Chandler and became a jay-hawker. Then Mother heard about it, and the next time I came home, she told me that it was wrong. And I quit. My mother always knew. The next year she died—and then I went into the army as a scout. I knew that was honorable."

"And then you came to St. Louis," I broke in.

"That's what I did. And a pretty girl slapped me in the mouth."

"Well, you know I didn't mean to."

"And said that my poetry didn't mean anything."

"Well," I answered truthfully, "I couldn't get much sense out of it."

"Maybe I couldn't put the sense into it," he said and rose abruptly. "You see, I haven't been so sensible lately. A man never is when he's in love. Good night."

He stepped down from the porch and went down the street without looking back. But I watched after him, making his way through the shadows, watched after him with the happy, confident knowledge that a girl can only have when she has suddenly awakened to the fact that she is in love with a man—and that the man is in love with her.

CHAPTER 2

However, the fact that I was in love with the man who later was to become Buffalo Bill did not mean that I had made up my mind to become his wife, if he asked me. I believe that neither of us were thinking of that then. In fact, in spite of our rather tumultuous entrance into a love affair, there was an element of steadiness about it all that we both realized and that we both understood. I had been reared in a convent. My range of vision had not been large, my scope of reading had always been toward the romantic and the adventurous, and I felt it natural that I should become fascinated by a man who had lived so eventful a life as William Frederick Cody. But whether subsequent events, new traits of character remaining to be discovered, other attributes of the nature of the man I loved almost before I knew him, would change my ideas toward him, I did not know, nor could I know until time had told its story. That was more than fifty years ago, as I have said. Time has since had its say, and today I feel toward the memory of Buffalo Bill as I did toward his living self that night on the porch in Old Frenchtown. He is still my ideal—yes, and my idol.

As for Will, something of the same sentiment no doubt existed in him. He had been for years on the plains, where he had seen few women he could even respect, much less care for. Just prior to the time he met me, he had been in the army and had seen no feminine person at all that he could meet on a social basis. And therefore he had his grounds for consideration as well as I.

And I must say that we occupied our time well in studying each other—though, of course, no one would have called our meetings exactly by that name. The next day Will was back at the house again, and the next after that. On the third day, I was sitting on the steps of the porch, dressed in my best, when one of the children of the block came to me and cuddled in my lap.

"Who're you waiting for?" she asked innocently.

"Oh, someone."

"Is it the tall one?"

"The tall one?" I parried evasively.

"Yes, with the black hair, who walks so straight."

I confessed. A second more and she was out of my lap and bounding toward the street.

"That's who she's waiting for," she cried. "I knew it was—I knew it was. She's waiting for the tall beau, the handsome one."

"Huh!" A boy who had been rolling a hoop stopped and looked toward me and my reddened face. "Lookit her blush. Eee—yeh—yeh—she's waiting for her handsome beau and—"

"Tommie Francesco!" I called out, "you stop this instant. Don't you dare—"

But he had already gathered reinforcements, and a line of children was on the sidewalk, pointing their fingers at me and crying:

> Louisa's mad
> And I am glad
> And I know how to please her!
> A bottle of wine
> To make her fine
> And her handsome beau o squeeze her!

Then they scattered—for the "handsome beau" was coming down the street—scattered, leaving only the urchin of the hoop behind. I had started from the porch to paddle every one of them and suddenly stopped, blushing and angry and trying to keep from laughing at the same time. Will's voice boomed forth:

"What's all this shouting down here?"

"Oh, it's these children," I answered, "I wish they'd stay at home and—"

"We didn't do anything, Mister," broke in Tommie Francesco. "We just asked her who was coming to see her tonight, and she got mad about it."

"Well," and Will chuckled, "you needn't ask her anymore. If you want to know, I'll tell you. I'm the one that's coming to see her, and if she'll let me, I'll be coming to see her every evening from now on. So run along and don't worry about it."

Then, little thinking that he had spread the news of a practical engagement through the whole of gossipy, interested Frenchtown, he came chuckling and laughing to the porch. I guess my eyes were blazing, because he stopped and looked at me queerly.

"Don't you know what you've done?" I asked.

"No—what?"

"Why, every one of those children will run right home and tell what you said."

"Well," he boomed, "let 'em tell. It's the truth, isn't it?"

And that was Will Cody, then and afterward. His faith in humanity was almost childlike in its sincerity; his belief in the wholeheartedness of others was founded upon his own wholeheartedness and his generosity.

Thus began our courtship—if we ever had one. I have often wondered whether a man and a woman who declare on their first meeting that they are to be married have a courtship or an engagement. Nevertheless, whatever it was, there were few hours of the day when we were not together during the month that followed his first visit to our house. He was at that time stationed in St. Louis, awaiting the mustering out of his regiment, and passes were easily procurable. The result was that every evening found me sitting on the bottom step of the porch and some child of the neighborhood hurrying along the walk to inform me that "my handsome beau" had just been sighted far down the street.

Then came May 30, and his discharge from the army. That night we said goodbye in the moonlight-splattered shadows of the old maples, and he hesitated as he started away.

"I want to ask you something—and if I asked you would you be mad?"

"No, I won't be mad, Will. What is it?"

"If I asked you to go back with me—"

"Wait," I told him and ran into the house. I found a photograph and wrote on it, "Maybe—sometime," and took it out to him. "Look at this when you get back to your hotel," I told him. And then, very discreetly and very formally, we shook hands in goodbye. As he went up the street—about a block away—I saw him take the picture out from beneath his coat and look at it under the streetlight, then go on again.

The next morning I got a letter, and it contained another poetic effort. But I'm afraid that it wasn't the best in the world—even though I thought it very pretty at the time. Will had tried to work in the thought of "maybe sometime" in verse, and it simply wouldn't fit into the meter. But, as I said, I thought it very good at the time, and never once did there enter into my mind the incongruity of a man who had earned a living by fighting Indians, and undergoing hardships, writing verse. Some way, it was the natural thing for him to do—for the West today is the best example I know that Buffalo Bill was a dreamer and a poet, and the free, wild life he led was only an expression of the yearning of a thing that could not bear fettering. The West today is Buffalo Bill's dream come true, and when he died, there were thousands who testified to it.

But in the spring of 1865, I was not thinking of those things, not stopping to analyze why an Indian fighter and a born adventurer should like poetry. I only knew that I was lonely and that I was in love and that I was falling more in love every day. Will had gone back to Leavenworth, Kansas, whence he wrote me of hunting and wagon-train trips, all made in the hope of gaining a little money for that "Maybe—sometime," and of the time when he could return to St. Louis. That time came sooner than either he or I expected.

It was a brisk morning in October that I answered a knock on the door, to find him standing before me, his eyes old, his face haggard. There were lines about his lips, and his features had the appearance of one who had seen deepest suffering.

"Charlie's dead," he said simply as he entered.

Charlie was his seven-year-old brother. Then, when we were alone, he told me why he had come to St. Louis.

"You remember that I wrote you how much Charlie always liked your picture?" he asked. I nodded assent.

There was a pause.

"The little fellow died with it in his arms," came at last. "He asked for it—for the pretty lady—and when I gave it to him, he held it tight and we couldn't take it away from him again. And it made me realize more than ever just what you mean—to me. I've come to ask you for your promise."

And I gave it. The next spring—March 6, 1866—we were married in the room where we had first met, with a few of the soldiers who had served in Will's company and a small number of my friends present. Then to our honeymoon—a boat trip up the Missouri River to Leavenworth, where we were to remain for a time at the home of Will's sister, Mrs. Eliza Meyers.

And with our arrival on the boat, the old spirit of fun became uppermost in Will's mind again.

"Haven't I seen that pilot before?" he asked me, pointing to the little deckhouse.

"Yes," I told him, "you met him at our house the first week I knew you."

"I thought so." Then a grin came across his features. "Listen, you go around this side of the boat and I'll go around the other. He doesn't know we're married, does he?"

"Why, of course not. How should he?"

"Oh, I don't know." He boomed it forth with such strength that I was afraid the entire boat would hear. "I just feel like the whole world ought to know I'm married. But we'll keep it secret long enough to have some fun. Hurry up around the side of the boat."

"And then what?"

"We'll meet just where he can see us and begin to flirt with each other and just see what he does."

"Oh, Will—but all right."

And around the boat I went, to meet him, pass him, drop my handkerchief and begin a flirtation of the most violent order. Nor was it long until the pilot was out of his little house, leaving the wheel in an assistant's hands until he could come downstairs and draw me to one side.

"Do you think that's quite the thing to do, Miss Frederici?" he asked in a fatherly tone.

"Oh, I believe you've made a mistake," came my cool answer. "I'm not Miss Frederici. I'm Mrs. William Frederick Cody, and the gentleman to whom you're referring is my husband!"

All of which was the beginning of festivities. Every boat in those days carried its musicians. Often they were the negroes who performed the heavy labor when the ship stopped at its landings. Nevertheless, with their banjos, and someone to thrum upon the piano, they could make good music, with the result that the pilot soon had arranged for the orchestra, had gathered all the passengers of the boat in the main cabin, and Will and I were ushered in and introduced. Then began the frolic, with a grand promenade to the "Wedding March," Will and I leading the procession.

A voyage up the river in those days was not a swift affair. The old river steamer plodded along against the swift current of the muddy Missouri, stopping here and there to take on wood, or to unload some of the freight that it had brought from St. Louis. It was all very new to me. I, of course, had seen the steamers at the levee in St. Louis, and had taken short excursion trips on them—but nothing like this.

It was like what I often have imagined an explorer's trip on some unnavigated river to be. For hours and hours we made our way up the river, around sandbars, through narrows and muddy, swirling whirlpools, with never the sight of a house for almost a day at a time, only the ragged banks and the bluffs and scraggly trees of the unleaved woods beyond. Now and then, of course, we would reach some town, like the old village of Boonville, or Jefferson City, perched high on the bluffs. But as a rule the day was spent only in a succession of wildernesses.

It all began to have its effect on me. Now I began to realize that I had said goodbye to civilization, that the old comforts and safety of St. Louis might be a thing of the past forever. I knew now that I was going into this vague thing called the West, this place where roamed the antelope, the deer and the buffalo, where Indians still regarded the white man as an interloper, and where death traveled swift and sure. In spite of the gaiety of the boat—for that evening dance had become a regular thing now—the thought clung to me and harassed me. And then came the climax.

We were nearing the end of our journey and had stopped at a small, wild-appearing landing. Some of the negro boys had lowered the gangplank and were loading wood from a pile on the bank, while the remainder still twanged at their guitars in the cabin. Will and I had gone on deck to watch the loading and to listen to the negroes sing, for never was there a duty to be performed without its accompanying chants by the hurrying roustabouts, working in tune to their weird, high-pitched songs.

Suddenly, we noticed a confusion on the bank, as of someone struggling. It was night, and the lamps of the boat threw only a faint glow upon the shore, the rest of the illumination being supplied by the swinging lanterns hanging from just above the gangplank, throwing us in the light as much as the shore itself. We heard cries, then shouting.

Will rushed forward to the rail, calling back to me that it evidently was a quarrel between some of the settlers and the roustabouts. A shot crackled, and I felt my knees become weak beneath me. Then again sounded a shot, followed by the cry of someone in pain, and I fainted.

When I recovered, Will was holding me in his arms, kissing me, and calling to me. The trouble below had been quieted; faintly I could hear the creaking and scraping of the gangplank as it was shoved aboard again. The steamer's whistle tooted hoarsely, the paddles began to churn, while I clung to Will and trembled. Then as the old boat plowed its way out into the middle of the stream, I gained more courage and tried to laugh away my fears.

A part of the returning courage, I must admit, came through the fact that the moon, which had been hidden by threatening clouds, came forth about that time, lighting up the muddy, swirling waters of the river and changing their dirtiness to a silver sheen. The ragged banks, softened by the shadows, took on a more inviting aspect. But I'm afraid that even my show of courage was not sufficient to persuade Will that he had not made a terrible mistake in taking such a little tenderfoot for a wife.

Together we walked to the end of the deck and stood there, watching the spray as it flew from the paddles in the moonlight. At last Will's arm went about my waist and he drew me to him.

"I'm sorry, Lou," he said slowly.

"For what?" I countered. "That I got frightened? I am too, Will. I—I tried not to be. But maybe it was just my nerves, and—"

Will was looking far out into the river, to where an old tree was floating down with the current. I'll never forget that old black carcass of the forest. I watched it, too, watched it with the realization that it was floating downstream, back toward St. Louis, back toward home, where there were lights on the street corners and policemen and horse cars and safety. For a long time both of us were silent, then Will's arm gripped me a bit tighter.

"Lou," he said, "I'm taking you into a new country, a strange country. I never thought about it much until—that trouble back there."

"Neither did I, Will."

"You won't have many conveniences out here."

"I know it."

"It won't be like it was back in St. Louis. There won't be many good women that you can associate with. There won't be many nice men. Everybody's pretty rough out here."

"So you've told me, Will."

"You're going to meet gamblers, and ruffians who have killed their man and who have mighty little in the world to recommend them except that they are helping to populate this country out here," he went on. "Maybe you won't understand it all at first—you may never understand it. You're going to be forced to live without a lot of the things that you have always had, and there may be times when there'll be dangers, Lou. That's why I want to talk to you about it now."

I was silent a moment, then I caught his hand in mine and pressed it tight.

"What was it you wanted to ask me, Will?"

"Whether—" and he hesitated, "whether you think you're going to be able to stand it."

He was looking down at me, and my eyes went up to meet his.

"I knew about these things before I married you, Will."

"That's true. But you were in St. Louis then—and all you knew about life out here was what you had heard. You've just seen an example of what it's liable to be. Not that I won't protect you," he added hastily, "because I will. I'll shield you all I can and I'll work hard for you and I'll try to be the husband that I should be to you—but this life out here is different from what it is in the cities. And—and I thought that if you were afraid—"

"What?"

He hesitated a long time. It seemed like hours to me. Then:

"If you think you're not going to be able to stand my life, I'll try to stand yours. I don't know whether I could do it or not—but I'd try my best. Out here's my world. I'm at home out here—I can breathe and live. I love it but I love you, too. And I love you enough, Lou, so that if you tell me that you don't want to go, if you don't want to take the risk, we'll go back."

If ever there came a test to me, it came then. I was homesick, I was frightened, I was going into a strange land. From a convent I was bound for a country where men often killed for the love of killing, where saloons and fights were common, where the life was coarse and rough and crude. I was going into a country where I would know nothing of the customs, nothing of the mannerisms, nothing of the best way in which to live my life and be free from the constant harrying of the environment into which I would be thrown. The tears came to my eyes. I wanted to cry to him that home was calling, that I cringed at the thought of what was before me. But instead, the heart of me gave an answer that I never regretted:

"Will, do you remember what the minister said when we were married?"

"Yes," he burst forth with a sudden laugh, "he waited a minute and then said: 'Give me the ring!' And my fingers were all thumbs, and I thought I never was going to get it out of my pocket."

"No, I don't mean that. I mean what he said about us being together always."

"Yes, I remember." And his voice was soft. "He said 'till death do us part.'"

"Well, that's what I say to you now. You've asked me whether I'll go out there with you and stand the hardships that I may have to face, and I tell you that we have promised to remain together until death do us part. I'll try not to be afraid again, Will."

"And I'll try to shield you."

And so we faced the new life together, standing there on the deck of the old river steamer, watching the spray as it flashed from the paddle wheels, Will making his pledge to watch after me in this new, crude world we were entering, I giving my word that I would endure and abide by the laws of No Man's Land. And as we talked of it, Will gave me a new insight into his nature, a straighter, clearer view of his heart.

"And it isn't all that this life out here is free," he said, "there's something more. The world isn't big enough for everybody that's in it. It's got to spread, and they'll want to come out here. Every day you can see the wagon trains starting across the desert. They're building the railroad through Kansas. They need men who are rough and ready and who can fight their way forward and clear the path.

"I know the West, Lou. I know every foot of it. And I've got to do my part. It isn't a very pretty place now, but there'll be towns someday out here almost as big as St. Louis, and I've got to help make the road clear for them. I'm working for tomorrow, Lou, and I want you to help me."

And again I gave my promise, while the old steamer plowed on, up the muddy Missouri toward Fort Leavenworth. And there, when the gangplank lowered, I found that Will had made his first step in trying to make my entrance to the West as easy as possible.

He had telegraphed ahead—the telegraph ran then as far as the Kansas Pacific had built—to his sister, to summon many of the officers and friends of the post to the landing to meet us.[1] And they were waiting, with carriages and flowers and greetings and happiness.

Instead of the Indians I had expected were cultured men and cultured women, persons I had made up my mind to forget had ever existed. So strongly had the thought of the lawlessness of the West fastened upon me that it had not entered my mind that there were others, just like me, who were making the fight for civilization, that there were men and women, too, whose sole thought in life did not concern itself with gambling brawls and dance halls. I was almost hysterical with happiness when I went down that gangplank and ran forward into the arms of Will's sister, then turned to receive the introductions of the others who had gathered to greet me. And as Will and I were bustled into a carriage, that old twinkle was again in his eyes and he squeezed my hand.

"It isn't so terribly bad—yet, is it?"

And I agreed that it wasn't.

In fact, it was all very wonderful. Leavenworth was glad to receive someone new, almost as glad as I was to know that Leavenworth did not consist wholly of stockades and hurrying soldiers rushing out to meet Indian attacks. There were dances and parties and carriage rides and—

"Will," I said one night as I smoothed out the flounces of my "best dress." "What's wrong with you?"

He looked at me quickly.

"Nothing, why?"

"Yes, there is," I answered. "And I want to know what it is."

He walked around the room a moment with his hands jammed deep in his pockets.

"I'll tell you after the dance tonight," came at last.

And so, when the dance was over and we were home again in Eliza's house, I asked the question once more. Will's look of worriment faded for a moment.

"Lou," he questioned, with that old twinkle in his eye, "are you glad you married me?"

"Why, of course."

"And did you like that hack we rode in down to the boat?"

"Yes, Will. But what's—"

"Did you have an interesting time coming here?"

"Certainly. But why are you asking all those questions?"

"Well." Then he smiled and walked around the room again. When he came back again, he stopped and looked straight into my eyes. "Well, because—"

Then he turned his pockets inside out. They were empty.

"Broke," he said quietly.

I stared.

"And we haven't any money?"

"Just enough for me to get out and get a job on, and for you to live until I can send you back some," he answered. "I've rented the old hotel down at Salt Creek Valley from Dr. Crook, and you'll stay there. I'm—I'm going to get a job pushing a wheelbarrow."

"Where? At the hotel?"

"No. On the Kansas Pacific. They're looking for men now, and I've got a family to support. But—" and he came forward quickly and kissed me, "I won't be pushing a wheelbarrow long. There's always something happening out here in the West."

CHAPTER 3

The next day we said our goodbyes and he started out for Salina, Kansas, then the end of the Kansas Pacific, where the road was being built on toward Denver. Long days intervened, and at last came a letter from him, saying that he had stopped at Junction City, where he had met his old friend "Wild Bill" Hickok, who was scouting for the government, with headquarters at Fort Ellsworth, and that he did not think he would stay long at the construction job, inasmuch as the government needed scouts, and that "Wild Bill" felt sure that he could obtain employment.

The next letter I received told me that he and "Wild Bill" had visited Fort Ellsworth and that my husband had obtained his position. So throughout that winter, I received letters now and then, telling me how he had guided General Custer from Fort Hays to Fort Larned, straight across a country that was without trails, and that the general had told him that if he ever was out of employment to come to him.[1]

"I think that was very nice of the General," he wrote, "and I thanked him, telling him that I was a married man now and that I always would need a job to provide for my family."

Then later came the news that Will had guided the Tenth Regiment in a terrific Indian fight near Fort Hays, in which a number of the soldiers, as well as Major Armes, were wounded, and a retreat was made in the face of superior numbers of Indians only with the aid of darkness.

All of which was not the happiest news in the world for a new bride. Nor did the fact that cholera had broken out at Fort Hays, where my husband often was forced to visit, relieve the situation. More times than once in that first year was I forced to grit my teeth and fight back the discouragement that almost overwhelmed me. Then came a new viewpoint to life in the person of our baby.

It was December 16, 1866, when she was born. Away out on the plains somewhere was her father, undergoing hardships, I knew, dangers of which I could only dream. But I was sure of one thing—that if Will was alive, if it were possible to reach him, he would come to me. I sent the word, by telegraph as far as the wires would carry it, by pony the rest of the way.

Days passed. Then came the sound of hurrying feet, the booming of a big voice, and I was in my husband's arms. His eyes were glistening.

"Boy or girl?" he bellowed with that big voice of his.

"A girl, Will," I answered.

"What are we going to name it?" He had taken the covering from the baby's face and was jabbing a tremendous finger toward her eyes, causing me to believe every moment that he would make a slip and ruin her features forever.

"What'll we name her?"

"Why, haven't you thought of a name?" I asked.

"Me?" he stared, wide-eyed. "Gosh, I'm lost there. The only thing I ever named was a horse, and none of those names'd do, would they?"

"Hardly. I've rather thought of the name of Arta."[2]

"Pretty name. Lo, Arta!" he roared—when Will became excited his voice was like a foghorn. Naturally, with this great being bending over her, shouting in his happiness, the baby began to cry. Will's face became as long as a coffin.

"Kind of looks like she ain't pleased," came his simple statement, and I couldn't help laughing at the lugubriousness of his expression.

"My goodness, neither would you like it if you had someone shouting in your ear. Now, don't poke your finger in her eye! Don't you know how to act around a baby?"

"Never got close enough before to take any lessons." he confessed, "How do you lift her up, anyway?"

And thus began a new lesson for my scout. He could ride anything made of horseflesh, he could tear a hole in a dollar flipped into the air and then hit it again with a rifle bullet before it touched the ground, he was at home in the midst of danger, and there had never been an Indian who could best him in a fight, but when it came to babies, I was the master.

He was a willing student, but it was a hard lesson. More than once he turned to me in utter discouragement.

"Crickets!" he would say, "but they're sure bundly, aren't they? I'm always afraid of squashing her."

"You ought to be, the way you're carrying her," I'd reply when I wasn't laughing at his great-hearted, clumsy efforts to amuse the tiny little thing, "if you're so tired why don't you give her to me."

"Uh-huh. No. I'm all right. We're getting along fine."

Then, when the baby would begin to cry, he would boom forth with that thunderous voice, singing the only lullabies he knew, something along the order of:

Shoo fly, don't bother me,
Shoo fly, don't bother me—

Whereat, at the resumption of new wails, he would mournfully hand her over to me and then sit watching, like a boy with a new knife that he has been forbidden to touch.

But the West called again, and he went away, not, however, before his education in the care and culture of infants had been somewhat bettered.

And when next I saw him—

It was months later that a wildly enthusiastic man entered the door. I stared for a second.

"Of all things, Will Cody, what's happened?"

"I've become a millionaire!" he shouted as he came forward to kiss me, and then turned to the baby. "Become a millionaire, that's what I've done! What's more, we're going away from here. We own a town now. Rome, Kansas. I'm a half founder of it."

"But—"

"Guess I'd better start at the beginning," Will said exuberantly. "I was scouting around at the end of the Kansas Pacific out by Big Creek when I met a fellow named Bill Rose, a contractor. Well, we got to talking about towns and all that sort of thing, and I kind of suggested to him that it would be a pretty nice thing if he and I could get up a little town of our own. He thought the same way about it, so we put our money together and bought up some land out there for about a dollar an acre, and then we put the beginning of a town on it."

"What's the beginning of a town?"

"Saloon and a grocery store." Will laughed. "You can't have a town without 'em. Where they are, the town will follow. And do you know that right now—" He slapped a knee with one hand. "We've got the finest little town that there is in the West? A hundred houses on it right this minute, and with us owning all the land, when things get settled down a bit and we can get started charging rents and all that sort of thing, we'll have money rolling in hand over fist! Yes, sir! And what's more, we wouldn't let that skinflint of a railroad man come in on it either."

"Who was that?" His information, in its enthusiasm, was rather coming in bunches. Will waved a hand.

"Why—a railroad man. Said he was with the Kansas Pacific and told us that, inasmuch as the railroad was building its line out there, it ought to have half the town. Know what we said? We told him that we were fixing things for the railroad company and doing it good and that it ought to be darned grateful that we'd gone and built up a fine town for it to come to. But some way or other, he didn't seem to take to it very much. But Bill Rose and I weren't going to give him half our town. No sirree!"

"I wouldn't either," I agreed. "What right has the railroad company to ask you for half your town?"

"None at all. That's just what I told him. You betcha we sent him hustling away all right. Guess you'd better start getting packed up. Certainly a fine town out there. Bill and I thought a long time over the name. We finally decided on Rome, because Rome's lasted for a long time and we want our town to be remembered in history, too."

"It's a beautiful name," I agreed enthusiastically. "When do we start out there?"

"Just as soon as we can get a few things packed up. Better not take too much out there at first."

So the packing began and then Will, the baby, and I started to make our first journey into the real West. At Saline, we left the Kansas Pacific, and I sighted long lines of great, cumbersome wagons, which waited by the side of the track. Will pointed.

"That's ours—the third one. Come on, I'll help you into it."

We made our way forward to the wagon, a tremendous thing, trussed and beamed, with a slope-shouldered, long-mustached man lounging on the front seat, the reins to twelve teams of mules hanging listlessly in his hands, his jaws churning with a tremendous cud of tobacco. One by one, Will boosted first me, then the baby into the wagon and turned.

"Bill Rose is around here somewhere waiting for us. Got his wife with him," he said as he started away. "I'll hunt him up."

I watched after him timidly, then looked again in the direction of the front seat. The black-mustached driver was still slumped forward, studying his mules, apparently thinking of nothing else in life. I looked out to see where Will had gone and watched in the direction in which he had departed.

Presently I felt something touch my shoulder, something gliding and creeping. Quickly I glanced, then screamed at the sight of a black, snake-like something that was gliding toward the baby. Then I turned, and there came a chuckling, rumbling laugh as the driver drew back his bullwhip and haw-hawed at me.

"'Taint only me, lady," he apologized. "Jest wanted t' tickle th' bebbe. Don't see many of them out here."

I smiled, still quivering with fright, then brightened at the approach of my husband and his companions, William Rose and his wife.

They climbed into the heavy wagon, the driver cracked the whip that had frightened me so much, and, rumbling and bumping, the start was made. For safety's sake, the wagons traveled in numbers, rarely less than a dozen, each with its long string of mules before it, its drivers shouting and swearing, its yelling riders, its whips popping like rifle shots. "J. Murphy" wagons was their title, capable of carrying seven thousand pounds of freight each, and with their beds as large as the room of an ordinary house.[3] Each was covered with two folds of heavy canvas, upon bentwood hoops, to protect the cargoes from the rain, and as I watched the ones traveling ahead of us across the prairie, they seemed like some great winding, fantastic serpent, whose vertebrae had become disjointed at intervals, writhing across the plains toward—where?

I watched a long time, noticing in a vague way that every man who rode past the wagon was armed with a heavy revolver on each side of his belt and a rifle slung across his saddle. Far away, at each side of the train, other men were riding, sometimes slowly and sometimes swiftly, and they too were armed. For a long time I did not realize the import of it all. Then it struck me—we were in the Indian country, and those outriders were there for a purpose, to keep their keen eyes ever on the outlook for the approach of Indians, and to fire the shot that would send the long wagon train into a hastily constructed circle of defense. I turned to Will.

"How would we know if there were Indians around?" I asked as calmly as I could. Will rose and pointed.

"Easily enough. See those spots over on the hills about a mile away?"

"Yes."

"They're cattle or buffalo."

"How do you know?"

"Because they either stay in one position or move slowly around. An Indian does neither. He bounces up and down—you'll see him for just a second and then he disappears."

"Why?"

"It's their method of scouting, and that's the thing that gives them away. Never worry about an object you can see right along. But if you notice something bobbing up and down, just showing and then dropping out of sight, you holler and holler quick."

And with my baby held tightly to me, I watched the hills, watched until the last rays of the sun had faded and the hills had disappeared in the darkness, without a sight of the thing I feared.

But the worst uncertainty was still to come. The wagons had been drawn into their circle for the night, and the campfires were blazing in the center, while the drivers and others were preparing the evening meal. With Mr. and Mrs. Rose, Will got out to stretch a bit and to assist with the work. I with my baby remained in the wagon, listening to the chaff of the men and to their conversation. Two came nearby.

"How does it look?" I heard one of them ask.

"Oh, all right," came the voice of the other. "We're pretty well protected—as well as possible, anyway. We've posted sentries everywhere."

"Well." The first driver took a hitch at his trousers. "I'll be glad when we're out of here, just the same. I never did like this Three Wells, even before the massacre."

Three Wells! The name told its own story. It had only been a matter of months since the Indians had swooped down upon an emigrant train here, killed the drivers and the passengers, burned the wagons, and driven off with the stock. Three Wells—I remembered how I had cringed at the horrors of the killings when I had read about them—even then a week old—in the newspaper at Fort Leavenworth. I had cringed then and been fearful. Now I was to spend the night on the very spot where that massacre had taken place.

By and by the dinner was cooked, and Will brought me forth, pale and trembling, from the wagon. He looked at me queerly in the firelight.

"Aren't you feeling well?" he asked.

"Fine," I answered, summoning a wan smile, "just . . . just a little tired, that's all."

"Hey—" He turned and called to one of the wagon-men. "Fetch my wife a little coffee, will you? She looks a bit weak."

But when the coffee came, I could not drink it. My mind was on only one thing, that somewhere, out there in the darkness, were the sunken spots of what once had been mounds of earth, where slept the victims of that massacre. The Indians had come in the darkness that night, silently crept forward until they had surrounded the train, then, with a sudden rush, killed the outposts and broken their way through to the inner defenses even before the men could reach their guns. And why should not tonight offer a chance for a repetition of it all?

The fact that many and many a wagon train had passed this spot since the massacre had occurred, and done so safely, did not in the slightest degree allay my fear. My food cooled on the plate before me, while my wondering husband sought to learn the cause of my indisposition. But I would not tell him. Back there, in our honeymoon days, I had promised that I would be so brave, that I would accept his life and go where he went, and now that the time for me to prove my promise had come, I did not intend to weaken. And so I smiled—smiled in spite of my dry throat, my fevered, parched lips, my anxious eyes that watched every shadow, my jangling, raw nerves that seemed to leap and jerk at the slightest sound.

And that was only the beginning. Hours followed, hours in which men slept and mules brayed, hours in which I remained awake, watching, watching, my baby held close to me, watching and praying for dawn.

At last the light dragged its way across the sky. The teams were again hitched to their wagons; once more the bullwhips cracked in the air, the drivers and riders swore, and we went onward. Then and only then, I dozed—safe at last from the ghostly, haunting memories of Three Wells.

Throughout that day, Will and Mr. Rose talked incessantly of their town, how it would grow, how brick and frame buildings would replace the shacks and tents that now stood there, and how the money would flow into their pockets in a never-ending stream. Night came again, with a moaning wind, and I slept fitfully, awakening with a start now and then, to rise from my bed in the old wagon, to gasp at the sight of the sentry, then to bury my head under the blankets and reason myself into a state approaching calmness, that I might sleep.

Again day, and again evening. The wagon train circled and left us just at the edge of a hill. I looked apprehensively toward my husband.

"Don't worry, Mamma." He had adopted that name when the baby was born. "The town's right over the hill. We're as safe as bugs in a rug. Come on."

Up the hill we started, toward our majestic entrance into *our* town of Rome. We made the top, and the two men dropped their arms, aghast. The moon was shining, shining down upon what once had been Rome, with its hundred or so shacks, and tents. But Rome—Rome, the glorious, had roamed away. Only the shack that sheltered the saloon remained, its lights glowing on the scattered debris of where a town once had stood. Rose turned, gasping.

"I—I wonder what's happened," he asked haltingly. Will rubbed his chin.

"This is the place, all right," he answered after a moment of gazing about him, "everything's here—there's the butte over there and—and everything. It's all here but the town!"

And certainly the town had disappeared. Hurriedly we made our way down the hill, Will in the lead, carrying the baby. He ran to the door of the saloon and banged upon it, finally to bring forth the bartender.

"What's become of the town?" he asked excitedly. The bartender grinned.

"Didn't you hear about it? It all moved away, about a week ago. The railroad started up a better town over by Fort Hays and let it out that it wouldn't come anywhere near here. So everybody pulled up stakes. This is the only place that's left."

Huddled in a wondering little group outside the circle of light, we heard the news. For a moment none of us could say anything. Will and Mr. Rose walked up and down looking at the bits of tenting, the scraps of tin, the scattered papers that told the story of their town that had disappeared. Then Mr. Rose came back to where his wife and I stood disconsolately waiting.

"There's only one thing to do, I guess," he said at last, "and that's to walk over to the fort."

I thought of the Indians.

"If Will's willing I guess we'll stay here," I said, "maybe we can find a tent or something."

Mr. Rose went back and talked to Will. Then he and his wife said good night to us. Will gave me the baby and went into the saloon for a moment. Then he hurried back to me.

"There isn't a tent around here," he told me, "but the bartender says that there's a cot in the back room. You can have that and I'll sleep on the floor. Come on—the door's around this way."

Together we made our way in the semi-darkness, to halt suddenly at the sight of a hurrying figure. A negro's voice came to us.

"Hello dar."

"Hello yourself. Who're you looking for?"

"Marse Cody."

"That's me. What's wrong?"

The negro hurried forward and saluted.

"Major Armes done sent me oveh heah t' see ef you kem, yit. He wants yo' at de fo't."[4]

Will turned and looked at me.

"Are you afraid?" he asked quietly. Again I summoned a smile.

"No, Will," I answered. "I'm not afraid."

"And I can go to the fort knowing that you'll not be worried—and that you'll feel that you'll be protected if anything happens?"

"I'm not afraid," I answered again. He brought something from his pocket.

"Here are the keys," he said, "one to this door and one to the door leading into the saloon. There are some bullwhackers and gamblers in there now. They may become noisy but they won't hurt you. And you're sure you're not afraid?"

I had to grit my teeth to summon the courage to say the words, but I managed it. Then Will opened the door for me, lit the dingy kerosene lamp, kissed the baby and me, and was gone. I was alone—alone in the back room of a frontier saloon.

For a moment, I could only stand and look about me, staring at the crude pictures on the walls, the dingy little windows, the rickety door. Then I gained enough courage to creep to the door leading to the saloon and assure myself it was locked. After that I locked the door leading to the outside, and, extinguishing the lamp, lay down on the cot, fully dressed, with my baby hugged tightly to me.

Outside in the saloon, men were talking and cursing. I could tell by the noise from the end nearest me that a gambling game of some kind had been established and that the men were drinking and quarreling as they played. Tremblingly I heard them shouting invectives at each other and cringed at the language. Then someone asked:

"How about that woman? Is she still around here?"

Another voice, evidently that of the bartender, answered:

"Cody's wife? No, they went over to the fort. A soldier was just in here and said that Major Armes had sent him to get Cody and that he'd met them just going in the door."

"I'm glad of that," came the first voice, "this isn't any place for women. I don't want 'em around here anyhow!"

And if he had only known how little I wanted to be there! But he had no chance of learning.

My strength had gone. All I could do was to lie on that rickety cot and hope for morning.

The noise soon began again, and the quarreling at the gambling table grew louder. Suddenly I leaped, straight in the air, it seemed. The sound of scuffling had come from the other room, followed by the bark of a revolver shot. It had been no worse than I had expected. My imagination told me what was outside the door—the crumpled body of a man, huddled on the floor, the revolver, its smoke trailing upward—blood—

Then the baby began to cry, and I was thankful for the cursing and yelling that was coming from the barroom. Vainly I tried to still her. She only cried the louder. And with her sobs, I dully realized that the noise from the other side of the door was lessening. Plainly I heard someone say:

"Listen—what's that?"

Then absolute stillness, except for the frightened screams of the child. It lasted for one of the longest moments of my life, followed by a muffled mumbling that I could not interpret. At last I heard the steps of men, as though they were on tiptoe, and a slight knock on the door. I did not answer. Again it came—and again. I struggled to reply, but, for a moment, the words simply would not come. At last I managed to get out:

"Who's there?"

"It's only us," someone called, in a voice that was trying terribly hard to be pleasant, "we didn't know anybody was in there. Where's Cody?"

"He's gone to the fort." I said it before I thought.

But the answer reassured me.

"We're plum sorry we made the baby cry. One of us got to scuffling around and his shootin' iron went off. Ain't nobody hurt. We're awful sorry we disturbed you."

The news that the killing I had imagined had not happened after all brightened my life considerably. And I knew from the tone outside the door that the barroom, tough and rough though it might be, was standing in humble penitence.

"That's all right," I answered. "The baby's stopped crying now."

There was another moment of apparent consultation. Then the knock came again.

"Mrs. Cody!"

"Yes."

"Be you dressed?"

"Yes."

"Do you reckon you could stand it t' let us in? We'd powerful like to see that baby o' Bill's."

Somewhat fearfully I rose and pawed about at the side of the old kerosene lamp, at last to find an old "eight-day" match and light it. Then I opened the door.

About ten men stood there, dirty, unkempt, bearded, their hats in their hands. They looked at me with a sort of bobbing bow as I faced them, then timorously, and even more fearfully than the way I had walked to the door, they stepped into the room. One by one they involuntarily lined up, somewhat after the fashion of persons passing a bier. Then they gathered near the cot where little Arta lay.

Silently they watched her a moment, their lips grinning behind their heavy, scraggled beards. Then, in a half-embarrassed way, one of them stuck out a finger. Arta reached for it, caught it, and laughed. The bearded one's face beamed.

"Look at the little———!" he exclaimed, then, suddenly realizing his oaths, pulled away his finger and faded into the protection of the rest of the group. The others looked about them with pained expressions, understanding for once that here was a place where profanity was not fashionable. At last, the bartender, being more of a man of society than the others, wiped his hands on his dirty apron and, turning to me with a wide grin, asked:

"Pretty baby, ain't it? What is it, a him or a she?"

"She's a girl," I answered as quietly as I could.

"Kind of thought it was. Kind of looked like it. Mind if we sort of dawdle around with her? Babies ain't much of a crop out here."

And so they stayed and "dawdled"—great, powerful children in the baby hands of the little child that lay on the cot. Then, one by one, they turned and thanked me, the bartender again wiping his hands on that greasy apron.

"We're plum sorry about making her cry," he apologized for the fourth or fifth time, "we thoughten you and Cody'd gone over to the fort. We're plum sorry about it. But you and the young 'un trot on to bed now. There ain't no business tonight anyway, and these fellows want to go back to the fort. I'll set up in the barroom."

"You goin' to shet down?" One of the group asked the question as though it were a sacrilege. The bartender wiped his hands again.

"Yep," he answered with an air of cold finality, "I'm going to shet down."

They turned and tiptoed out, the bartender closing the door behind him as he apologized for the last time. For a moment or so, I heard the group loitering about the saloon, evidently taking their last drink for the night. Then came their goodbyes, and the slamming of the front door. Finally, only the steps of the bartender echoed through the place, and at last the scraping of a chair as it was tilted against the wall. The bartender, true to his promise, was "setting up," and there Will found him the next morning, snoring in his chair.

Will's news was not the best in the world. He had been out most of the night on a scouting expedition, and the Major had informed him that morning that he would like, if possible, to have him accompany him on a hunt, as meat was getting scarce at camp and some buffalo had been sighted nearby. Our home in Fort Hays, he told me, must be a tent for a while, until we could go to the Perry Hotel, every room of which was at that time occupied. So to our tent in Fort Hays we went.

That domicile was near the camp of the soldiers, members of a negro regiment. For several days Cody remained there, and then came the order for the hunt, while Major Armes designated twenty men who were to act as guards about my tent and protect me. But for some reason, the guards did not perform their duties.

It was late one night when I was aroused by the sounds of shouting and quarreling. Some members of the regiment, passing my tent, had met another contingent with which they had quarreled previously and had decided to fight it out.

Perhaps the guards were there, perhaps they did their best—all I know is that almost before I realized it, my tent was the center of the struggle and forms were all about me, tearing at each other, knocking the tent down about me, and constantly placing me and my baby in danger of being trampled to death. I reached for a revolver that Will had presented to me, which he had given me some instructions in aiming during our old courting days in St. Louis. Hurriedly I picked up the baby in one arm and, fighting my way clear of the folds of the canvas, made my way into the open.

"Get back there," I cried. "I've got a gun and know how to use it. Now get back!"

A soldier turned and struck at me, knocking the gun from my hand. From across the way, an old man, seeing my predicament, ran to my assistance, only to be knocked down and kicked into insensibility. Vainly I cried and screamed for help—it seemed that it would never come. I sank to my knees then struggled to my feet again.

From down the street came the shouting of orders and the blurred forms of men. Almost in an instant the milling figures about me started to run as a detachment from the fort hurried after them to put them under arrest. But the damage had been done as far as I was concerned.

The limit of my endurance had been reached. I had held my nerve as long as holding it was possible. I had striven my best to keep the word I had given on the boat, back in the days just after our wedding—I had tried to be brave, but the force of circumstances had been too much for me. Will returned from his hunt to find me collapsed from the strain, hysterical and nerve-racked. Furiously he set out to gain vengeance on every man who had participated in the fight—but that was impossible. Then, white-faced, trembling with anger, he returned to my bedside.

"Mamma," he told me, "it's a good thing I didn't find them. I would have killed them. I'm sorry."

"Will," I answered, "you don't need to be sorry. It wasn't your fault." I reached out and took his hand. "I just couldn't hold up any longer. I tried to be brave—honestly I did."

"You were brave," he said, and there was a tenderness in his voice that gave recompense for all I had endured, "braver than ever I dreamed. And I'm as proud of you as I am sorry that this happened."

I was in the hotel now, having been taken there by the guard detachment that had insisted on a place for me, and Will proclaimed to the management, with a forcefulness not to be resisted, that there I would stay, congestion or no congestion. Will had his way as he usually did when he narrowed his eyes and set his head square on his shoulders, with the result that the days that were to come were to be far happier ones, in many ways, than I had known for months.

And especially were they happy in the fact that I had passed through my baptism of fire, that I had seen the West in some of its worst attire, and that, with the exception of the breakdown following the fight around the tent, I had managed some way to pull through. Greater, even than that, was the knowledge that I was to be near my husband, that I would know by courier if accident should befall him on any of his hunting and scouting trips, and that I would not be subject to nerve-racked weeks until a letter should tell me whether he was alive or dead.

CHAPTER 4

And there were happy days to come, days that were full of brightness and enjoyable incident, in spite of the fact that my health had been broken by the nervous strain I had undergone, in spite of the hardships of the life, and the tatterdemalion excuse for a town in which Will and I made our home. Fort Hays—or Hays City, as it now is known—was not a choice metropolis in those days. Like my husband's unfortunate town of Rome, it had grown practically overnight, from a short-grassed stretch of prairie to a conglomeration of tents, shacks, frame buildings, gambling, whiskey, and soldiery. The population had swelled from nothing into hundreds, gathered from the plains and from the farther West: scouts, hunters, men who had stopped on the way to the West, and those who had dropped from the trail on the way back east after their failure to glean the gold of California or the wealth of Colorado.

A sort of clearinghouse for the best and for the worst was Hays in those days. The Perry Hotel, in which Will and I made our home—if a shell of a building, with partitions extending only partway to the ceiling, with no carpets, with clapboarded walls and scant furnishings, it could be called a home—was the place of registration for high army officials, famous plainsmen, gun-toters and man-killers, soldiers of fortune and soldiers of the regular army, gamblers, early-day get-rich-quick-Wallingfords, professors, ne'er-do-wells, college graduates, railroad men, hunters, and every other phase of humanity. The streets were only openings between rows of shanties and tents, where, in every third habitation, men crowded about the rough-boarded bars or heaped their money upon the gambling tables.

Toneless, clanging pianos, appearing miraculously from nowhere, banged and groaned in the improvised dance halls. Men quarreled and fought and killed. The crowded little streets, with their milling throngs, suddenly would seem to be cleared by magic—except for two men, one standing with his revolver still smoking, the other a crumpled heap in the dust. Then a rush for a horse, the soft clud of hoofs, and only one form would be left an object for the consideration of a quickly assembled coroner's jury, and a verdict of:

"Death from gunshot wounds."

And not always did the winner of the duel seek safety in the number of miles placed between him and the pursuing posse. More often, in fact, he would wait until the street filled again, and the friends of the loser carried away the body. Then he would turn to the half-admiring crowd with the simple statement:

"It was either him or me, boys. Had to do it. I guess it's time for me to buy. Let's have a little red liquor and forget it."

Whereupon another notch would find its way into the handle of a killer's gun, one of the many canvas-covered saloons would do a rushing business for an hour or so, and the next day there would be a new grave in the little cemetery just out of town. One man, more or less, made little difference in the West of those days. Each played his own game, each made his own laws, as long as he could enforce them, and each apparently was accountable to only one thing—Death.

Strangely enough, in spite of my nervousness, and the weakened condition in which my ordeal in the tent had left me, I found myself little affected by all this. I had accepted the West; I had learned that these conditions existed and that there was seemingly no cure for them but time, and no attitude to assume except that of indifference.

Not that I did not realize the status of the environment into which I had been thrown, nor that Will did not know and understand what it all meant. We both knew and we both understood, and never was a woman more carefully guarded, more thoroughly shielded than I. Through Will's efforts, orders had gone forth that I must never leave the hotel without the company of an officer and a competent guard, and that should any harm come to me, through the laxity of that guard, it would be cause for a general court-martial and the strictest disciplinary action. The result was that I saw all that Fort Hays had to offer in the looseness of its lawless youth, yet suffered none of the consequences.

My fright and the shock to my nervous system had left me weak physically and with little nervous resistance. Will watched over me with all the tenderness and care that a mother would exert over her child. Incidentally, one of the first things that he had done was to procure for me the services of a young Vassar graduate—and how she had ever chosen Fort Hays as a place in which to live is more than I can understand—to care for Arta and to take from my mind all the worry and care of the baby.

By special permission, Will's hunting and scouting trips had been shortened considerably, with the result that he was seldom gone from Hays City for more than a few days at a time. In those days I would sit by the window of the rickety little hotel, watching the life of the tented, shack-lined streets, listening to the crack of the bullwhips as the heavy wagon trains rumbled through, to the banging of the pianos from the dance halls, to the shouts and laughter from the saloons and gambling "palaces," waiting, waiting for Will to come home again. Then would come the clickety-clud of hoofs, the sight of a rushing figure, the form of a man who swung from his saddle and was on the ground even before his horse had stopped, the booming of a big voice as a giant figure came up the stairs—and I would be in my husband's arms again.

Then would follow glorious, happy days, in which he would put a sidesaddle on his favorite horse, Brigham, and we would ride far out into the prairie. There Will would bring forth his heavy, cumbersome six-shooter from its holster and hand it to me.

"The next time anything happens," he said, more than once, "I want you to shoot—and shoot to kill. Now, let's see whether your aim's improving. Bang away!"

Whereupon he would select a target, which to me seemed miles away, and with the most bland, childlike expression tell me to hit it.

"Hit that?" I would ask. "Why, Will, a person couldn't hit that with a rifle, let alone a six-shooter."

Will's eyes would open wide, and a half-smile would come to his lips.

"Give me that gun," would be his answer. A swing, a sudden steadying of the wrist, and a burst of smoke. Then Will would turn to me with a courtly bow. "Please go look at the target," he would ask. And invariably there would be a bullet hole in its center.

But the same thing did not happen when I shot. It was true that he had taught me something of the art in St. Louis and in Leavenworth—but did you ever try to swing a heavy .44 caliber six-shooter through the air, bring it down to a level, get your aim, and pull the trigger in less than a second? Will would not let me shoot any other way.

"It's quick work out here in the West," was his constant reminder. "You don't shoot unless you have to—and then you shoot quick. Now, try it again."

Following which I would bang away with the old gun until my wrist, my arm, even my shoulder would ache from its terrific kick. Day after day we went to the target "range," with the inevitable result that gradually I learned the knack of assembling several faculties simultaneously and executing the aiming of the gun, the pulling of the trigger, and the assimilation of the recoil, all at once. The targets began to show more and more hits. Then, one day, Will nodded approvingly.

"From now on," he said, "you'll shoot on the run. Let's see you hit that target with Brigham going at a gallop."

And so, a new school of instruction began—and then a new one after that. Even little Arta did not escape the rigors of the schooling that my husband had determined to give me. As soon as I had learned to shoot from the back of a horse, and to shoot both deliberately and by simply snapping the hammer, Will gathered the baby in his arms one day and took her with us.

"Put Arta on your lap," he ordered. "Now—that target over there is an Injun. You've had to take a ride, and just as you come home, this old Red Pepper bobs up on you. I want you to spur Brigham into a gallop and put a bullet through that old reprobate's head."

"All at once?" I asked vaguely.

"Why, of course," my husband answered as though it were the most natural thing in the world. "You know, if that Injun's out for business, he ain't going to wait for an invitation before he starts shooting. Gad!" He had caught the expression from a college professor and was using it in almost every sentence. "I'll bet a buffalo hump you can do it the first time."

But Will was a bad better. I missed the first time, the second, and consecutively up to about the hundredth, while Arta, laughing and clapping her hands—yet shivering at every blast of the old six-shooter—called for more. Will looked at me ruefully.

"I guess there's only one thing for me to do. That's to get rich. I'll never pay for your cartridges any other way. Try it again."

I did—and this time I nicked the target. Then began a system of hit and miss, until at last I could gallop by the target at full speed and put a bullet so near it, at least, that it would not have been comfortable for a human being. Even Will was satisfied. "I'll feel easier now, when I'm away," he said simply as we made our way back to town, and I knew what was in his mind. He still was thinking of that day when he had come home to find me screaming with hysteria, as a result of the attack of the soldiers. And, I must admit, I felt a great deal more comfortable myself.

So were the days spent. At night the "lobby" of the little hotel would be filled with officers and scouts, and the few women of the town who occupied a social position that goes with the term "a good woman." I am afraid that in those early days of Fort Hays, just as it was in every other frontier town of the West, the good women were few and far between. But, in spite of the fact that we who clung to the conventions and who took pride in the fact that we held a position in our own esteem were far fewer in number than the painted, bedizened persons who leered from the doorways of the dance halls and who, more than once, played one man against the other for the sheer joy of seeing the swift flash of revolvers, the spurting of flame, the crumpling of a human form, and the spectators who would point her out as a woman for whom one man had killed another; in spite of these conditions, there were enough of us to have our little sewing bees, our social functions, such as they were, and to "go round," when the dining room of the Hotel Perry was cleared of its rough tables and rickety chairs for the weekly dance.

And such dances! High on a hastily improvised rostrum would be the fiddlers and perhaps some wandering accordion player, squeaking away for all they were worth, their fiddles—they could, under no stretch of the imagination, be called violins—scratching out the popular music of the time, such as the "Arkansas Traveler," "Money Musk," and the other quickstep music of that day, while out before them would be the most energetic person at the dance, red faced, his arms waving, the veins standing out on his neck, his voice bawling:

"Ladies-s-s-s-s right, gents left! Swing-g-g-g-g yo' podners, one an' all, do-se-do an' round th' hall!"

It was just before one of these dances that Will came hurrying to our room, his eyes bright with excitement.

"Put on your best bib and tucker," he announced. "We're going to have some celebrated visitors at the dance tonight."

"Who?" I asked.

"Texas Jack and my old pardner, Wild Bill Hickok."[1]

"The killer?"

"Yes. He don't dance much, but he said he was going to dance with Bill Cody's wife if he broke a leg. And I want you to look your prettiest."

"For a killer? Why, Will, I'd be afraid to death of him."

Will shrugged his shoulders.

"Wait 'till you've seen him first."

I must admit that my toilette that evening was not accomplished with any great joy. The stories of Wild Bill Hickok had been many and varied. The notches on his gun were almost as numerous as the accounts of his various battles. Wild Bill Hickok had never been known to snap the hammer of his revolver without a death resulting. And I had been promised to him that night for a dance!

For one of the few times in my life I was angry with Will Cody, my husband. I pouted all through the evening meal, and when Will asked me the trouble, I told him without much equivocation. But Will, humorist that he was, only grinned.

"Just like a woman," he said with a chuckle. "Get mad at her poor husband before she knows all the facts of the case." Then he became serious. "Lou," he said, "do you remember that time in St. Louis when I was telling you about my boyhood? Remember how I told about the man who had protected me when the bullwhackers of the wagon train had made up their minds to make my life miserable? If you remember that, you'll also remember the fact that the man who came to my assistance was Wild Bill Hickok. When I saw him today, he asked for a dance with you. Could I—or should I—have said 'no'?"

My little fit of anger was over.

"Forgive me, Will," I answered. "I'll dance with him—even—even if I will be afraid every second that he'll pull out a revolver and start killing everybody on the floor."

Again Will chuckled. And he was still chuckling when he reached the room—nor would he tell me the reason.

The hours passed. The fiddlers ascended their rostrum, the caller took his place, and the dance began. Chills were running up and down my spine—I was soon to dance with a man who had a reputation for killing just that he might see men die, and who was supposed to have defied every law ever made by God or man. A dance went by, hazily. Then two and three. Suddenly there was a craning of necks, and I saw Will, as though from a great distance, talking to some man who had just entered. A moment more and Will had hurried to my side.

"Come with me, Lou," he ordered.

I obeyed dully, hardly seeing the faces about me as I walked forward.

Then suddenly I blinked. Will was speaking, and a mild-appearing, somewhat sad-faced, blond-haired man had bent low in a courtly bow. Faintly I heard Will say:

"Allow me to present Mr. William Hickok, Wild Bill."

And this was Wild Bill! I had looked for a fiendish-appearing, black-haired, piercing-eyed demon and had found a Sir Walter Raleigh. Almost gaspingly I told him I was glad to meet him—and I was most assuredly glad to find him a different sort of man from the one I had supposed. In a mild, quiet voice, he told me that he had made a request of my husband—and then added:

"But, of course, you're the final judge. Do you think that you could manage to dance a quadrille with me?"

"Most assuredly." And I meant it. I could have danced the Highland Fling, I believe—so happy was I to find mildness where I had been led to believe would be the most murderous of persons. Instinctively I looked for revolvers. There were none—not even the slightest bulge at the hips of the Prince Albert he wore. I was happier than ever.

We danced. And I must confess that we danced and danced again until Will laughingly put a stop to it. And, of course, it was just like Will to say:

"And you said you wouldn't dance with a killer!"

"Will!" I broke in, for the eyes of Wild Bill had turned with a sharp, quick look, the look of a man when he realizes his reputation and feels the shame of it. There was a moment of silence. Then Wild Bill looked at me with a little smile.

"You've been hearing stories?" he asked.

"Yes," I confessed.

"Do I look like the kind of a man who would shoot unless he had to?"

"No," I confessed, and I meant it. And what was more, that was the truth. More than once, throughout the West, I have found persons who have talked of Wild Bill as a killer of men who was not happy unless he saw the body of a human being huddled before him. But that was not the truth. Now that my interest was aroused, I learned Wild Bill's real story from those who knew him, and the only murder in his life was the one in which he himself was killed—he was shot in the back during a card game at Deadwood, South Dakota.

He was a gambler, it is true. So were they all in the early days of the West. A gunfighter, a dangerous man once his anger went to the steaming point, and as deadly with his revolver as a cobra with its bite—such was Wild Bill. Many were the notches on Wild Bill's gun for the reason that he never missed, that when he pulled the trigger his opponent fell, never to rise again.

Perhaps, all this, coming from a woman, sounds hard and cold and heartless. It is not. It is simply the echo of days that are gone, days in which one was obliged to follow the customs of the country or leave. I had seen my share of lawlessness; gradually and surely it had been forced upon me that I was living in a country where Death came swiftly and frequently, and where human life was of little worth. Viewed from a cold standpoint, it might be compared to the rate of exchange in a foreign country where the unit of money is of small value. One does not have the same respect for it that he does for his own unit of wealth. Had these same things happened in a place of civilization, I would have been in constant terror. But I was in the West now, a different land. And I accepted it all.

I was growing a little stronger physically, and Will now and then would venture to take me out to the races, which were a constant occurrence in Fort Hays. Naturally, they were not such races as one sees today, with great grandstands, silk-clad jockeys, Paris-gowned women, and the thousand and one evidences of luxury. They were in keeping with the West, built upon Western lines and—but let the description come in its proper place. It all began when Will rushed to me with a great idea.

"Just happened to think of something, Lou!" he announced. "I want to make a good showing when you come out to that race Saturday, and I just happened to think that there ain't a soul in town that can sport a jockey suit."

"So I'm to make you one?"

"That's just it," he said enthusiastically. "Look! I've already bought the goods!"

He dragged a parcel from beneath his arm and pulled away the paper. There, flaming up at me, was the brightest, most glaring piece of red flannel that I ever had seen in my life. It simply seemed to blaze—almost as much as the enthusiasm in Will's eyes.

"I guess that'll make 'em know that there's somebody riding in that race!" he announced proudly. "And, Lou, make those pants so tight I'll have to take 'em off with a bootjack!"

When I finished laughing, I examined the goods. It was flannel, red flannel—and for one jockey suit, made extra tight, Will had bought fifteen yards of material!

"Just wanted to be sure that you'd have enough," he explained when I cut off the amount I would need. "Thought if there was any left over, you might make a dress for Arta or something of the kind."

"Oh, you go on!" I laughed at him. "The rest of that's going right back to the store. So bundle it up and take it back and tell them you want a refund."

"Oh, Lou!" His face was almost piteous. "I—I don't want to go back there. You—you take it back."

"No sirree. You bought it."

"But—but—"

"Now, hurry along, Will. Or I just won't make this suit for you. So there."

Will looked lugubriously out the window, hugging the piece of red flannel tightly under one arm. A long time he stood there, for all the world like a man striving to screw up his courage to do something he feared. Then, hesitatingly, he turned, kissed me like a man going to a funeral. I had to relent.

"You dear old coward!" I chided him. "Afraid of a little thing like that! Never mind. I'll go."

His face beamed.

"Gosh!" he broke out. "That's sure a relief. I'll kill Injuns any day, ride pony express, do most anything. But, Lou, Mike Gordon's wife's got the hardest face I ever saw in my life—and she's working up in the store now and—and—what'd I done if she'd said she wouldn't take it back? You can't pull a gun on a woman!"

So, even the bravest can show fear—sometimes. Will had faced death, exposure, trials, tribulations, and, more than once, disaster—but he couldn't face Mike Gordon's wife. So I had to face her for him, then I hurried back to the making of the suit, while Will, like a small boy awaiting his first pair of boots, sat humped on a small chair, awaiting the ordeal of "trying on."

It was a wonderful concoction that we eventually conceived—made in the greatest secrecy. A flowing blouse, skin-tight trousers, a cap with a visor so long that I feared it would tickle the horse's ears, all ending in a pair of cowhide boots. William Frederick Cody, in this regalia, was the most wonderful specimen of human foliage that I ever had seen. We both laughed until the tears came. But the suit had been made—and Will wore it.

Perhaps it is best to explain that horse racing in those days, in the West, at least, was an entirely different matter from the racetrack style. Each man rode his own horse, and no matter whether he weighed a hundred pounds or two hundred, the odds were the same. Every scout who rode the plains possessed some horse that had saved him more than once from Indian attack, and in which he placed every confidence in the world. There was little opportunity for competitive judgment, with the result that a group of scouts would gather, begin to extol the wonderful performances of their horses, start an argument—and end the whole thing by arranging a horse race, which the whole city of Hays would attend.

And so it was that on Saturday, with Will's wonderful suit concealed beneath a long linen duster, we journeyed out of town toward the racetrack. That, incidentally, was only a name. There was no turf, simply a stretch of level ground in a valley where someone had paced off a mile, and where the townsfolk could gather all along the track to cheer on the victors and console the losers.

We were late and the valley was thronged. Here and there were groups of men, arguing, announcing, in speeches that bore no sign of softness, the prowess of their various mounts. Money was changing hands from the betters to the stakeholders. Here and there, scattered along the mile track, were little tents—the inevitable traveling barrooms that accompanied every gathering of people in the West. Will and I stepped from the carryall and quietly approached the largest group. Then unostentatiously Will removed that linen duster.

It was as though a meteor had dropped into the valley. The arguments ceased as if they had been cut off with a sword. The bar-tents emptied, horses were forgotten, bets were neglected, while the population of Fort Hays and environs gathered about me and the resplendent William Frederick Cody. Very quietly Wild Bill Hickok, a wad of money still clutched in his hand, where it had been interrupted in the placing of a bet, came forward and looked intently at Will.

"I don't guess I'll race my horse today," he said quietly.

"What's the matter?"

"That's a good horse," said Wild Bill as he turned away. "I'm not going to risk him going blind from looking at bright lights."

That was the beginning of the joking and chaffing. But behind it all was envy, deep, galling envy. For where is the true westerner of the old days who will not confess a failing for color and plenty of it?

Suddenly, however, the joking stopped temporarily. The Major had interrupted.

"We'd better be holding our races," he announced. "Some of the men have reported Indians in the vicinity and—" He looked at Cody. "If anything can draw them here this afternoon, it's that prairie fire that Bill's wearing. So will the ladies please take their stations?"

"Stations?" I asked.

Will turned to me.

"Forgot to tell you," he said. "You're the only ones that work out here. We depend on you to keep your eyes out for the Injuns."

I knew what that meant, to constantly watch the hills that hedged us in for the sight of bobbing figures. That had been one of my first lessons on the plains—on the road out to Hays City—to know that an animal simply moves along in a straight course, that a man on horseback can be seen traveling in a straight line, but that an Indian raises and lowers his body constantly.

So, out we went to our stations, a few hundred yards from the racetrack, where we could have a commanding view of the hills. Now and then, as I watched, I could see the crowds milling about Will and could see his arms gesticulating at intervals with some vehemence. At last he turned from the crowd and came toward me.

"Lou," he said with a smile, "you've got to do a lot of wishing."

"Why?"

"Because if I don't win this race—"

"Yes?" He had hesitated.

"Well, you see," came his qualifying answer, "the boys all said I'd taken an unfair advantage. They said that this outfit I've got on will dazzle any horse that gets behind me, and that it'll burn my horse so that he won't know which way he's running. And I told 'em that if they had any money to put up to the effect that this wasn't the best jockey suit in the world and guaranteed to any old kind of a race, I might be interested. And there sure appeared a lot of money."

"And did you bet?"

"Everything," answered Will.

"All your money?"

"Money?" he boomed with laughter. "Shucks, Lou, that was just the beginning. I've bet this suit, I've bet my clothes, I've bet that sidesaddle you're sitting on, I've bet my rifle and my six-shooter, and I've even bet Brigham!"

CHAPTER 5

I laughed too. So thoroughly had I absorbed the genial, happy-go-lucky attitude of this man of the plains that I could even face the possibility of absolute poverty as the result of a horse race and joke about it! But that did not mean that either Will or I was anxious to lose.

Someone shouted from the track and Will turned away. I watched his comical red figure, with that flowing blouse, those skin-tight red trousers, and the heavy cowhide boots, go along the trail and toward his horse. A moment more and he had swung into the saddle, to jog down the track toward the starting point, while I resumed my task of watching the hills.

However, I could not keep my eyes entirely away from the race-track. When everything one possesses is at stake, even the thought of Indians cannot keep one from taking a little peek once in a while—and so, now and then, my eyes would leave the hills and wander far away, a mile down the track, to where the forms of horses and men were milling about, preparatory to the start.

A sudden spurt, and I saw that the race had begun. Everything was a jumble of hazy figures except one—the red-clothed Cody stood out on those plains like a lighthouse. And, worst of all, I could see that he was not in the lead.

Hastily I turned for a look at the hills, saw that everything was serene, then looked back again. Another horse had passed Will, and he was now fourth in the race. Already more than a quarter of the distance had been covered—and if he kept dropping back that much every quarter, where on earth would our earthly possessions be?

But in the next quarter of a mile or so he seemed to hold his same position, as though that would help. I couldn't see any joy in the fact that only three horses would beat him. Everything we had, even the horse that Will Cody was riding, depended on his being first, not fourth. I watched intently, forgetting my task of lookout, forgetting everything except that my husband was fourth in that race and that—

"Mrs. Cody!" It was the voice of a woman at my side. "Do you see anything moving over on that hill?"

I turned abruptly. A second passed. Then, far away, I saw a speck show against the horizon for just an instant, then another, and another.

"Indians!" I cried.

We whirled our horses toward the crowds and started on a gallop, screaming our warning as we went. The eager watchers of the race suddenly forgot their bets. Men ran toward their mounts. A big revolver boomed forth its warning, and down on the racetrack the riders swerved from the straightaway, out into the plains, dragging forth their guns as they made the turn, the race a thing of the past now.

Hastily the men rode toward us and received what information we could give them. Then came the barking shout of one of the plainsmen, for all the world like some sort of caller for a square dance:

"Ladies toward town; gents toward the hills!"

We obeyed, while every soldier, officer, scout, and plainsman made the rush against the Indians, who undoubtedly had been attracted by the brilliant hue of Will's Little Red Riding Suit. As we hurried along, we could hear the barking of guns in the distance, and, safely at the edge of the valley, we paused to await the outcome. For there was not one of us who did not have a husband up there where the guns were sounding, a husband who might fall victim to the musket ball of some old Indian rifle or be stung by the barb of an arrow.

Anxiously we waited, then brightened, for the sounds of firing faded from the far away, and soon we could sight the forms of the returning Indian hunters. The rest of the women sought vainly to identify the men they loved, and I tried to help them. For my heart was easy. The first thing I had seen, distant though those horsemen might be, was the glaring red of Will Cody's jockey suit. And then indeed was I truly grateful for the wonderful idea of the boyish, rollicking plainsman who had brought it into being.

Gradually the men grew closer, and at last they reached us, with the information that the Indians had departed without a fight, followed by sundry revolver bullets fired at long range. There had been only one casualty—and that was the horse race. All the horses were fagged now; it would be an impossibility to get a spirited contest out of them. The bets were returned, and once again I could count our possessions as our own.

I looked upon it all as a stroke of great fortune. I sang and hummed as Will and I rode side by side back toward town. But Will's face was like a coffin. I leaned toward him laughingly.

"Cheer up, Willie," I said, "maybe Brigham was just having an off day."

"Huh?" he stared at me.

"Next time," I continued, "he'll be running in form and—"

"That's just it," came his answer, "he was running in form today."

"But what of it? You didn't lose."

"But I did."

"Do you mean"—a quick fear shot through my heart—"that anybody could want a bet on a race that wasn't finished? They couldn't make you pay for—"

Will rose in his saddle.

"Lou," he said with a sad smile, "I don't guess you understand horse racing. I lost today because I didn't win. When that Injun scare bobbed up, I had all the money in the world, right in my hands. All I needed was the home stretch and Brigham would have shot out like a skyrocket. Why, I hadn't even let it run fast enough to turn a hair!"

And I had given the alarm that had spoiled the race! But, even so, I was just as happy. Risking everything you own upon the running qualities of a scout horse is not an enjoyable thing. For once I was glad there were Indians on the plains.

But all the races were not so tempestuous. Of course, it would not have been a western affair if money had not changed hands, but, as a general thing, moderation was used. For to the horse owner, a horse race won was a vindication of good judgment, and that was reward enough for the man who loved that horse as a thing that had borne him and saved his skin more times than once.

Many times afterward I went to the little valley, and more times than one I gave the Indian alarm again. My eyes were particularly keen, and I came to be depended upon as an Indian lookout—an Indian lookout who only a few years before had been a romantically minded girl of old St. Louis, without even a dream that she someday would see adventures far wilder than those of the imaginative novels she so eagerly devoured.

An Indian lookout—but just the same, the old thought of St. Louis still lingered and grew stronger as my health began once more to fail and my nerves to become frayed and raw. I never had fully recovered from the effects of my nervous shock, and now the tired nerves were beginning to call for the comforts of home, the little luxuries that were impossible to obtain out here in the West, the niceties that were invariably lacking.

It all was a perverse viewpoint, for in truth I had come to like the West as I never had liked the closeness of the city. I had come to love the free, bright, clear air, the crispness of the atmosphere in the morning, the broad stretches, the great splotches of wonderful coloring at sunset; yet with this love in my heart, and particularly the love for the man who typified to me all that was good and wonderful in this great, open country, some Imp of the Perverse within me called continually:

"The city—the city! The smooth, paved streets, the trees, the sidewalks. The pretty windows of the stores, the fine dresses—the city, the city! That's where you want to be!"

I was homesick—homesick for something I did not really want. Such are the vagaries of one's nerves. Then, it all took definite shape, in a definite longing for one thing—something that would typify the city, that would typify luxury and comfort and ease: the straight lines of tree-fringed streets, a silly thing, perhaps, but all things are silly except when viewed by the person who believes in them. And I believed in this: I wanted a buggy, a soft-cushioned buggy with light springs and a patent-leather dashboard and a place to carry a whip. And I wanted that buggy more than anything else in the world.

But such things were not plentiful in Hays City. Kansas City was miles away, and it was from there only that such a thing could be procured.

More, I knew that my husband had no money to buy such a luxury. And so I wished in silence.

Then came the great chance. It was late one afternoon when I heard Will bounding up the stairs, three at a time. He threw open the door, and as I rose to kiss him, he lifted me in his great arms as though I were a child.

"Honey," he shouted, "we're rich! That's what! We're rich! Guess what's happened!"

"You've founded a new town!" I joked.

"Nothing like it. I'm going to get five hundred dollars a month for doing nothing."

"For w-h-a-t?"

"For doing nothing—just fooling around a little bit and using up a little ammunition. I've made a contract with Goddard Brothers to furnish all the meat for the Kansas Pacific. All I've got to do is kill twelve buffalo a day!"

"Is that all?" I laughed.

"Shucks! That's nothing at all."

And for Will Cody it *was* nothing. Those were the days when buffalo rode the plains in great herds, ranging anywhere from fifty head to five hundred, and more than once, Will had killed twenty and thirty buffalo out of a herd while on a casual hunt. Therefore, with buffalo hunting as a business, it seemed a simple matter for him to procure an average of twelve a day.

And it was. There were often stretches of two and three days at a time when Will did not stir out of Hays City. The weather was cool, permitting the meat to be kept fresh, and a large herd of buffalo invariably meant days of rest for my husband, at a salary of five hundred dollars a month. And while this lasted, the old nerve-sadness was far away.

Then came a stretch of lean days, when the buffalo roamed far from Hays City, and when it was necessary for Will and the wagons that were to transport the meat to travel day and night to procure the necessary meat for the workmen of the railroad. Then, too, the road was building farther on, and there were often camps where Will would make his headquarters instead of making the long trip back to Hays City.

And on those days, the silly, insistent call would come again for that trinket, that plaything—a buggy.

And when Will came back from his next hunt, I asked him for it. His face took on a queer expression, and he just stood and looked at me for a moment.

"Why do you want it, Lou?" he asked.

"I don't know, Will," came my answer. "I've just got a craving for it—like a person would have a craving for fruit or for water. I—I guess I'm a little homesick."

"Then I'll send you home for a visit."

"But I don't want to go home," I answered with that perversity so common to nervous prostration. "I—I just want that buggy."

"But . . ." Will's voice was slow and serious. "You would want to drive out into the country with it."

"That's just it," I broke in. "I want to go out in the evening and watch the sunsets, and feel the cool air and be free. And when you are not here, I want to go alone—just Arta and me. Will, I never go anywhere except under guard. There is always someone watching, watching all the time. I know it's for my safety—but you understand, don't you, Will?"

He came to me and patted my cheek.

"Of course I understand," he said gently. "And it's just because I understand that it hurts me. If I didn't. I would simply tell you that you couldn't have it, Lou. Buggies are slow, honey. Indians are swift. You would never escape."

"But, Will—I won't drive far."

He smiled, as though he knew that he would yield in the end.

"I'll order the buggy from Kansas City tomorrow," came his quiet reply, and the question was settled.

While we waited, Will asked me to come with him to one of the extended camps of the railroad, and I did so. The creaking old train reached there early in the morning and, leaving me in the care of the commissary steward, Will saddled his horse and hurried away. Soon a wagon appeared in the distance, and I heard a voice calling to the cook.

"Hey, Red! Something coming in. Looks like the buffalo wagon."

"Buffalo wagon, huh?" came the shouted answer. "Bill with it?"

"Nope."

"Guess it must just have a few on it then. Probably bringing 'em in while old Buffalo Bill chases the rest of the herd."

The commissary steward laughed.

"What'd you call him?"

"Buffalo Bill," answered the cook.

"Where'd you get that up?"

"Oh, it ain't mine. Got a fellow working down on the section that made up a piece of poetry about it. Runs something like:

> "Buffalo Bill, Buffalo Bill,
> Never missed and never will;
> Always aims and shoots to kill,
> And the comp'ny pays his buffalo bill!"

The commissary man doubled with laughter.

"That's shore pert!" he chuckled. "I'm going out and recite that to the bunch around here. They ain't heard it or I'd known about it before this."

Then, repeating the doggerel over and over again to be sure of memorizing it, he started forth, little knowing that he was about to perpetuate a name that would travel around the world, that would be repeated by kings and queens, presidents and regents, and that would eventually become known to every child who breathed the spirit of adventure. For thus was Buffalo Bill named, named for the buffalo that he killed that he might buy a buggy to appease the fancy of a nerve-strained, illness-weakened wife.

And how that name traveled! That afternoon, when Will, with "Lucretia Borgia," his old buffalo gun, slung across his saddle, came back from the hunt, he was greeted by grinning workmen who shouted the new title at him—nor was Will ever anything but proud to be so designated. Buffalo Bill he became that day, and Buffalo Bill he remained even after death, the typification of the old West, when the buffalo roamed the short grass and when the New World was young.

Even before we could return to Fort Hays, the name had traveled there and struck the fancy of everyone. The hotelkeeper spoke it with a smile when we came home again. The rangers and cowmen and scouts and gamblers shouted it at him along the streets. Will Cody, famous though he had been as a scout and as a hunter, now suddenly found himself invested with a new power and a new glory—through the application of a euphonious nickname.

And the name spread through the days and weeks that followed. Everyone insisted on using it, even the station agent when he came to the hotel to announce that the long-looked-for buggy had arrived. And like two children with a new plaything, Will and I went down to watch it uncrated.

A beautiful, shiny, soft-cushioned thing it was, and I was as happy as a child with a new toy. Will was quiet, his eyes serious, in spite of the joy that he took in my happiness.

"We'll go driving tonight!" I announced. Will shook his head.

"I believe we'd better wait," he said slowly.

"Maybe we'd—we'd better drive it around town for a while, until we get used to it."

"Foolish!" I laughed. "Get used to a buggy? Whoever heard of such a thing?"

"Well, Brigham's not used to it," he fenced. "And besides—"

"Will," I said plaintively, "I want to go driving this evening. Won't you take me—please?"

He turned.

"Lou," he said, "there are Injuns around—plenty of them. Every scout that comes into the fort brings some kind of a story about a brush with them. I—"

"Please, Will. We'll only go out a little ways."

Will's face suddenly took on an expression that was unlike anything I ever had seen before.

"Very well, Lou," he said quietly, and three hours later we were driving out into the country.

Will was silent—in a silence that went entirely unnoticed by me. For I was happy and chattering about everything I saw, clucking to Brigham, who seemed a bit nervous in his new outfit—he had been driven very few times in his life—humming and happy. At last, Will touched me on the arm.

"We'd better turn here," he urged.

"Oh, no. Let's go on up to the hill there. I want to watch the sunset."

"It's safer to turn here."

"But—"

"Lou, I've been a scout a good many years—"

"Yes, and you go out and risk all sorts of dangers and never worry a minute about yourself. But if I take a little buggy ride—it's just up on the hill, Will," I begged, "it's only a little ways."

I saw Will turn anxiously in the seat and look back toward town. Then he settled down again, more watchful than ever.

"Be ready to turn at any minute, Lou," he told me.

But I laughed at his fears. I was in a new world—one created by a foolish four-wheeled contraption—and I was looking at the world through rose-colored glasses. At another time, it all might have been different. But now—

I clucked to Brigham and we went on down the twisting road to the hill and started its steep ascent. The sun was just setting and, letting the reins lag, I watched it, watched the play of the colors, the changing hues, the violets merging into the lavenders, the gold and soft grays and softer pinks—only to swerve suddenly as Will jerked at the reins and, with a sharply spoken order, turned Brigham almost in his tracks. Then the whip cut through the air, lashing down upon the back of the horse and causing it almost to leap out of its harness. A cry of excitement came to my lips, only to be stifled by the voice of Cody, lapsing into the vernacular:

"Injuns! Take these reins."

Brigham was galloping now, galloping in harness, the buggy swaying and careening behind him as he rushed down the hill and on toward the winding road beyond. Will shifted in his seat and raised himself on one knee. I felt his elbow bump against me and knew that he was reaching for his revolver. Then he bent over and kissed me on the cheek.

"Lou," he called above the noise of Brigham's hoofs and the bumping of the buggy, "I want you to know that I love you better than anything else in the world. That's why I may have to do something that—that—"

"Will!"

I looked up hurriedly. Something had touched my head. It was Will's revolver, and he was holding it, pointed straight at my temple. I screamed.

"Will—Will!"

My husband looked down at me, his face old and lined and hard.

"They've got rifles," he said shortly. "I've only got this revolver. They can outdistance me. I want to be ready—so that if they get me, I can pull the trigger before I fall. It's better for a woman to be dead, Lou—than to be in their hands."

The breath seemed to have left my body. I wanted to scream, to laugh, to sing, anything except to realize that at my side was my husband, nerving himself to fire the bullet that would kill his own wife rather than allow her to fall into the hands of the pursuing enemy. On and on we went, the buggy rolling and rocking, dropping into the hollows and gulleys of the road, then bounding out again as the faithful old Brigham plunged on. Up above me, I heard Will talking to himself, as though striving for strength to hold to his resolve. With all the strength I had, I placed the reins in one hand then, with the free one, reached outward. I touched Will's arm. Then I felt his left hand, icy cold, close over mine. We sped onward.

A quarter of a mile. A half mile. Then from the distance a faint thudding sound. Will bent close to me.

"Remember, Lou," he said again, "if the worst comes—it was because I loved you."

I pressed his hand tightly and the rocking, leaping journey continued. Alternate fever and chilling cold were chasing through my veins. My teeth were chattering, my whole being aquiver. On and on, while the thudding sounds from the distance seemed to grow nearer. Then, suddenly, I felt Will swing from my side and turn in the buggy. I saw him raise his revolver and fire, straight into the air. He waved his arms and shouted.

"Hurry, Lou!" he boomed, "a little more and we're safe! Hurry—hurry!"

Again the whip cut through the air. Then, far ahead, I saw the forms of men, urging their horses forward.

"It's some of the boys," Will called to me. "I asked them to ride out along the road if we didn't get back on time."

The forms came closer. Cody waved and shouted to them and pointed to the distance. A clattering rush and they had passed us—on toward the hills and the place where a pursuing band of Indians now would become a fleeing, scattering group of fugitives. Weakly I sank forward. Dully I felt Will take the reins from my hands. Then the world went black. The slender thread of my resistance had snapped.

When consciousness came, I found myself back in the hotel with Will and a doctor by my side. I heard something about St. Louis and the necessity for waiting a few days until I should gain a little strength. Then I learned that the verdict had been passed, that the physician had ordered me home. And I—well, I cried, cried like a child who had lost her doll, cried because I felt that, after believing my battle won, I had allowed myself to be defeated.

A week later, we went back to St. Louis, Will and Arta and me. Again, in Old Frenchtown, Will said goodbye to me, there on the little veranda where first he had told me the story of his boyhood, and told me:

"I'll be waiting, Lou—but you must not come back until you are well and strong again. You'll promise?"

"I promise," was my answer. But the promise was not to be fulfilled for many months, and then only for a visit.

It was more than a year afterward that I went downtown one afternoon, suddenly to be halted by a glaring poster, flaunting forth from a wall:

GRAND EXCURSION
TO
FORT SHERIDAN
KANSAS PACIFIC RAILROAD
BUFFALO SHOOTING MATCH

FOR
$500 A SIDE
AND THE
CHAMPIONSHIP OF THE WORLD
BETWEEN
BILLY COMSTOCK (The famous scout)[1]
AND
W. F. CODY (Buffalo Bill)
FAMOUS BUFFALO KILLER FOR THE
KANSAS PACIFIC RAILROAD

And with that, all the pent-up longing for the West that I had resisted so strongly during the months of illness that had followed my arrival in St. Louis surged up again in me. There, in that glaring sign, the West called to me, the wide stretches of the prairie, the twisting, winding roads, the faint sight of wagon trains in the distance, and the jackrabbit bobbing over the soapweed. I wanted to go back home—for the sudden realization came over me that St. Louis no longer was home, that it was a quiet, staid, tame old city, that it was cramped and crowded, that even the trees that lined the streets were prisoners of the sidewalk and the curb, prisoners just like me.

I wanted to be where the smoke did not hang in the atmosphere on gray days, where the sun shone bright and keen and where life was as free as the air. Quickly I changed my course. Within fifteen minutes, a telegram was traveling to my husband, telling him that I believed I had improved sufficiently to allow me to visit him and to attend the match. And when the excursion train, with its flare-stacked locomotive, pulled out of the station at St. Louis, it carried two passengers as eager to reach the end of the journey as the man who awaited them was anxious to receive them. Arta and I were Westward bound once more, traveling toward Fort Sheridan, to see Buffalo Bill, our Buffalo Bill, shoot bison for the championship of the world.

CHAPTER 6

The excursion consisted of about one hundred men and women from St. Louis—travel to Kansas in those days cost a great deal more than it does even in these days of advanced railroad rates. The journey was a long one, and a tiresome one, but not one of us regretted it. This was especially true of me. I was going back to the West.

For forty-eight hours the old train dragged along, then it stopped twenty miles east of Fort Sheridan. There wagons and horses awaited the excursionists, and an anxious buffalo killer sought out Arta and me. It was early morning, and soon after the greetings, we were on our way to the buffalo grounds.

The bison were especially plentiful in the vicinity of Fort Sheridan, the reason this place had been selected. Billy Comstock was a famous scout and buffalo killer from Fort Wallace, and as usual, it all had started in an argument. So now, in front of visitors from hundreds of miles away, the matter was to be settled.

Not that the buffalo were to be run before the spectators and killed á la carte. A sight of the various "runs" might perhaps mean miles of trailing far in the rear of the hunters, until the sound of the guns should give the signal that the shooting had begun and that the buffalo were too busy to notice anything except the hunters who had pounced upon them. And every one of those hundred excursionists was more than willing to make the trip.

However, the journey was not as long as had been expected. Hardly a mile from the starting point, Will sighted a herd of nearly two hundred buffalo, and the excursionists assembled on a hill from which they could watch practically the entire operation of the first "run," as the onslaughts were called. Referees were appointed, their watches set together, and the two contestants given a certain amount of time from the moment they ran their horses into the herd, separating their groups, to kill as many of the great, hulking animals as possible. Will was riding Brigham and carried the old gun that had served him so well on his hunts for the Kansas Pacific, "Lucretia Borgia." Comstock was on a horse that he prized as much as Cody prized Brigham, and he carried a gun in which he believed with equal faith. The two men struck their mark. The referee waved a hand.

"Go!" came the shout. The horses and riders plunged forward, the referee and his assistants hurrying behind, while tenderfoot men and women from St. Louis gripped their hands in excitement, and while my eyes followed the man I felt sure would win—my husband.

The herd was grazing in a slight valley and did not notice the approach of the hunters until they were almost on them. Straight into the center of the throng of shaggy beasts rode Cody and Comstock, separating the herd, Comstock taking the right half and Cody the left. Then, as the two halves started in opposite directions, Comstock began firing as he worked his way swiftly to the rear. Three buffalo dropped. Will had not fired a shot.

"Something's wrong with his gun—something must be wrong with it! Why doesn't he shoot?"

The queries were coming from all around me, but I only smiled to myself and held Arta close to me, to conceal the excitement I felt. Too many times had Will told me of the plan he had formed for hunting buffalo and slaying them in large numbers—and I knew that now he was making his arrangements for the carrying out of exactly that method. Comstock had gone to the rear of his herd and was driving it, firing as he went. Already he was far down the valley, leaving a string of four more buffalo behind. And still Buffalo Bill's gun was silent.

Then suddenly came a shout and pointing fingers. Cody had worked his way ahead of the herd and slightly to one side. Quickly he swerved and, riding straight past the beasts, fired as quickly as his gun would permit him. The leaders were dropped in their tracks, stopping the rush of buffalo from behind, and causing the whole herd to mill and hesitate.

Just as quickly, Will circled again and came back against the herd. Those were not the days of the repeating and automatic rifles. Firing was comparatively slow. A shot, then the gun must be loaded again, and while this was going on, the milling of the herd still held the target in place and awaiting death. Again and again the crack of old "Lucretia Borgia" sounded. Again and again the buffalo dropped, always in a place that would impede the progress of the herd and cause it to hesitate in its plunging rush as it sought a new avenue of escape. Now ten buffalo showed on the plains as a result of my husband's marksmanship. The number went to fifteen, to twenty, to twenty-five, to thirty, to thirty-five, to thirty-six—seven—eight—

A wave of the arm. The referee's assistant, following my husband, had called time. Three miles away, where the other assistant followed Comstock, time was being called also. And when the count was made, it was found that, in those three miles of chasing the herd, Comstock had killed twenty-three buffalo, while in a space of hardly three hundred yards, Buffalo Bill had killed almost twice as many.

A short rest came then, while from the wagons came a miraculous thing. It was champagne, and great hampers of dainties, brought out from St. Louis by the rich excursionists and served there on the plains, with dead buffalo lying all about—the dainty confections of the approximate East in the atmosphere of the West.

An hour, then Cody and Comstock started forth again. This time the search was longer, and the guns had been booming for some time when the excursionists came in sight of the hunters. The herd had been smaller this time, and just as the scene came into view, Will was finishing the last three buffalo of his half, while Comstock was vainly trying to prevent the remainder of his herd from escaping him.

Suddenly the herd swerved and plunged straight at him and his referee. Comstock, by a quick move, escaped, but the referee did not have the same good fortune. A second later, white-faced men and screaming women saw the horse of the referee lifted on the horns of a great bull buffalo, tossed high into the air, then dropped, writhing in its death agonies, while the referee, dusty and limping, dragged himself up from the spot where he had been thrown, fully thirty feet away. Comstock's run was ended—and we did not approach the hunting field. We had seen almost enough.

However, there was one more run yet to come, and with the exception of some of the St. Louis women who, white-faced and weak, returned to the train, all of us stayed to watch it. Will, with his inevitable love of the theatrical, suddenly beamed with an inspiration.

"I just think," he announced, as he crammed down a dainty sandwich and reached for another, "that I'll see if I can't even up this score a little. It's getting terribly one sided."

"Oh, don't sympathize with me!" Billy Comstock was helping his referee, who insisted on officiating again, in loosening up his wrenched ankle. "I'll manage to get along all right."

Will smiled.

"Well, then, you'll let me have a little enjoyment for my own sake, won't you?"

"Go ahead and kill yourself if you want to," came the joking reply of his contestant. "But I'm going to kill buffalo."

"So am I," answered my husband. "But this time I'm going to do it with a horse that hasn't either a bridle or saddle."

There were gasps of astonishment—and I believe that the loudest came from me.

"Will!" I begged, "please don't. Please—"

But Will only grinned and patted my hand.

"Shucks, Mamma," he said, "Old Brigham knows more about killing buffalo than I do myself."

"But if you should get caught in the herd—"

"Old Brigham will get me out again."

And while the crowd—and that included me—waited excitedly, Will quietly removed the bridle and saddle from Brigham and calmly examined his rifle.

Meanwhile, scouts showed on the horizon, with the information that a small herd of buffalo had been sighted about four miles away, coming in this direction. A leap and Cody was on Brigham's back. Comstock reached his horse and mounted it. The referees took their places and the hunters were gone; the excursionists, their wagons bumping along the road, following as fast as they could. As for me, the wagon seemed fairly to crawl. My husband, riding without saddle and without bridle, guiding his horse only by oral commands, was fading farther and farther in the distance, while, like some prisoner going to an execution, I was following, perhaps to see him killed or maimed. Yet I wanted to be there—if accident should happen, I could at least be near him, at least be where he could speak to me and I to him.

The slow ascent of a long hill—then the wagons leaped forward with a rush. Far down in the valley, the two hunters were galloping toward the herd, to separate them and to start their "runs." I looked for Will—he was slightly in the lead, Old Brigham carrying him swiftly and safely forward toward the objects of the hunt.

A sudden blurring as the two horsemen struck the herd, to be lost to sight for a moment. Then Comstock showed, turning his half of the herd and driving it before him, while he struggled to urge his tired horse to enough speed to reach a sure shooting distance. I strained my eyes, but for a moment I could not see Will. My heart seemed to stop beating. My hands, tightly clasped, were cold and wet and lifeless.

Then a cry of gladness came to my lips. Out from the side of the herd, where he had almost been lying on his horse's back to conceal his presence from the buffalo at the rear, shot Will and Brigham, swinging far in front of the plunging beasts, then suddenly turning. The thudding pop of a rifle sounded from far away, and we saw the buffalo pile up as they stumbled and plunged over the body of a fallen comrade; stop, wheel, and start in another direction.

But Cody was there before them. Old Brigham, bridleless though he might be, was working at the best game he knew, a game he had played practically all of his equine life, and he needed few orders. My fears departed. The worst was over, the herd had been reached and separated.

x "My husband will kill every one of them!" I prophesied. And my opinion was correct.

One after another they fell, until only one was left, a great shaggy bull that plunged forward with a speed that equaled Brigham's, and that seemed intent on coming straight toward us!

Nearer and nearer he approached, with Cody hurrying along in the rear. The half mile lessened to a quarter, then to an eighth, while nervousness began to make its appearance everywhere, and while Cody still raced along on Brigham, his rifle hanging loosely in his hand, his eyes intent on the buffalo. Suddenly fear appeared.

"Why doesn't he shoot?"

Someone asked the question spasmodically. Immediately panic began to reach the brains of the spectators.

"Maybe he's out of ammunition. Maybe—"

The buffalo was only a few hundred yards away now. Women were screaming, men helping them into the wagons. Others were running. But I stood in my position and laughed. I knew that Will Cody would have headed off that buffalo and started it in another direction if there had been danger. I was there and Arta was there, laughing and clapping her hands as she watched her father race after the plunging bison.

The hundred yards or so changed to a hundred feet, while spectators screamed and shouted. Then, just as the buffalo headed straight toward the wagons, Will Cody raised his rifle and fired. The beast leaped high into the air. Its heavy, shaggy shoulders seemed to unbalance its body. It somersaulted, rolled, struggled a moment, then lay still in death, at the very tongue of the first wagon.

Meanwhile, far in the distance, the forms of Billy Comstock and his referee showed themselves, coming back after a wild chase. His buffalo had scattered, with the result that from his end of the herd he had been able to kill only five, while my husband had added thirteen more to his score, making a total of sixty-nine against Comstock's forty-six and adding a new record to the name of Buffalo Bill.

That night, in Fort Sheridan, Will and I sat in our room in the hotel. He had Arta on his lap and was fondling her and chucking her under the chin, his big voice booming, his every action as fresh and bright as though the killing of sixty-nine buffalo in a day was nothing more than a bit of morning exercise. Suddenly, as with a sudden thought, he looked up.

"Mamma," he said, "how do you like being Mrs. Buffalo Bill?"

"Land sakes, Will," I answered him, "whatever made you ask that question? You know I'm as happy as a bug in a rug."

"Oh, I know that," he bantered, "but I mean the 'Buffalo Bill' part."

"Fine," I said, "but why did you ask?"

"Oh," he joked, "I just happened to think that you can't very well be Mrs. Buffalo Bill without being able to say that you've killed a buffalo."

"You mean for me to kill a buffalo? Well! I wouldn't be afraid to."

"Huh? What's that?" Will had straightened. I had known that he had expected me to be afraid. And so I had just taken the opposite angle. "You wouldn't be afraid to kill a buffalo?"

"If my husband can kill them, I can too."

"Well, I'm a son of a sea cook! By golly!" He let out a roaring laugh and jiggled Arta high in the air. "I'm just going to see whether you'll be afraid or not. Want to go along, Arta? 'Course you do! I'll strap you right on your mother's lap and let you take part in the festivities too! That's what! How's tomorrow?" he asked, turning to me. "Think you'd kind of like to take a little buffalo hunt in the morning?"

"I—I—" The denial was on my lips, but I checked it. I had gone this far and there was no turning back. I smiled, as though the killing of a buffalo were nothing in the world. "Why certainly. Just any time you want to go, Will, I'd be delighted!"

"You—would?"

"I'd just love it!"

But when bedtime came and the lights were out and I should have been asleep, I was wide-eyed and staring into the darkness, watching imaginary buffalo herds as they circled about and plunged toward me, their great shaggy shoulders rocking and bounding, their heavy heads lowered and menacing. I tried to sleep—but sleep was impossible. In the morning, I was going to hunt buffalo, with my baby strapped on my lap. And I didn't like that part of it.

Will awoke early the next morning, but I was up before him, cleaning my revolver, which I had dragged out of my trunk, and wishing for the time to start. Now that I was into it, I wanted to get it over just as quickly as possible. As for Will—

"What've you got in your mind, anyway?" he asked as he stopped and watched me.

"Killing buffalo," I told him and smiled.

Whereupon he chuckled and walked away, picking up Arta as he went along and carrying her on his shoulder. At last he turned.

"Are you really serious?" He grinned.

"Are you?" I countered laughingly. Daylight had brought me a good deal more courage.

"Well, I asked you first."

"And I asked you."

So there things stood. Will chuckled again, lowered Arta from her exalted position, and started for the door.

"By golly," he said with one of his sudden resolves, "I just believe you're gritty enough to do it! And I'll be darned if I ain't going to see if you will! Trot down to breakfast, while I go get the horses."

A half hour later we were making our way out of town and toward the broad stretches of the plains. I was riding Brigham, with a sidesaddle, and Arta had been strapped securely to my lap with broad straps that went around the hooks of the saddle and then about my waist. At my side hung my big revolver, one that Will had given me after I had demonstrated my ability to use it. And strangely enough, many of my apprehensions had vanished. I was on Old Brigham, and I knew that my sole task would be to fire the shot with the proper aim behind it. Brigham would do all the necessary thinking and maneuvering.

However, the nearness of the hunt was beginning to have the opposite effect on Will. When we had started from town, he was laughing and joking and whistling, but now, as we neared the buffalo grounds, he became more and more serious. Suddenly he started and rose in his saddle.

"Buffalo," he said shortly.

A thrill went through me, but strangely enough, it was not the thrill of fear. I suppose there is something about the hunt that gets into one's blood—for years, several years, at least, I had lived in the atmosphere of it, hearing about the exciting adventures, about the plunging beasts and the zest of it all, without absorbing it. But now I was at the very edge of that excitement myself, and it was like wine in my veins. I reached to my holster to assure myself of the presence of my revolver. Then I called to Will:

"I'm ready whenever you are."

"You're sure you're not afraid?" he asked quickly.

"Honestly, Will. I—I was last night. I was just joking when it all started, and I was scared to death last night. But now—honestly, Will, I want to see if I can kill a buffalo."

He rode close to me and leaned and kissed Arta and me.

"You're absolutely sure?"

"Absolutely," I answered.

"All right, then," came his reply. "You'll be safe. There's very little danger unless you get rattled and lose your head. Let Brigham handle the situation and don't try to ride him anyplace he doesn't want to go. Keep your whole mind centered on shooting. And remember to put the bullet right under the left shoulder."

"I'll remember," I said.

We started forward. A mile farther and we approached the buffalo herd, which was grazing and paying little attention to our approach. Will swerved to me again.

"I'm not going to let you hunt the whole herd. I'll scatter them and bring some toward you. All right. *Pronto!*"

Our horses leaped forward and we sped to the herd. A few hundred feet away from the bison, Will sped ahead of me and drove his horse straight into the mass of shaggy beasts. They split and fled, while Will cut out four or five and began to circle them toward me. Then he waved his arm, the signal for me to begin my hunt.

My heart was pounding like a triphammer. The whole world was hazy—hazy except for those plunging buffalo, upon which my every attention was centered. I knew what to do—Will was on the opposite side of the beasts, his rifle ready for an instant shot should anything go wrong, his horse keeping pace with the fleeing animals, his eyes watching their every movement.

I gave the word to Brigham and while Arta, strapped to my lap, laughed and gurgled and clapped her little hands, we galloped forward.

One great, heavy humped buffalo had moved out a few yards from the rest of the stragglers, and Will waved an arm to me to indicate that this was the one I should down. I turned Brigham toward him, and the chase began.

For nearly a mile we raced, gradually cutting down the distance between the buffalo and me. Then slowly we began to overtake him.

Only a few rods separated us, and I raised my revolver as though to fire. But Will anxiously waved me down.

"Closer!" I could not hear the word, but I could see his lips as he framed it. Even Old Brigham seemed to understand that I was about to make a mistake, for he suddenly plunged forward with a new speed, cutting down the distance between the speeding bison and me. Soon the distance was cut in two. Now to a third. Again I raised my revolver, and this time Will did not object. There was a puff of smoke, the booming of the heavy gun, and then—

Then, with a thrill that I never again shall know, I saw the buffalo stumble, stagger a second, and fall headlong. From behind came a wild sound, and I saw Will standing in his stirrups and whooping like a wild Indian.

"You got him, Mamma," he shouted. "I knew you could do it—knew it all the time!"

As for Arta, she was laughing and patting her little hands and having the time of her young life, while I—well, I must confess that I laughed a little hysterically and that my hand was shaking as though with a chill. I had killed my buffalo and with the first shot. Will sent his horse plunging to my side.

"Don't stop with one," he called to me, "make a record for yourself. Let's go after the rest of them."

I agreed, and once more Old Brigham broke into a gallop, as Will and I started after the other stragglers of the herd. Soon we were abreast of another, and once more my revolver was raised.

But this time my aim was unsteady. I still was nervous from the excitement of the first killing, and the gun would not hold true. Here and there it bobbed while I, seeking to steady my aim, let second after second pass. Vaguely I heard a voice shouting:

"Shoot—shoot!"

I pulled the trigger and then cried out with happiness. For again a buffalo had plunged and tumbled, pawed uncertainly at the ground, then lain still. Proudly I turned to Will.

"I guess that's pretty good shooting," I said haughtily. My husband's lips began to spread in a wide grin.

"Certainly is," he agreed. "Some of the best shooting I ever did in my life."

"That *you* ever did?"

"Uh-huh," came his solemn answer. "I had to time it pretty well to make it fit right in with your shot, but I did it. Yes, sir, that's pretty good shooting, if I do say it myself."

I stared.

"Why, Will Cody," I asked, "what on earth are you talking about."

"Killin' buffalo," he answered. "You see, I could tell from the way that shooting iron was wobbling around in your hand that you were liable to make a miss. And I knew that if you did that, you'd probably wound that old bull just enough to make him rambunctious. So, when you shot, I shot too, just to make things sure. And by golly, from the looks of things, I was right."

We were at the side of the dead buffalo now, and I could see the blood still flowing from two wounds. One was a jagged, rough affair below his neck, where the bullet from my revolver had torn its way along, just under the skin, doing nothing more than to make an ugly flesh wound. The other hole was clean and sharp, driving under the left shoulder and in a position to pierce the heart. Will grinned again.

"Come to think of it, Mamma," he chuckled, "we ain't such a bad team, are we?"

But my reputation as a buffalo huntress had been tarnished, and I said so. Will was for going home, but I wanted another chance—and he gave it to me. The main herd of bison had stopped its flight about a mile and a half away, and we rode toward it, this time attacking the whole herd, Will riding just a few feet behind me on the inside, next to the plunging animals, and ready at any moment to protect me with a quick shot, in case of accident.

But this time I needed no help. I had reloaded my revolver, and, riding close to the herd, fired at the nearest animal. It dropped. Then, as the bison behind it hesitated at the sight of the toppling beast before it, I fired again. This time the shot went slightly wide of its mark, and I pulled the trigger twice more before the animal could turn to plunge at me. It also fell. Then, as the herd went milling away, I restored my gun to its holster.

"There," I said proudly, "I guess that vindicates Mrs. Buffalo Bill."

"It sure does!" Will agreed happily. "I'm kind of thinking of taking a few weeks' vacation and letting you do the hunting for the family!"

But it was I who took the vacation, for, while I had greatly improved physically, both Will and I knew that a further rest back in St. Louis would do me no harm.

More than that, the Kansas Pacific was building farther and farther west every day. There were few accommodations now, and it would have meant a life of camping on the plains, with the accompanying dangers of Indian attacks, were I to remain with Will. Not that I would have feared these risks to have remained with my husband—but both Will and I had something else to consider—Arta, the baby. And when there was no necessity, we felt that we should not face the danger. So the baby and I went back to St. Louis, to wait until my husband should finish the contract that had given him his title, that of Buffalo Bill.

The conclusion of this took nearly six months longer, with the result that in May 1868 Will ended his career as a professional buffalo hunter, after having killed, with the rifle, 4,280 bison in a space of about eighteen months. And when I look back upon it, I cannot help reflecting how things have changed in this country of ours, how the waste of yesterday has given way before the enforced economy of today—and how much might have been saved to this generation if the West had only known and understood that the glorious days of plenty would not last forever.

Of those 4,280 buffalo that Will killed, only the humps and hindquarters were used, the rest of the bodies, with the exception of the heads, being left to rot on the plains. The heads Will always took in to the Kansas Pacific, where they were forwarded to a taxidermist for distribution throughout the country. And today, when you look upon the great, shaggy head of a buffalo in the railroad offices of the lines that succeeded the Kansas Pacific Railroad, you are looking on the head of one of the victims of old "Lucretia Borgia," for my husband, Buffalo Bill, furnished practically every one of those souvenirs of the West.

As for the parts of the bison that were left to rot . . . A buffalo rarely weighed less than 1,000 pounds, in edible meat. Of this, less than a third was taken for the consumption of the laborers on the Kansas Pacific. That meant, out of the hunting that my husband alone did in those eighteen months, nearly three million pounds of meat was left on the plains. And only a half hour ago my butcher coolly informed me that steaks had taken another jump, and that my favorite cut would henceforth cost 55 cents a pound!

CHAPTER 7

When the contract with the Kansas Pacific ended, Will resumed his vocation as a scout, this time serving under General Sheridan in his campaigns against the Indians in western Kansas, Colorado, and even in what is now New Mexico.[1] Arta and I, of course, were in St. Louis, and there we remained, while I gained strength and health for what was to be one of the really strenuous periods of my life. But that comes later.

It was during the few months that Will served under Sheridan that he made the ride that won him fame through the West as a dispatch bearer and a man who could stand the utmost amount of fatigue without giving way beneath it. Letters, which long ago became yellowed and brittle with age, told me the progressive story of that ride, letters that I read in the shade of the old trees that fringed the street in front of my home in old St. Louis, and which caused me to thrill with a homesickness for the West. For I was a Western woman now as I never had been before. I was growing strong and healthy, and I wanted the West. I wanted to feel the spring of a horse beneath me, the thrill of danger—yes, even the horror of fear, for that had become a part of my life. So, I waited for those letters as one would wait for the installments of a thrilling novel. And they had an unusual story of bravery and stamina to tell.

It was just after an encounter with Indian warriors under Old Santanta, a vicious Kiowa chief, that my husband rode into Fort Larned, Kansas, to learn that Captain Parker, the commanding officer, had been seeking him anxiously to carry some messages to General Sheridan, then in Fort Hays.[2] The country was full of Indians, fugitives from the Camp of Santanta, which had been broken up by the soldiers and scouts under Will's command, and the ride meant danger.

However, Will took the dispatches, slowly worked his way through the Indian country, rode straight into an Indian camp in the darkness, stampeded the horses that were tethered there, got out again before the savages could assemble enough horseflesh to pursue him, and at break of day delivered the messages personally to General Sheridan at Fort Hays. Then he rode over to the Perry Hotel, where formerly we had lived, took a nap of two hours, and reported back to the general.

General Sheridan, in the meanwhile, had found the necessity for sending some dispatches to Dodge City, ninety miles away. These Will volunteered to take, and within an hour he was in the saddle and away again. At ten o'clock that night he reached the fort and delivered his messages to the commanding officer, only to learn that there had been fresh Indian outbreaks on the Arkansas River between Fort Dodge and Fort Larned, about sixty-five miles away, and that other scouts had been reluctant to carry the messages because of the dangers attendant on the ride. Cody asked for a few hours for rest, then he reported to the commanding officer that he was ready to make the ride, and that all he wanted was a fresh horse.

But there were no fresh horses available. The only thing that the post could offer was a government mule. Will took him, jogging out of the fort and urging the tough-mouthed old beast along as fast as he could—which was hardly express speed. Everything went well, however, until Will reached Coon Creek, about thirty-five miles from Fort Larned, where he dismounted and led the mule down to the stream to drink. As he did so, the contrary old government animal jerked away from Will, showed the first burst of speed since the start at Fort Dodge, and ran down the valley. Will followed, hoping that he would stop—but there was no stopping for that mule. Finally he got back on the road again and started a jogging trot toward Fort Larned, while Will trailed along in the rear. And that procession kept up through the night, Will walking the thirty-five miles with the sight of a riding animal always just before him, but always out of reach.

Will, when he got really and truly angry, didn't have the sweetest temper in the world. And by the time the sun rose, he was just about ten degrees higher than fever heat in his attitude toward that mule.

Suddenly, the soldiers in Fort Larned heard the sound of a shot about a half mile away. Then another and another and another. When they reached the place where the shooting had occurred, they found Will standing over a dead mule, cussing energetically.

"Boys," he said, "there's the toughest, meanest mule I ever saw in my life. He made me walk all night and I decided that he wouldn't ever do that to another fellow. So I executed him, and I'll be jiggered if it didn't take six shots to make him stop kicking!"

Will delivered his messages, but his work was not yet over. There were rush dispatches to go back to General Sheridan at Fort Hays, and the next morning Will rode into the general's office and presented them, after having ridden, horseback and muleback, and walked 355 miles in fifty-eight hours, and with practically no rest. And all of this following a day and a night in the saddle during the trailing of Santanta's Indian band and the battle that followed! Is it any wonder, therefore, when I look back upon such accomplishments as this, that I feel a pride in having been the wife of Buffalo Bill, an honor that can be equaled by few women in the world?

By this time Will had the rank of colonel and was chief of scouts wherever he served. It was not long until he was transferred by General Sheridan to the Fifth Cavalry, under Brevet Major General E. A. Carr, as the chief of scouts, in the campaign of that regiment against the "Dog Soldiers," a group of renegade Indians that was wandering about the country, destroying settlements and killing pioneers throughout the entire western district of Kansas.[3] A winter campaign was made, then one in the summer, and it was during this time that the battle of Summit Springs occurred.[4]

Back in old St. Louis, I picked up the paper one morning to see the name of "Buffalo Bill" staring at me from the headlines. There had been a terrific battle in the West; a great Indian camp had been attacked by General Carr's command, just after the discovery had been made by Buffalo Bill of the burning of a wagon train. Tracks had been seen leading away in the sand, which showed that the Indians had captured two white women and that they were being taken to the Sioux camp. The Fifth Cavalry had followed, an attack had been made, and one of the women, a Mrs. Weichel, the wife of a Swedish settler, had been rescued. The other, Mrs. Alderdice, had been killed by the squaw of the Indian chief, Tall Bull.[5]

And, according to the story in the newspaper, the rescue of Mrs. Weichel had been thrilling. Tall Bull had her by her hair and was just raising his tomahawk, when there suddenly sounded the rush of hoofs and the banging of a gun in the hands of Buffalo Bill, with the result that another renegade had traveled to the happy hunting grounds.

So much for the story in the newspaper. Just the other day I picked up a history of the West, and there again read the account of that rescue and the blood-chilling killing of Tall Bull. But sometimes, even history can be wrong. For instance—

It was not long afterward that I heard the booming of a big voice, and I rushed out of the house, followed by Arta, to the embrace of my husband's great, strong arms.

"Got a month's leave," he announced. "Couldn't stay away any longer, Lou. And what's more, I've got big news! We're going to have a home!"

But I could only stare at him. It was my husband, and yet it was not my husband. Where the close-cropped hair were long, flowing curls now. A mustache weaved its way outward from his upper lip, while a small goatee showed black and spot-like on his chin. Even the news of a home-to-be could not take away the astonishment.

"What on earth have you done, Will?" I asked.

"Just grown whiskers and a little hair," he announced. "Like it?"

"It isn't a bit becoming," I said with a woman's air of appraisal. "What on earth did you grow it for?"

"Why, I had to," he explained boyishly. "It's the fashion out West now. You're not a regular scout unless you've got this sort of a rigout."

He pointed generally to himself, and I noticed the beaded buckskin coat, leggings and beaded cuffs. But I had seen all that before. It was the arrangement of hair that had stunned me—there was a womanish something about it all. Perhaps I had been too long in St. Louis.

"Well, I can't say it's very becoming," I objected again. Will appeared pained.

"If—if you don't like it, Lou," he said lugubriously, "I'll cut it off. Only—only I'd be kind of out of place with the boys, and—"

I had caught the disappointment in his eyes and was laughing.

"Oh, go on, Will," I prevaricated, "I was just fooling you to see what you'd say. I really think it's quite nice."

"Honest?" He brightened.

"Of course I do. I wouldn't have you cut it off for the world!"

And if I could have looked ahead into the years that were to follow, when that long hair was to turn to white, when that goatee and mustache and countenance were to be known to every boy and girl throughout the United States, and a great share of the world, there would have been a great deal more of sincerity in that sentence. I'm afraid that even with the stories of his prowess on the plains, Buffalo Bill would not have been Buffalo Bill without that long hair, without that mustache and that little goatee—at least, he would not have been the unusual-appearing character that he was, nor would he have been as handsome. And sometimes, as I look at his picture now—and long for the time when I can be with him again—I shudder a little at the thought of what a woman's whim might have done.

As for Will and me, the subject of coiffures was quickly lost in the news he had brought. He was going to be sent to Fort McPherson, to be stationed permanently there as long as he desired. He still was to carry the title and rank of colonel, and already the soldiers were building a little log cabin, just outside the fort, that was to be our home. Before long, I could again turn my face toward the West, this time to stay.

It was during this visit that I got out the newspaper that told the story of the battle of Summit Springs and of the killing of Tall Bull.

"I'm terribly proud of that," I said as I showed him the clipping. Will read, then that amused grin came to his lips.

"Only one trouble with it," he told me at last, "and that is that I didn't do any rescuing. But, Lou, I sure did get a wonderful horse!"

"But what's the horse got to do with the killing of Tall Bull?"

"Well, just about everything in the world. I'm not going to work myself half to death to kill an Injun just for the fun of it. You see, after I'd found those footprints and all that sort of thing, we made an attack on the camp and all the Injuns ran away. Well, we got the body of Mrs. Alderdice buried and Mrs. Weichel fixed up all right—the old squaw had chopped her up some with that hatchet—and then, all of a sudden, I saw the Injuns coming back. The next thing we knew, we were all fighting fit to kill and there were more Injuns flying around there than you could shake a stick at.

"Then, all of a sudden, I noticed an old chief yapping around and begging his warriors to fight until they died, and, Lou, he was riding the most beautiful horse that I ever saw in my life. So I just said to myself that I'd get that horse.

"But I didn't want to take a chance on wounding it. There was a gulley right along the battlefield, so I started to sneak down it. An Injun up on the hill saw me and began pecking away at me with his gun, and I had to turn around and shoot him before I could get any peace and quiet. Then about a hundred feet farther on, another one bobbed up and started to make motions with his gun, and I had to put him away too. By this time I was getting pretty near disgusted. And then, when I slipped on a rock and skinned my knee, I just sat down and cussed.

"But I kept on, and finally I picked myself out a place where I knew that Injun would pass if he kept on exhorting his warriors the way he had been. I was pretty much inside the Injun lines now, and most any minute one of those tomahawkers might come along and begin carving on me—but I wanted that horse. And, by golly, I got him. First thing I knew, along sailed old Tall Bull, talking and yelling fit to kill, and I decided to stop the whole shooting match right then and get some peace around there, to say nothing of that horse. So I just up and banged away, and, Lou, I've got the finest riding horse now that you ever looked at."

So that is the story of the killing of Tall Bull that Buffalo Bill told me, his wife. Many times afterward he laughed at the historical account of the killing—one out of the many heroic things with which he is credited that he did not accomplish. Nor did he ever claim it.

A glorious, happy month there in old St. Louis, then Will went away again. But we were to meet soon, this time not to part for years.

It was late in August 1869 that I stepped off the train in Omaha to find Will awaiting Arta and me. Then together we made our way by rail and wagon train out to Fort McPherson, on the forks of the North and South Platte, twenty miles south of which is now North Platte, Nebraska.

Only a frontier trading post it was, with the houses of the few settlers and traders a few hundred yards from the fort proper. And there, in the trading post of William Reed, we stayed until the log house was completed.

A wonderful thing it was, according to the standards of the West in those days. The commanding officer of the fort had allowed Will to take a number of tents that had been condemned, and with these the walls had been lined, after a chinking of mud had been placed against all the logs. An old army stove had been procured somewhere and set up in the kitchen to serve as a combination instrument of heating and cooking. Then, with the first wagon train from Cheyenne, bearing the furniture that Will had ordered, we moved into our new home.

But Will seemed worried. Something was missing. Piece after piece of furniture, such as it was, we unpacked; bundle after bundle we opened, but the object of his search did not make its appearance. At last there was nothing left to investigate, and Will straightened up from his work.

"Guess I've got to ride into Cheyenne and get it myself," he said with an air of finality.

"Get what?" I asked.

"Not going to tell you," came his answer. "It's a surprise. Of course, they had to go and leave it out. But never mind, I'll bring it back."

Cheyenne was far more than a hundred miles away, but Will kissed the baby and me and walked out to his horse like a man going down to the drug store for a cigar. Soon he had faded in the distance as his horse scurried over the sandhills, not to appear until days later. Then, dusty, but radiant, he dropped from his horse and lugged a bundle into the house.

"There it is!" he proclaimed proudly. "There's something worth looking at!"

I opened the bundle. It was wallpaper!

It was not exactly what he had wanted, to be sure. The flowers were small, and the background placid. But it was wallpaper and that was all that counted. Will looked about him appraisingly.

"Got any flour?" he asked.

"Plenty."

"Put some of it on the stove and heat it up—you know—with water. Think I'll do a little paper hanging."

"But, Will, can't the soldiers—"

"Nope! Any wallpaper that I have to go to Cheyenne to get, I'll paste up. Might as well make it a good job all the way around."

Whereupon, while I prepared the paste, Will departed for Mr. Reed's store, to return a few moments later lugging a rickety stepladder and a broad paintbrush. Then he spread a roll of wallpaper on the floor and began to sop it with paste.

And from then on, things happened. Will got paste in his eyes; he got paste in his hair and paste in his mustache. One strip would hang beautiful and straight; another would take a sudden notion to curl and crinkle, while Will, balancing himself on the rickety stepladder, would sing and whistle and say things to himself—and now and then I would walk out into our little yard and let him get the cuss words out of his system that I knew were seething there. Then I would come back, Arta at my side, to watch the wonderful operation of papering our home.

Had Will continued at the job, it undoubtedly would have been a marvelous piece of work. Sometimes the flowers matched; most of the time they didn't. Sometimes the paper was cut too short and sometimes too long. Often it curled and crinkled like some old, dried piece of parchment and positively refused to take any definite position on the canvas whatever. But Will persisted at his self-appointed task, and it was not until the rickety old ladder, groaning and grunting under his weight, finally brought him, his brush, and half the wallpaper clattering down upon the floor that he decided to retire from the field of operations.

Carefully I unwound the paper from about his neck and shoulders, where most of it had settled, sticking to his buckskin coat with a tenacity that it had never shown on the wall, whitening his mustache and goatee and hair, and giving him much of the appearance that one sees in a motion picture after the throwing of the fateful custard pie. Just as carefully Will arose and stared at the wrecked result of his efforts as an interior decorator. He rubbed his brow with a pasty hand.

"I guess I'm more of a success as an Injun killer," he mused, and the job was left to the soldiers.

They showed more aptitude, with the result that Will and Arta and I soon had a cozy, happy little home. Fall was coming, and with it the cold snap of the wind and now and then a flurry of snow, or the sweeping swirl of a sandstorm. But we did not mind. We were happy and comfortable and warm, sitting by the fire o' nights, Will with Arta on his lap, telling her stories of the days when she was a wee, tiny baby, and when her mother was a tenderfoot straight from the big city, and oh, so afraid of the West. Will always loved to tell those things—and all for the reason that he knew that I would answer him with a story on him, such as his race on Brigham when he wore the Little Red Riding Suit, or the time when he rode "mule express" and walked all the way. No man ever lived who had a greater sense of humor than Buffalo Bill, and the best part of it all was the fact that the story he loved the best was the one which had him as the butt end of the joke.

We were very happy. The Indians were giving little trouble, game was plentiful, and there was rarely a night that Will was forced to spend away from me. But as winter came on and the plains grew white with snow, the inevitable change approached.

Outside the cabin, the wind was screaming and whining one evening, as Will and Arta and I sat before the fire, talking and laughing and joking as usual. Now and then a flurry of snow would sift against the little windows, indicative of the blizzard that was sure to come during the night. And as we sat there—a shouting voice. A clattering knock on the door. The call of:

"Cody! Cody!"

Will leaped to his feet. A second more and he had opened the door, to find one of the scouts there, fidgeting, anxious.

"Injuns, Bill!" came his sharp greeting. "They've gone on the path. Sioux!"

Already I was at Will's side with his heavy coat, his cap, his gloves, and his rifle. A hasty goodbye and he was gone. Ten minutes later I heard the faint call of "boots and saddles" from the fort, then the sound of many horses as the soldiers rode forth. And I knew that far in front of them, riding hard and fast against the wind, was my husband, facing the dangers of darkness, of snow, and of cold, to take up his position in the advance and to give the warning that would lead to battle.

But the same sort of thing had happened before in my life, and I took it as I had always taken it. Long before Will had told me never to worry, never to fret for him.

"It's bad luck, Lou," he had said. "I'm always the first one to go out and I'll always be the first to come back. If I know that you are worrying about me, that will make me worry too—and someday it may make me lose my head, just when I need it worst."

I had promised and kept my word—and Will had kept his also. Galloping always in the advance of a command, that he might scout out the country and report the signs of Indians, Will inevitably was the first to hurry forth on the call to action. But just as he had said, he was always the first to gallop back into camp after the fighting was over and the troops returning, that he might bring the news of the engagement and assure me of his safety.

And so I did not worry, except for his comfort and for his health. The wind became sharper and colder, and with the change the flurries of snow changed to a straight driving sheet of white that fairly seemed to cut through the air, heaping itself up against the window ledges, sifting through the tiny chink beneath the door and through the one or two wee holes that had been left where the window sashes had been set into the logs. For a long time I sat in front of the fire, Arta in my arms, until she went to sleep. Then I put her to bed and went back to my chair, to doze a while before retiring.

It was an hour or so later that I awakened with a start. Someone was at the door, pounding hard against it and calling. I answered the knock, and a snow-whitened soldier hurried in out of the wind.

"The Major would like to see Colonel Cody, please."

"Colonel Cody is out scouting. He went out with the detachment that left here early in the evening," I said.

The soldier appeared puzzled.

"But that detachment came back, Mrs. Cody."

"Back?" A quick fear shot through my heart. "How long ago?"

"About an hour and a half."

"Well, then, maybe the colonel is over at the fort. Did you look?"

"Yessum. At the officers' club and everywhere. Nobody'd seen him. So I thought—"

My hands were clasped until they were white. The detachment had come back—but somewhere, out in that blizzard, was my husband. And I knew he was in danger! I seized my greatcoat and hurried toward the fort with the soldier. Just as we reached the dim lights of the gate, I saw a group of men gathered about something. I hurried forward. It was Will's horse, which had just come in—riderless!

"Boots and saddles" was being sounded again—and I knew that this time they were calling for aid, aid for my husband, somewhere out there in the blizzard. Perhaps already he was dead, perhaps a victim of a lurking Indian's bullet; no one knew. The command of the party had deemed it wisest to turn back, so that undoubtedly the Indians would be forced to seek cover from the storm and hunting them would be useless with the blizzard covering every track, every mark that could give an indication of their progress. And with the turning back, Cody had, as usual, forged ahead. But here was his horse, without its rider.

There was nothing to do but to go back again and wait—back to the little log home where we had laughed and joked by the fireside only a few hours before—back to wait until some word should come from the searchers, and information as to whether Will, my Will, was alive or dead.

And oh, the agony of waiting! Waiting without the knowledge of what is happening out there somewhere, without the faintest hint of the accident or the disaster that has befallen the man you love! Nothing! Just empty nothing, with the moaning of the cold, cutting wind to send a thousand fears clutching at your heart, the sifting of the snow to remind you that out on the plains the drifts are heaping higher and higher, and that one of them might conceal the body of the great-hearted boy—and that is just what he is—who is yours.

My throat was dry and parched, my whole body burning as with a fever, yet I was cold—cold with fear. Dully I heard the soft thudding of hoofs as the men rode forth on their cold mission; anxiously I awaited the same sound that would tell of their return, and perhaps some news for me. But it did not come.

The minutes lengthened to hours, while I stood at the window, wiping the frost away and watching the faint swirl of the snow, extending only as far as the light from within extended, yet watching nevertheless. I at least was looking into the outside world, and that world contained my husband.

Waiting—waiting! You who live the peaceful life of today, with comforts all about you, with telephones, with every convenience, have little idea of what that word means—waiting, while men rode out into the trackless prairie where the snow whirled and sifted, where every track vanished almost as soon as it was made, waiting without even the knowledge of what I was waiting for—such was my night. The hours dragged by, ever and ever so slowly. Then, as daylight came, and I could stand the strain no longer, I wrapped myself in my greatcoat and started out into the snow.

I had hardly gone more than a hundred yards when a cry came from my lips, and I started forward. Away off in the dull gray of the distance, a form was stumbling forward, falling, rising, then stumbling on again. I called, but there came no answer. Again I called as I ran forward, and I saw the figure faintly raise an arm and endeavor to wave. Then it sank to the snow again. It was Will, my husband.

Hurriedly I reached his side and helped him to rise. His features were blue from the intense cold, his lips chattering from the fatigue and exposure. My strength suddenly became superhuman; small as I was in comparison to his great frame, I put my arm about him, and my shoulder beneath his armpit, and almost carried him to the cabin, there to support him to the bed, where he fell unconscious.

Hurriedly I ran to the fort and summoned the doctor, returning with him just as the first of the searchers came in with the news that they had trailed the tracks of a man to the cabin and inquired if Will had gotten safely home. It was with happiness and fear that I replied in the affirmative. Happiness for his return, fear for what the doctor might say, and what might follow as the result of his exposure.

Will was conscious when we reached him, and as I rubbed his half-frozen hands with snow, he told of the accident that had nearly caused his death. He had been hurrying home to me, and he had not watched his progress as closely as he should. Soon he realized that he was off the trail, traveling blindly in the darkness and fast-driven snow. Then a rocking crash, a fall, and when he again became conscious, it was with the realization that he lay at the bottom of a ravine into which his horse had stumbled, and that the horse was gone. And through the night he had wandered in the blizzard, at last to strike the faint, snow-covered evidences of the trail again, and to fight his way homeward.

While he talked the doctor made his examination, anointed the bruises, bandaged the torn flesh resultant from the fall in the ravine, and then gave his verdict:

"He'll be all right again in a few days."

And then my tears came, tears of happiness, to eyes that had been dry and staring throughout the long night. Of such, sometimes consisted the life of the wife of a winner of the West.

CHAPTER 8

In fact, life on the plains had many a diversity. Will's adventure in the blizzard became history within a week or so, and he was once more up and out on the range, driving the Indians off the warpath, while I drove them away from the house in which we lived. For I had my Indian battles as well.

Some of them are laughable now, as I look back upon them from the safe distance of many years. But in those days they were serious affairs, to say nothing of being vexatious. It's not the cheeriest feeling in the world to be sitting in the old rocking chair, with your daughter beside you, comfortably sewing in the radius of heat thrown out by the old army stove—then suddenly to become aware of the fact that someone is staring at you through a window, and look up to find that someone is an Indian. That happened more than once.

And more than once they ran away, more frightened at the sight of Pahaska's wife than of Pahaska himself. With the growing of that long hair, Will had become the recipient of a new name from the Indians, that of Pahaska, or "the long-haired man," and as Pahaska's wife, I had plenty of Indian victories to my credit—as well as a good many defeats.

In the little circle in which we lived were just six log huts, the nearest of which was the one occupied by William MacDonald, a trader. The result was that when Will was out on a scouting expedition and Mr. MacDonald was busy with the work of his trading post, Mrs. MacDonald would come over to my house, and together we would do our sewing or laundry—for servants were an unknown quantity at Fort McPherson. On these visits, I always noticed that Mrs. MacDonald would bring a package that I could see contained a bottle and place it within easy reach.

"Indian medicine," she explained the first time, as though I would understand, and then said no more about it. Nor did I question.

Time after time she visited the cabin, finally to look out toward the ravine just back of the house one day as we were ironing and leap to her package.

"Indians," she exclaimed, "they're coming right this way."

I hurried to the window.

"Sioux!" There was fear in my voice as I noticed their headgear, their dress, and their accoutrements. They were sneaking along, taking advantage of every gulley, every natural hiding place—a band of raiders, creeping in as close as possible upon the fort to steal what they could, then to make their escape. I heard Mrs. MacDonald take the wrapping from the package she always carried, then turn in my direction.

"All right," she called. "Take it—quick!"

I looked at her, to see her waving a hatchet in one hand and holding forth a bottle of what looked like whiskey in the other. I gasped but she smiled quickly.

"It's only cold tea," she said hurriedly. "Indians are afraid of a drunken woman. So we've got to be drunk—quick!"

I felt like a tenderfoot. And yet, I had never been in a situation just like this before. There came a slight sound from the other part of the house, and I turned apprehensively with the thought of Arta, my little daughter, whom I had left asleep in the next room. Just then the door opened and she came trotting in, to stop staring as she saw Mrs. MacDonald. I hurried to her.

"You must appear frightened, honey," I said quickly. "Indians!"

She began to cry, and we encouraged her in it. Then, with one sweep, I pulled my hair over my eyes and grasped the bottle of cold tea that Mrs. MacDonald had thrust in my direction, just as the first of the Sioux approached the house. Mrs. MacDonald screamed like an insane woman.

"Give me that girl!" she cried and started in my direction, swinging the hatchet. Wildly she waved it in the air and crashed it down on the ironing board, ruining a perfectly new blanket and splitting the board from end to end. Arta cried more loudly than ever. I reeled about the room, the hair hanging over my eyes, acting as though I were trying to drink from the bottle and was too intoxicated to do so. And as I staggered toward the window, I saw a face that was more frightened even than that of my daughter.

It was a Sioux chieftain standing there, his eyes popping, his mouth hanging wide open. Only a moment more did he stare, then I saw him leap away and gesticulate wildly. Hurriedly, three others joined him and, from a distance, stood a second, looking in on our masquerade. Then came a guttural warning:

"Wanitch! Lile sietche! Lile sietche!"

Perhaps my spelling is wrong, after all these years, but I'll never forget the words. Again the warning sounded, telling the others that we were bad, bad, worse than bad, and that it was time to move. A hurried pow wow, then down the ravine raced fifteen or twenty bow-legged Sioux warriors, running as hard as they could from two women and a little girl. I gathered Arta to me as quickly as I could and soothed her fears. Then Mrs. MacDonald and I sank into the two chairs that the room afforded, took one look at each other, and laughed until our sides ached. Truly there never existed two more maudlin-appearing persons than she and I seemed to be just at that moment. Our hair stringing about our faces, our dresses splattered with the contents of the cold tea bottle, Mrs. MacDonald still with that hatchet clutched tightly in her hand, and the smashed ironing board leaning all awry—realism appeared everywhere. And in spite of the fact that we were quaking from fright, we laughed until we almost rolled out of our chairs.

So passed my first real visit from the Indians. I was to have many more, of a different type. The Pawnees, friendly though they were, had just been mustered out of service as United States soldiers, and they naturally felt that they still had the right to go and come about the fort as they always had done. Coupled with this was the fact that restrictions had been removed from them and the watch that had been kept on them while they had been in uniform had lessened in a great degree. Therefore the houses of the settlers outside the fort soon began to feel their presence, mine especially.

They were the ones who peered through the windows, or who more than once simply stalked into the house, bobbed their heads and grinned, said, "How kola" and proceeded to make a grab for anything eatable in sight. I don't believe I ever saw a Pawnee Indian in my life when he wasn't hungry. At least, none of them ever showed themselves about the Cody cabin. And I remember one time when they were particularly gifted with hunger, while I—

Well, Will had come to me, all excited, with the light in his eyes that always glowed when something wonderful was about to happen. Hurriedly he surveyed my little pantry then grunted.

"Guess I'd better start making tracks for the hunting grounds," he exclaimed. "Fine people coming, Mamma. We're going to entertain royalty!"

"Royalty?" I blinked. "In this little log house?"

Will looked at me and chuckled.

"That's why they're coming here," he answered. "A log house is just as much of a novelty to them as their big houses would be to us. Just got the word up at the fort. They're going to be here day after tomorrow. Where's my gun?"

He already had it in his hand and was examining it carefully. He started toward the door then stopped.

"I'm just going to bring in an antelope and some sage chickens and stuff like that," he announced. "It'll just be that sort of a dinner and—"

"But, Will," I begged, "I don't even know who it's for yet."

"That's right!" He cocked his head. "Got so excited that I forgot all about it. It's Lord and Lady Dunraven from England, and Lord Finn from Australia.[1] They're coming out here to see what the West looks like and, of course, it's sort of our business to entertain them. They won't live here—" He laughed as he looked at the rather meager furnishings of the little home. "But we'll have a spread for them. So I'm going out now to get the fixings."

He kissed me goodbye, lifted Arta in his great arms, swung her high in the air, and planted her on the floor again. Then with a booming goodbye he was gone, while I faced the problem of entertaining royalty in a log cabin.

As soon as I could, I hurried to the person who was always my good friend, Mrs. MacDonald. Together we schemed and devised, and in her kitchen we cooked the pies and cakes that must accompany the dinner. The next day Will came home lugging sage chicken and an antelope slung across his saddle. We took the choicest, tenderest portions and planned the great meal.

And what a meal it was to be! Mrs. MacDonald and I were up at five o'clock in the morning and at work in that kitchen, roasting and basting, flying about here and there, trying to do impossible things with the cooking utensils we possessed, hurrying to and from the trading post, and rushing about as though it were our last day on earth. Gradually we began to get the meal assembled, after we had lugged almost everything that the trading post possessed over to the little cabin, to make the place presentable for the great guests. The hours passed. Mealtime came and, with everything warming on the stove, we shut the kitchen door and went into the "setting room–dining room" to receive the guests.

Soon they came, Lord and Lady Dunraven first and Lord Finn following. Mrs. MacDonald and I had been trembling somewhat with excitement—and this, accompanied by the booming excitement of Will as he told them about the building of the cabin, his attempts at hanging wallpaper, and the various vicissitudes we had undergone in trying to make our home out here on the plains made the moments pass far more quickly than I had imagined. At last, however, I started slightly at a punch on the knee from Mrs. MacDonald, and I turned to see her nod in the direction of the kitchen. I rose.

"Now if you'll just all take seats," I announced, "Mrs. MacDonald and I will serve the dinner. You see . . ." I laughed. "We don't have servants out here like you do in England."

Lady Dunraven smiled and rose.

"Can't I help?" she asked.

"I wouldn't think of it! Besides, there isn't so much to bring in. Now, you all just sit down here and be comfortable. Mrs. MacDonald and I will look after all the fixings. Better begin to whet up that knife, Will!"

"That's what I had," boomed my husband. "Tell you right now, Lord Dunraven, you may have a lot of things over in England that we haven't got out here in the West, but you haven't got the game. No sirree, bob! Just wait 'til you taste that antelope. Killed him myself when I heard you were coming and—"

I lost the rest of it. I had opened the kitchen door to stand a moment aghast, then to rush forward in white anger, seize the big coffeepot, and slosh the whole contents of it across the room. For where the dinner had been was now only a mass of messy, mussed-over dishes! The kitchen was full of Pawnees! And the Pawnees were full of the dinner that had been cooked for royalty!

Wildly they scrambled as the hot coffee scorched them, waving their arms and jumping and struggling to get out the door. A long stick of wood lay in the corner and I seized it, calling for my husband as I did so. Then, without stopping to see whether or not he was coming, I lit into those Indians!

"Get out of this house!" I screamed at them, pounding away with my club. "If I ever catch you in here again—"

"Yes, don't you dare ever come near this house!" A slapping, banging sound, and I realized Mrs. MacDonald was beside me, whanging away at them with a broom. And above all of it we heard the sound of heavy, rumbling laughter and:

"That's right, Mamma! Give it to 'em! That's right—that's right!"

I stopped and turned.

"Will Cody!" I snapped. And then the tears came. Will's laughter ceased immediately. Hurriedly he came forward and put his arms about me, while their Lordships and her Ladyship watched somewhat surprisedly from the door.

"There, there," he comforted me. "I'll get those Injuns tomorrow and scalp every one of 'em!"

"They—ate—up—my—dinner!" I sobbed. Will couldn't hold back a chuckle.

"Well," he answered, "a part of it was mine. So I guess we've both got cause to get mad. But don't worry, Mamma. There's plenty to eat up at the fort."

Thus went glimmering our first attempt at feeding royalty. I took one last tear-dimmed look at the sodden remains of my feast, and then we all went to the fort for the food that should have been served on the Cody table. But just the same, while I saw a good many Indian faces after that, I never saw one of the group of Pawnees that sneaked into my kitchen and ate the food of royalty.

So went my life, day after day—and sometimes there were incidents in my "Indian campaign" that were far from ludicrous.

As I have said, there was a ravine just back of our little home through which the Indians often sneaked in their raiding expeditions on the fort. The Pawnees rarely frightened me, for they were a friendly, good humored lot as a rule, grinning and foolish and thieving, and it was nothing to run them away. But when the Sioux came—!

Arta and I were sunning ourselves in the big chair one afternoon and dozing. Will had left for the fort only a short time ago with Texas Jack, who had stopped in from one of his scouting expeditions. Everything was peaceful and quiet, when suddenly I heard the slamming of a door from the other part of the house and the hurried swish of moccasined feet. I leaped from my chair and ran into the other room, leaving Arta behind me.

"Get out of here!" I cried as I sighted the first of a number of Pawnees crowding into the kitchen. But they did not obey. I started forward, suddenly to come face to face with Old Horse, one of the Indians who had served in the army and who could speak English. He stopped me.

"Sioux!" he exclaimed, pointing excitedly out toward the ravine. "Sioux! Heap mad Pawnee. Pawnee run—no want fight. Hide here. Sioux go by!"

"Go by?" I questioned in a voice of excitement. "If you think so, look!" I pointed out through the window, toward where the first of the Sioux band was making its way out of the ravine.

"They're coming here—and you can't stay! They'll find you—"

"We stay here!" Old Horse crossed his arms and shook his head. "This Pahaska's tepee. No come here!"

But I knew better. The Indians were circling the cabin now, and I rushed into the other room and, throwing a shawl around Arta, opened the window and lifted her through it.

"Run!" I told her. "Run just as fast as you can and get Papa. Tell him there are Indians here—Sioux!"

The little girl did not even whimper. Her lips pressed tightly, and she clenched her little hands.

"I'll get Papa," she said confidently, and her little legs were paddling even before she touched the ground. A moment more and she had dodged behind a slight rise in the ground and was speeding as hard as she could toward the fort, while I turned to see the first of the Sioux entering my cabin.

"Go away!" I commanded them. But the leader only looked at me and kicked at the door leading to the kitchen. Around at the other side of the house, I heard other sounds that told me the Indians were banging away at the entrance to the kitchen, trying to gain entrance there. A gun lay across the room and I strove to reach it, but the Sioux were too quick for me. One of them, a great, burly warrior, simply picked me up in his arms and carried me across the floor, planting me in one corner.

"You Pahaska squaw," he said quietly. "Sioux no hurt Pahaska squaw. Me fight Pawnee!"

A glimmer of hope came to me with the realization that he could speak and understand English.

"But there are no Pawnees—" I got that far and stopped. Will had told me never to lie to an Indian. I began again on a different strain. "Pahaska get heap mad!" I cautioned him. "Pahaska kill!"

"Me know Pahaska!" came the answer. "Me fight Pawnee."

By this time one of the Indians had picked up the rifle and was examining it. A moment more and he had shot through the door, while I stood screaming in the corner. If Will would only come, if—

Far away, up at the fort, I heard the faint call of a bugle. I knew that call—a call that sent the blood racing through my veins. "Boots and saddles!"

But the Sioux did not seem to hear. And it would mean a good ten minutes before those soldiers could mount and reach the house. Unless something should happen before that—

A crashing sound, as the door at the rear of the house began to give way. A shot sounded, then another. Again I screamed then, suddenly forgetting my fear, raced to the window at the sound of hoofs.

Two men on horseback were approaching. One was Will, my husband. The other was Texas Jack. I whirled and pointed.

"Pahaska!" I cried. The Sioux leader shouted a guttural command. A moment more and they were piling out of the house and into the little yard, where they faced the revolvers of Texas Jack and my husband. I heard a clear, commanding voice.

"Now, you Injuns make tracks—quick! Jack, ride around to the other side and help hold this bunch 'til the soldiers come—they're just starting from the fort now." He called the last part of the sentence to me, standing trembling in the door. Jack swung his horse about and rounded up the recalcitrant Sioux, keeping his revolvers ready for instant action, while Will upbraided them. For, it seems, this was a small band of Sioux that had presumably made peace and had been granted government stores on the condition that they keep out of trouble. For a long time he harangued them in Sioux, then he suddenly veered in his position, as a number of cavalrymen galloped up.

"We'll just take these fellows out in the hills and give them a good start," he commanded. "Now—"

"But, Will!" I called from the door, "the house is full of Pawnees. They were fighting each other."

Will jumped from his horse.

"Jack," he ordered, "you and some of the men take these Injuns off to the north. I'll handle the Pawnees."

A command and a number of the soldiers started away, driving the Indians before them. Will came into the house, paused just long enough to kiss me, then opened the door to the kitchen. The first Indian he saw was Old Horse and, reaching forward, he caught the Pawnee by the collar of his leather jacket.

"You old bag o' bones!" he shouted, "I'll teach you to come into my house!"

He whirled him around—and then he kicked! I never saw an Indian move so swiftly in my life; it was as though he had been lifted by a catapult, straight out the door and on to his face in the pebble-strewn yard. Will did not even stop to see what had become of him. He was too busily engaged in dragging out the other Pawnees and kicking them individually and collectively out of the house.

There the soldiers corralled them and started away with them in the direction opposite to that which Texas Jack had taken with the Sioux. Five hours later, Jack and Will were back, after having separated their various charges by a distance of about ten miles. But it did no good.

Late that night a wounded Pawnee limped into camp and asked for the aid of the soldiers. Again "boots and saddles" sounded and the cavalry, Will and Texas Jack leading, galloped out on the plains. This time the battle had been in earnest. Somewhere, those Indians had procured enough firearms and ammunition to go 'round, and the Sioux had trailed the Pawnees until they had met. When the cavalry reached there, practically every member of the Pawnee band was either dead or wounded, while the Sioux had hurried on at the first warning of soldier aid, once more to take to the warpath. It was poor diplomacy to trust a Sioux in those days, and even Will learned that.

There were, of course, many of the Indians who regarded him as more of a friend than an enemy. It was not Will's policy to kill Indians simply for the fun of it, or simply because an Indian on the warpath meant legitimate game. Will's idea was a far different one. He realized that the Indians had their claims, that they had their rights, and that it more than once was the fault of the government itself that they were forced to the warpath. And whenever he could, Will sought to impress upon them that the fighting game was a hard one to follow, that there were thousands upon thousands of white men who could be brought against them to exterminate them, even as the buffalo was being exterminated. He tried to teach them that the white man would help them if they would allow themselves to be helped, and that when things went wrong in the governmental way of running things, it did not always mean that the Indian was being forgotten; that there were those, like himself, who would strive always to aid and to make the Indian's life on the plains a bearable one. It was thus that he won the friendship of such Indians as No Neck and Woman's Dress, and Red Cloud and Sitting Bull, and others who, in turn, helped Cody more than once.[2]

But he also experienced the sad rewards of being a missionary. Will had been buying horses and, among them, he had purchased a racing pony that he called Powder Face. One night, as we sat in the little log cabin, Will scowled and looked at his fist.

"That's what I get for trying to be good to an Injun," he announced. "Skinned my knuckles knocking the stuffing out of him today. He tried to run away with Powder Face, after I'd brought him into the fort so that he could see that soldiers wouldn't hurt him. I—"

He jumped out of his chair. From down at the corral had come shouts and the crackling of a revolver. We both knew what it meant—Will's entire herd of horses had been stampeded.

He was out of the house in an instant and on the way to the fort for the soldiers. A short time later I heard them clatter by the house, and then the sounds faded in the distance. For a long time I waited, but there came no sound of shots, no evidence of conflict. The chase was to be a long and hard one.

It was not until late the next afternoon that Will came home again, tired, bedraggled, but grinning. Over his saddle hung two war bonnets, their eagle feathers trailing nearly to the ground. I called to him as he approached.

"Did you find Powder Face?"

"Find him?" he shouted back. "That horse was over the Great Divide before we even got started. But I made a record. Two Injuns at one shot!"

"Two what?" I asked in astonishment as he descended from his horse and came to the door, trailing the war bonnets behind him. He chuckled.

"Two Injuns. We caught up with most of the bunch about daylight this morning. Two of the critters were riding one of my horses, and I knew there was only one way to get 'em off. So I just pulled the trigger and I'm blamed if the bullet didn't go through both of 'em!" Then his face grew long. "We got all the horses back but Powder Face. I'm sure sorry about him. He'd have won me all kinds of money when the racing started in the spring."

"And he might have lost some for you, too." I laughed. For betting his last cent on the horse of his pride was Will's greatest amusement. And sometimes he lost!

CHAPTER 9

However, right then, there were things to take Will's mind off the loss of his favorite pony. One of them was the fact that midwinter had come and that Christmas was only a few weeks off. For Will had been deputized by the soldiers and officers to be the official messenger who should go to Cheyenne and return with the necessities of the Christmas season.

And what excitement there was about it all! In that great camp, where lived the men who guarded the West, were only three children—three girls: the bandleader's child, Mrs. MacDonald's little daughter, and Arta. And for them the soldiers had saved their money that they might have a real Christmas, and Will was to be the official messenger to Santa Claus.

I'll never forget all the conferences that were held. Night after night, Mrs. MacDonald in her little cabin, the bandleader's wife up at the fort, and I would lead the thoughts of our children around to Christmas, that we might learn the things that they most desired. Certainly that was not a hard thing to do, and one by one we gained the information we sought. Some of their wishes were entirely beyond the range of possibility—but where is the child who does not desire the impossible? And so it was with Arta and her two little comrades.

However, at last Will made his start toward Cheyenne, with the whole long list, and with a face that was longer. He was going to face that worst of ordeals—shopping. However, he was brave about it.

"Don't know what they're going to say when I walk in out there and ask for chiney dolls and all those other things out of *Godey's Lady's Book*," he announced. "But I'll do my best. I'll bring back the bacon or bust!"

And so he rode away, while we three women turned our attention to the plans for the Christmas Day entertainment.

Of course, there must be speaking, and each of us picked out the piece we wanted our little girls to recite. I chose "The Star of Bethlehem" and, night after night, while Will was away, I trained Arta in her recitation, outlining each little gesture, showing her how to emphasize every word. I was terribly proud of her, for I felt that her piece would be the prettiest of all—and, well, you know the natural pride of a mother.

Therefore, it was with glowing eyes that I greeted Will when he came back from Cheyenne, loaded down with packages, to say nothing of the wagon that followed him. It was two days before Christmas. Up at the fort the soldiers had been working, sending out details into the plains to find the prettiest little pine trees possible, to be placed about the big assembly hall—and I knew that the whole setting would be wonderful for my little triumph.

So, when Will had shown me all the presents he had brought for Arta from the big trading post: the rag dolls, the bright bits of silk, the little train of cars and the inevitable fire engine; the woolly dog and the other gee-gaws that had found their way into the Far West, I told him of my accomplishment. Then I added:

"Now, Will—" I stuffed the copy of the poem into his hand. "You'll just have to look after the final training. If Arta doesn't study right up until the last minute, she'll be just like all other children. She'll get up there to speak her piece and then won't remember it. That would be awful, wouldn't it?"

"Sure would," he agreed earnestly. "But why don't you do the rehearsin'?"

"Because, silly, I'll have to work up at the hall. My goodness, all those soldiers have been piling stuff in there for a week, and land only knows what we're going to do with it! They think that all there is to fixing up Christmas decorations is to go out somewhere and cut down a tree. Only women can look after those things properly; besides, there's the popcorn to string and the trees to decorate, and everything like that! Gracious, we'll be worked to death looking after everything, to say nothing of all the cooking to 'tend to. And you haven't a blessed thing to do—so you can just finish teaching Arta that recitation."

"But suppose the Injuns break out?" he asked lugubriously.

"Well, that'll be different. But, so far, they haven't broken out, and, Will, you've just got to help me. Now won't you?"

He bobbed his head with sudden acquiescence and began to stare at the paper that I had shoved into his hand.

"'Til start tomorrow," he promised faithfully. The next morning I went to the fort to help the other women with the decorations for our first really big Christmas on the plains.

How we worked! How we schemed and contrived to make that big hall look like a Christmas back home! All in one day, there was everything to do—and very little to do it with. This was different from the land of civilization. There was no store to run to for an armful of tinsel, no decorator's shops to furnish holly and mistletoe and Christmas wreaths. The wreaths that hung upon the walls we made ourselves. The bright red berries that spotted them here and there were hard-rolled bits of red paper; the greenery everywhere had come fresh from the buttes and knolls of the plains, with here and there a few cactus spines thrown in to make things more difficult.

The popcorn had long lain in the bins at Charlie MacDonald's trading post. It burned, it parched, it did everything but pop. A hand-picked proposition was every puffy ball that went upon the strings, gleaned from skillets full of brown, burned kernels that had persistently refused to pop, to do anything in fact but scorch and smoke and instigate coughing and sneezing. But we were determined to have a regulation Christmas, and a few difficulties were not going to stop us.

All day long we worked, and far into the night, hanging the various bits of greenery, cooking on the old range that slumped in one end of the hall, or decorating the trees. The soldiers, gawking here and there about the big room, did their best to help us, but where is the man who is a particle of good at Christmastide? Every time we would make a gain on the popcorn, one of them would come along and steal a handful, and then we would have to run them all out of the hall, laughing in spite of our vexation, and start all over. We knew the feeling in the hearts of those men—they were children again, children back home, preparing for Christmas!

Late into the night we cooked and slaved, while our husbands waited for us in a nodding line at one side of the hall. At last it all was nearly done, and with Will I started home.

"How did Arta get along with her piece today?" I asked.

"Oh, fine!" Will looked straight ahead. "I taught her and taught her."

"She won't forget it?"

"No sirree! She's got it down line for line."

I went to bed happy and expectant. Arta would look so sweet tomorrow. Will had brought her a pretty little plaid dress from Cheyenne that fitted her wonderfully well, considering that a man had picked it out. Of course, there was the necessity for a little taking up here and a little letting out there, but I could get up early in the morning and do that before time to hurry to the hall again.

So at dawn I was at work and, finally, awakened Will with breakfast and with the information that he must be the one to dress Arta and bring her to the hall. I would be working there until the very last minute, and I simply wouldn't have time to come back to the house. Will did not object.

"I'll have her dressed up like all get out!" was his cheerful announcement. "I sure want her to make that speech today!"

"And so do I. Goodness, won't it be just too lovely if she's the best one there?"

"If?" my husband questioned. "Why, there ain't any doubt about it. I bet Arta gets more hand-clappin' and shoutin' and that sort of thing when she does her little trick than both of those other children put together. Now, just you watch her! I'm handling that end of it, and she's got all those lines down pat!"

"Well, don't you forget to go over it two or three times," I ordered as I kissed him and hurried to the door.

"Oh, we'll go over it a lot of times!" he assured me. "Just wait 'til you hear it!"

I rushed to the hall, again to work, again to scheme and devise. Then, somewhat flustered, I seated myself as the time for the entertainment approached and the soldiers thumped into the hall. Will, dressed in his usual buckskin and flannel shirt, found me sitting near the rear of the long lines of chairs and immediately assisted me to my feet.

"What?" he asked. "Sitting back here? No sirree! We're going right up with the mourners!"

"Mourners?"

"Well, you know what I mean. Up on the front row where everybody can see us when Arta makes that speech. Got it all down pat, haven't you, Arta?" He beamed down at her.

"Yes, Papa," she lisped, and a feeling of great pride swelled through me. Up to the front row we went, while the hall filled, and the Santa Claus of the fort, resplendent in a red flannel shirt hanging straight from the waist, a pair of riding boots that reached above his knees, and cotton whiskers and hair, filched from the post surgeon, distributed the presents. One after another they were called out, first the presents for the children, and then the ones for the soldiers. There were paper dolls and baby rattles and a hundred and one foolish things that Will had bought in Cheyenne and packed across the weary miles: bottles of beer with vinegar in them, tiny kegs labeled in chalk: "Finest Whisky," and disclosing when opened only carpet tacks, and everything else foolish that men can think of. One by one they were all doled out, and then, following the booming of the post quartet, the singing of a solo by the bandleader's wife, and a speech on Christmas by the Major, the recitations began.

Mrs. MacDonald's little girl came first, and had I not known what a really wonderful presentation Arta would make, I would have been really jealous. Then followed the bandleader's daughter, with her little recitation, and then—

Arta!

Her father carried her up to the platform, squared her around, patted her on the cheeks, and hurried back to his seat. My heart thumped with excitement. It was Arta's first recitation. Prettily she made her little curtsy, and then, with a quick glance toward her father, she parted her lips.

But the words that came forth! My pride changed to apprehension and then to wildest dismay. For Arta was reciting something that I never had heard before, something only a few lines in length, that ran:

> The lightning roared,
> The thunder flashed,
> And broke my mother's teapot
> A-l-l-t-o-s-m-a-s-h!

Then she laughed, clapped her little hands and, running to her father, leaped into his lap. Will was almost rolling off his chair. The tears were running down his cheeks, his face was as red as a boiled beet, and he was shaking with laughter from head to foot. As for the rest of the big hall, it was roaring like a summer thunderstorm, while I, like Cardinal Wolsey, sat alone in my fallen greatness. For a moment there was only blank dismay. Then I looked at Will and understood.

"Willie!" I exclaimed dramatically, "I'll never speak to you again as long as I live. Never! Never I Never!"

But a moment later, as he choked down his laughter to boom out a lump-de-de-lump to the tune of "Rock of Ages," the closing song of the celebration, I reached over, took his hand, squeezed it—then pressed tight my lips to keep from laughing myself. But never again did I entrust to Will the task of rehearsing a child in its recitations!

However, there were plenty of times when the laugh could go around the other way, when it would be I who would chuckle at the troubles of my husband. One of them came shortly after Christmas, and with it arrived my revenge.

Will had come home all excited—just as he invariably did when something new happened in his career. This time he was staring at his buckskin clothes and at his high riding boots.

"Mamma," he announced, "guess I'll have to be getting some different duds. That's all there is to it—different duds for a man of a high-up station. I'm a judge now."

"A judge of what?" I was busy with the cooking. Will straightened and pounded his chest.

"Why, a judge—a regular judge, you know. One of those fellows that sits on a bench and doles out the law. Reckon I'll have to get along without the bench, but it'll be all right. I'll—"

"How about getting along without the law?" I laughed over my shoulder. Will swelled his chest.

"Oh, that'll be all right. I know as much law as I need to know around here. It's just white man's law against Injun law, and you give the fellow what you think's right. That's the way they explained it to me up at the fort. You see, there isn't any justice of the peace here, and so they thought I would make the likeliest one out of the bunch; so here I am, Judge Cody."

I didn't say anything just then. And I didn't remind Will of the fact that he had been a judge for only several days. But I had said a good many things to a young soldier and a young woman who I knew had been thinking about getting married.

Among the things that I pointed out to them was the fact that not everyone could have the distinction of being married by Buffalo Bill. It took. A few days later Will walked into the house to find the soldier and his wife-to-be waiting, while I stood at the girl's side, ready to give away the bride.

"Will," I announced, "we've been waiting for you."

"For—for what?" I could see Will begin to appear a bit worried.

"Why, these young people want to get married. And there isn't anybody here that can marry them but you."

Will blinked for a second. Then he nodded his head and led me over to one corner. I followed him very seriously.

"Isn't there any way out of this?" he asked.

"I don't see how, Will. They're here and—"

"Well . . ." He pressed his lips tightly together. "Guess I've got to go through with it. Say, we got married once. What did the minister say?"

"He said for me to love, honor, and obey. That's about all I remember."

"And wasn't there something about 'till death do us part'?"

"Of course."

"Well," and he reached for the copy of the *Statutes of Nebraska* that had come into his possession with the judgeship. "I guess I'll make out. Anyway, it ought to all be in here."

But evidently it wasn't. There were statutes on limitations of grazing lands, statutes on almost everything that went with a young state, but there wasn't anything on marriage. A slow sweat began to break out on Will's forehead. Now and then he looked up anxiously, and his tongue scurried over his lips. Once he excused himself, and as he walked into the kitchen I saw him reaching for something in his hip pocket; he returned licking his lips. It was one of the few times that Will was ever forced to resort to Dutch courage. Hurriedly he planted himself in the middle of the floor and, holding the *Statutes of Nebraska* upside down, made the pretense of looking at them.

"Line up!" he ordered. The soldier and his bride-to-be came forward. Will poked his head toward the bridegroom.

"Look here!" he questioned, "this is all in earnest?"

"Why—why, of course."

"And there isn't any monkey-fooling about it anywhere?"

"No—no, sir."

"All right, then. Because this thing's got to stick. I take it you two want to be hitched to run in double harness the rest of your life."

"Yes, sir."

"Fine. You're going to take this woman to be your lawful wedded wife and support her and see that she's got a house to live in and everything like that?"

"I do!" By this time the bridegroom was so flustered that he would have given an affirmative answer to anything. Will turned to the bride.

"And you take this man to be your lawful wedded husband and you'll love, honor, and obey him and cook his meals and tend to the house?"

"I do."

"That just about settles it. Join hands. I now pronounce you man and wife. Whoever God and Buffalo Bill have joined together, let no man put asunder. Two dollars, please, and—" Will ran a finger about the collar of his buckskin coat. "If you'll please pardon your husband for just a minute, he and I will go and have a drink!"

However, that was simple in comparison to the next task that faced Will as a justice of the peace. This time it was not a question of joining two persons in wedlock, but of breaking the bonds that held them.

They were a man and woman who recently had come to camp, and their quarrels had been frequent ever since their arrival. At last came the day when they knocked on the door of our little cabin and came stalking in, glowering at each other. The man stared hard at Will.

"Bill Cody," he snapped, "you do lawin', don't you?"

"Off and on," said Will. "What's wrong?"

"There's a hull lot. Me and her ain't agreein'. We want a divorce."

"A who?" Will had craned his neck forward.

"A divorce. I ain't satisfied with her and she ain't satisfied with me. It's pull an' tug, tug an' pull, all th' time. And we want t' get unhitched."

Once more Will reached for his *Statutes of Nebraska*. Once more he thumbed the pages. He turned the book foreside, backward, upside down, over, and around again.

"What was it you said you wanted?" he asked again, this time more anxiously.

"A divorce. We want to get unhitched. Ain't that it, Sarah?"

Sarah agreed emphatically that it was. Will nodded his head judiciously and moistened a finger.

"Um-humph," he grunted. "Divorce—divorce, page 363, paragraph 6. Um-humph." The pages turned again. Then Will squared himself. "'No divorce shall be granted,'" he read, "'unless'—humph! Guess maybe we'd just better leave out that 'unless.' 'No divorces shall be granted.' That sounds pretty good. Says so right here in the book. 'Course they shouldn't. 'Tain't natural. Now, look here, Charlie, you ain't as bad off as you think you are. Sarah cooks good meals, don't she?"

"Larrupin'," agreed Charlie.

"And—Mamma!" Will turned suddenly and called to me, "take Sarah off there in the corner and talk to her. I've got a few words to say to Charlie."

Obediently I led Sarah away, while Will dragged Charlie over behind the stove. Long we argued, while Sarah told me the story of all her troubles, stopping now and then to remark that everything Charlie was saying to Will was the finest collection of falsehoods ever fabricated. An hour passed. Then the tears began to flow as Sarah detailed the difficulties of sailing the matrimonial sea with Charlie as the pilot. Will took one look at her then, reaching out one great paw, he seized Charlie by the coat collar and yanked him to his feet.

"Look at that!" he shouted. "Look at her crying! Now you just hit the trail over there and make up!"

Charlie stood and sulked.

"I'll go halfway," he announced finally. Will turned toward me.

"Give Sarah a push!" he ordered.

I pushed and they met in the center of the room. For a moment there was silence, then a resounding smack of lips. Another great law case had been settled, and Will once more had established himself as an attorney of record. And, what is more, the last I heard of the soldier and his bride and of Charlie and Sarah, they still were making their way along life's road, agreeably hitched in the Cody brand of "double harness."

And most of Will's cases turned out in about this way. Of statutory law there was very little, but of common sense there was a great deal. And when argument failed—

I remember a little matter that concerned the theft of a horse. Two men claimed it, and one asserted that the other had stolen it. Will reached for old "Lucretia Borgia" and went out with the claimant.

He found the new possessor of the horse only a few miles from the post.

"Turn over that horse," he ordered.

"Sure," the man had taken one look at the gun. Will continued: "Now, listen, there ain't any place at the fort that ain't full up. Haven't got any regular jail, and I'm blamed if I'll put you up at a regular house. So you're fined right now. Fork over a hundred dollars."

"For what?" The horse thief—if he was one—was becoming obstinate.

Will shifted his gun.

"Time and trouble of the court in coming out here after you, and costs of lawin' in Nebraska."

"And what'll you do if I don't fork over?" The defendant was preparing to dig the spurs into his own horse. Will looked blankly at the sky.

"Oh, nothing much," he announced. "I wouldn't kill you. T'wouldn't be right, seeing there's some dispute about this horse and you really didn't steal him, just sort of took him, as it were. So I won't kill you. I'll—just shoot a leg off."

And when Will came home, he brought with him a hundred dollars in gold, "costs of the case." Thus was law administered in the childhood days of the broad and brawny West.

CHAPTER 10

All this time, Will was becoming more and more famous throughout the East. The summer before, while guiding a party of eastern hunters, he had met Elmo Judson, a novelist who wrote under the name of Ned Buntline, and had given him permission to write stories of Will's experiences in fiction form.[1] It was exactly what the eastern public had been waiting for, and now, every week, some new thrilling story, in which Buffalo Bill rescued maidens in distress, killed off Indians by the score, and hunted buffalo in his sleep, appeared in the romantic magazines. Much of it, while founded on fact, was wildly fantastic in its treatment, and the most surprised man of all would be Will himself when he got the month-old periodicals and read of his hair-raising adventures. But it all had its effect. The East began to call for Buffalo Bill—to demand Buffalo Bill. But Buffalo Bill had just attended a horse race—time had now gone on toward midsummer—and Buffalo Bill had guessed on the wrong horse. Then with the winter came another visit from royalty.

This time it was the Grand Duke Alexis, who, with his retinue, traveled westward for a real shot at a buffalo.[2] A month before his coming, while Will was out on a scouting expedition, I determined that there would be no more visits from Indians and that, this time, my kitchen would have some protection. I went to the fort.

"Major," I said, "I'd like to have some wood."

"For what?"

"I want to build a fence."

The Major leaned back in his chair and laughed.

"Why, Mrs. Cody! Every finger will be black and blue! Don't you know that a woman can't handle a hammer?"

I laughed.

"Well," I answered, "the last time Will was out on a scouting expedition, and I wanted something to pass the time, I built myself a kitchen table. And if I can do that, I can build a fence."

"But I'll send some soldiers down to do it."

"Send the soldiers down with the wood and I'll attend to the rest."

The Major scratched his head.

"Blessed if there's any wood in camp," he said at last. "Except—well," and he smiled, "whiskey comes in wooden barrels, and the canteen seems to be doing a rushing business. I might let you have some barrel staves."

So thus it was that our little log cabin came to have a picket fence in honor of the visit of Grand Duke Alexis. And every picket in that enclosure was a barrel stave! What was more, everyone had been firmly put into place by Buffalo Bill's wife—I wanted to be sure that no Indians were coming in to eat up my cakes and pies and game meats this time!

It was a wonderful day at the fort when the grand duke and his retinue arrived. By cramping every foot of space, we managed some way to get them all about the table in our little log house, but when it came to the reception that followed, that was a different matter. We had to hold it in the yard, in the confines of the picket fence—although such a thing as boundaries made little difference. The day was balmy, and everyone at the fort was there at one time or another.

Finally the grand duke and his hunting party went out on the plains—and the grand duke killed a buffalo. It was the greatest achievement of his life. Will could have anything—anything in the world. And Will named the one thing that had entranced him as much as the thought of killing buffalo had entranced the grand duke. He wanted to go back East. Grand Duke Alexis announced that the wish should be granted.

Back toward New York went the grand duke, and then, six weeks later, came a letter. Will opened it and stared, half frightened, toward me. A long strip ticket was in the envelope. It was a railroad ticket—a ticket back East, all the way to New York, and a pass from General Sheridan. Will, my husband, was about to have his Biggest Adventure!

Somewhat wildly he looked at his clothes, his buckskin coat, his fringed leggings, his heavy revolver holster and red flannel shirt.

"Mamma," he exclaimed woefully, "I can't wear this rigout. I'll— I'll have to have something else."

With that started a feverish week for Mrs. Buffalo Bill. Hurriedly we procured some blue cloth at the commissary and, sewing day and night, I made Will his first real soldier suit, with a colonel's gold braid on it, with stripes and cords and all the other gingerbread of an old-fashioned suit of "blues"; dear, patient, boyish Will sitting anxiously to one side, then rising to try on the partially completed garment, getting pins stuck in him, squirming and twisting, then sitting down again to wait for another fitting. More than once as he waited his eyes would grow wistful, and there would come a peculiar downward pull to his lips as he stared out the window into the faraway.

"Mamma," he would say time after time, "I wish you were going along with me. I'm going to be as scared as a jackrabbit back there! I wish you were going along."

But there was a beautiful little reason why I could not accompany him; and so, the sewing completed, the last basting thread pulled out of his new uniform, I accompanied him to the stage landing and watched him ride away. And never did Buffalo Bill riding out to the danger of death look like the Buffalo Bill who rode away that day. He held me tight, so tight that his fingers bit into my arms, as he said goodbye. And then—

"I sure wish you were going along."

A kiss. A cloud of dust as the horses galloped away. A waving hand, fading in the distance. My husband had gone, gone to a land uncharted for him, unfamiliar and strange.

Two months and he was back, booming and happy. He pulled the free air into his lungs like a bellows. He patted my cheeks, he kissed me, and he walked away, hurried back, and kissed me again.

"Mamma!" he exclaimed, "they almost scared me to death back there. They swished me here, there, yonder and back again; they took me in places where the lights were so bright that I could hardly see, and where women looked at me through spyglasses like I was one of those little bugs that What's-His-Name, the professor, used to look at so much through that telescope last summer. Gosh, I was scared. Couldn't say a word. Just couldn't say a word, Mamma, only just stand there while they stared at me. Guess they expected me to pull out a couple of shootin' irons and put out all the lights. Gosh, I was scared!"

And so it was that when a letter came from Elmo Judson, telling Will how much money he could make by going on the stage, Will simply laid it aside and whooped.

"A whole hall full of women looking at me through those spyglasses!" he exclaimed. "Not much! Out here in the West is good enough for me. Why, Mamma, I'm such a tenderfoot right now from being away, that I'd run if I even saw an Injun!"

But a few days changed all that. At the next call of "boots and saddles," there was Will, home again, leading the galloping procession as it raced out upon the plains, the fringe of his buckskin flying in the wind, his broad hat flapping, his eyes as keen and as bright as ever, his finger ever ready at the trigger for the sight of the Enemy of the Plains.

It was while Will was out on one of these expeditions that the reason that had kept me from going to New York became a reality. Will returned to find the house full of soldiers and the women of the settlement, all of them excited with an event far greater than that of the biggest kind of an Indian raid. It was a tiny little baby boy, and already the suggestions for names had run all the way from Archimedes to Zeno. Will's voice had a new note in it as he came to my bedside, and the visitors drew away that we might be alone with our newest treasure. Gently Will touched the baby's cheek then kissed me.

"A boy," he said softly. "A boy! I want him to grow up to be a real man, Mamma. A boy! He'll carry on the work when his daddy leaves off. He'll be the one to see the West that his daddy wants to build. A boy!"

I really believe it was the greatest moment in Will Cody's life. He was to meet kings, he was to be entertained by royalty all over the world, he was to become the idol of every child who could read the name of Buffalo Bill, but never did a light shine in my husband's eyes as shone that day in the little log cabin, as he gently kissed our baby's cheek and repeated over and over again:

"A boy! Daddy's boy! Daddy's boy!"

Soon, however, the assembled Fort McPherson decided that we had been alone long enough. There were great things to be mastered, such as a selection from the hundred or more names and, above all, the proper arrangements for a christening. Babies were indeed far between in the West of those days, and especially brand new ones. Already couriers were making ready for a hurrying trip to Cheyenne for a rocking crib, for the proper amount of baby rattles, teething rings, and playthings. And by this time, Will had joined in on the general excitement of seeking a name.

"Tell you what!" he announced with a great inspiration, "we'll name him after Judson. That'll tickle Judson to death. Yes, sir; that's it. Elmo Judson Cody! That's what we'll name him."

"We won't do anything of the kind, Will," I announced with the woman's prerogative. "You know you always said you liked the name of Kit Carson."

Will stopped and stared.

"'Course I did. Whoever started this Judson idea? Hello, Kit!"

A big finger was wiggled in the baby's face, and the name was settled. However, that didn't mean that the christening was over. Far from it. Two weeks of preparation and the inhabitants of the fort again gathered in the assembly hall where I had met my Waterloo as a manipulator of "speakin' pieces." Gravely the soldiers lined up while Cody and I carried the baby before the Major. And thereupon the child was officially announced to be Kit Carson Cody. And with the last words—

"Aw-w-w-w right! Grab yo' podners for the quadrille!"

Up on the rostrum the band began to blare. There were not enough women to go 'round, but a trifling deficiency like that made little difference. Where places were vacant, soldiers filled them, and the dance went on, while Will, bouncing our new baby in his arms until my heart almost popped from my throat with fright, took his "spell" at relieving the dance caller, and the bandmen played until their eyes seemed to fairly hang out upon their cheeks. And right in the midst of it all—

"Tya-tay-de-tya—!"

"Boots and saddles!" Will rushed toward me and planted the baby in my arms. Soldiers left the hall by doors and windows. A second and the place was empty except for the women of the fort, while out upon the grounds the first of the cavalry already were beginning to clatter into position. A few moments more, band, dance caller, proud father, christener, and all, they were galloping away, while we poor women had to walk back home, our celebration gone glimmering. Indians were a nuisance in those days!

In fact, they continued to be a nuisance, for soon came another of their sporadic outbreaks on the warpath. Time after time Will was called out, while I waited to watch for him at the window, only to see at last his great form leading all the others as he hurried home to Arta, Kit Carson, and me. But at last came the time when he rode slowly and lowered himself gingerly from the saddle. One quick, flashing look and I was out the door and hurrying to his side. There was blood on his face!

"Thought I was Injun-proof!" He laughed weakly. "Guess I was fooled. Didn't know Injuns could shoot so straight."

Fearfully I took him into the house and awaited the visit of the army surgeon. However, before medical aid could get to him, Will had regained his strength, washed the blood from the scalp wound in his head, tied himself up with a Turkish towel that made him look like some sort of East Indian, and was bellowing away at a song, Arta on one knee and Kit Carson on the other. It was the one and only wound that my husband ever received, in spite of the fact that never was there an Indian fight in which he participated that he was not in the hottest of it, never a brush with the savages that he did not return with a new notch to his gun. Once upon a time I sought to keep track of the number of Indians that "bit the dust" as a result of my husband's accurate fire. But I lost count long before his fighting days were over.

But withal, it was a happy, carefree life we led, with just enough of the zest of danger in it to keep it interesting, just enough novelty to put an edge on the otherwise dreary life of the plains. And when novelty did not come naturally, Will made it.

Thus it was that one day he asked me to accompany him on a buffalo hunt. I left the children with Mrs. MacDonald then mounted and started forth with my husband, only to notice that his rifle was missing. In its stead was a smooth, coiled rope, hanging over the pommel of his saddle.

"Going to try something new today," he announced. "That's why I thought I'd better have you along with a gun. I'm going to lasso a buffalo."

"But, Will!" I exclaimed, "it can't be done!"

"You mean that it hasn't been done," he corrected me then urged his horse forward. In the far distance was the black smudge that presaged a herd of buffalo.

Fifteen minutes of hard riding, and we were upon them. Swiftly Will gave me his commands, for me to follow at an angle from which I could ride swiftly forward and shoot if necessary, while he plunged into the herd. He touched the spurs to his horse and shot forward. A moment more, riding as hard as I could, and I saw that Will had cut one buffalo out from the great mass and was pursuing it in an angling direction to me, his lariat beginning to circle over his head.

Wider and wider went the loop of the lasso. Then a wide, circling swing and it started forth through the air.

It wavered. It hung and seemed to hesitate. Then a quick, downward shot and it had settled over the heavy bull neck of the buffalo, while Will's horse spraddled its legs and prepared for the inevitable pull and tumble.

A great jerk, while the rope seemed to stretch and strain. Then the buffalo rose in the air, turned a complete somersault, and was on its feet again. Once again Will tumbled it, and again, while I circled about, ready for the fatal shot in case the lariat should break and the maddened animal turn on its roper. But when the bison rose from its third tumble, its fight was gone. Placidly it allowed itself to be led to a tree and tied there, while Will sat atop his horse and chuckled.

"T'wasn't so hard now, was it?" he asked. "Shucks, I thought I was going to get some real excitement!"

CHAPTER 11

Thus passed a year. Then another big event happened in our lives. In fact, two of them. One was the birth of a third child, the second to see the light of the West through the windows of our little log cabin. Again, came the usual excitement at the fort, the usual christening and the dance. This time the baby was another girl, and we named her Orra.

The second great event was a series of letters from Mr. Judson (Ned Buntline), each more pressing than the other and all telling of the fortune that could be made if Will would only come back East and be an actor. During the time of Will's visit to New York, he had attended the performance of a dramatization of one of the stories that Ned Buntline had written about him. Will had been pointed out in the box, with the result that the audience had called on him for a speech, and with the further result that Will had arisen, flushed, stammered something that he couldn't even hear himself, and seated himself again, worse scared than any Indian who ever faced his rifle. And so now that Ned Buntline was really suggesting that he, Will Cody, appear on the stage as an actor, the task appeared even more difficult than ever.

But there was constant temptation in the thought of the money. Letter after letter came to our little log cabin, telling of the hundreds and thousands of persons who were waiting to see Buffalo Bill portrayed in some wild Western play, and portrayed by the original of the character. Letter after letter also spoke of thousands of dollars as though they were mere matters that would simply flow into the Cody coffers with the arrival of Buffalo Bill in the East. And the more Will and I read, the more we were tempted. But just the same—

"Mamma, I'd be awful scared," he said to me more than once. "I'd get out there and just get glassy-eyed from looking at those lights. I couldn't do it. I'd just naturally be tongue-tied."

"Oh, you could do it all right," I answered with that confidence that a wife always has in her husband, "but is playacting just the right thing?"

"Shucks, playacting's all right and—" Then he stopped and looked at the children, Arta growing up to young girlhood; Kit Carson, his ideal and his dream, just at the romping age; and Orra a tiny baby. "And," he said at last, "if there was money, it would mean a lot for them, Mamma. It would mean that we could send them to fine schools and have everything for them that we wanted. You know, I didn't get much chance to go to school when I was a boy. And I want them to have everything I missed."

With that, the great problem of whether or not Will Cody should become an actor was settled. It was further disposed of when Texas Jack roamed down to the house, heard that Will was seriously considering the Buntline proposition, and immediately decided that he would like to go on the stage himself. Will, wavering, was strengthened.

"Guess I'll write to Ned and tell him we're just about ready to be roped and hogtied," he announced, more to himself than anyone else. Deliberately he sat down and scratched for an hour, finally composing a letter to his satisfaction. Then he sent it away on its long journey, and in the meanwhile—

There was an election. And who, at the last minute, should be decided upon as a fit and proper person to represent the Fort McPherson district in the state legislature, but my husband! There wasn't any campaign; Will simply announced that it was true he was running, but that he didn't know which way. There were not many voters—every one of them knew the "Jedge," as they sometimes jokingly called him, personally—and there was no competition. Will was just elected and added an Honorable to his name without even taking the trouble to make an election speech. And hardly had he been elected when there came a letter from Buntline saying that everything was rosy in the East, and that a fortune awaited Will and Texas Jack almost the minute they stepped into Chicago. Will looked at the letter and then dug up his certificate of election. Carefully he weighed the careers, that of an actor in one hand, that of a Solon in the other. Finally he looked at me and chuckled.

"Mamma," he said, "I know I'd be a fizzle at legislatin'. I don't know just how bad I'd be at actin'. I guess maybe I'd better find out."

Whereupon his fate was settled as a public servant. As for Texas Jack, never was a person happier, for Texas Jack had absorbed the stage fever; he wanted to be an actor, and, what was more, he was going to be an actor whether the audiences said he could act or not.

What excitement there was after the decision was made! What selling off of horses, of furniture, even to the kitchen table at which I had hammered and banged away during the long days in the little old cabin. What sewing and hopes and dreams! Will resigned as a scout, as a colonel, as a justice of the peace, and as a legislator. We packed our grips and "telescopes," and when the stage pulled out one afternoon, late in 1872, there we were, piled in it, Will and Texas Jack, me and the babies, bound for the adventures of the unknown.

And if Will and Jack only had known what was to happen when they reached Chicago, I don't believe that stage would have carried us ten feet. Neither of them ever had seen more than a dozen stage plays in their lives. They had no idea of how to make an entrance or an exit, they did not know a cue from a footlight, and they believed that plays just happened. The fact that they would have to study and memorize parts never entered their heads. And what was worse—

"All right, boys!" It was Ned Buntline, greeting them at the station in Chicago. "We'll do a little quick work now and have this play on by Monday night."

"Monday night?" They both stared at him while they weren't gawking at the crowds, the sizzling, steaming engines, and the great trucks of baggage passing by. "Ain't—ain't that rushing things a little?"

Buntline smiled.

"It is going a little fast, but you fellows ought to be accustomed to that. Come on now. We'll go over and fix up for the theater."

Texas Jack scratched his head.

"I thought that'd all be arranged for."

"Nothing of the kind. The owner's got to see his stars first. So come on."

"But—who all's going to be with us in this rigout?"

"The company?" They were in the hack now, bound for the amphitheater. "Oh, I haven't given that a thought. But there are plenty of actors around town. Don't worry a minute about them."

But both Jack and Will did a good deal of worrying. Evidently the manager of the amphitheater felt the same way about it.

"When are you going to have your rehearsals?" he asked after Buntline had outlined a possible contract to him.

"Tomorrow."

"Why tomorrow? There's no one on the stage this afternoon, and time's getting short. This is Wednesday, and if you're going to open next Monday, you'll have to do a lot of practicing. So I'd suggest a rehearsal just as soon as you can get out the parts and—"

"Well." Buntline smiled. "That's just it. You see, I haven't written the play yet!"

Will gasped. So did Texas Jack. And so did the manager. More than that, he refused to make a contract on a play that was not written for two stars who never had been on the stage before. Buntline grew angry. He dragged a roll of bills from his pocket.

"What's the rent on this theater for a week?" he snapped.

"Six hundred dollars!"

"Taken—and here's three hundred in advance. Give me a receipt. Thanks. Come on, boys."

Out he swept, while Jack and my husband followed him somewhat vaguely over to the hotel, and to Buntline's room. The dramatist pointed to two chairs.

"Sit there!" he ordered, and they sat. Whereupon, dragging out pens and paper, he shouted for a bellboy.

"Tell every clerk in this hotel that they're hired as penmen," he ordered quickly. The bellboy stared.

"As what, sir?"

"Penmen. I'm going to write a play and I'm going to do it quick. Haven't got time to fool around. These are my two stars here, Buffalo

Bill and Texas Jack—and we're going to give a play in the amphitheater next Monday night. And now I'm going to write the play, and I'll want someone to copy the parts. So hurry them up!"

Perhaps the bellboy stared the hardest. Perhaps not, for he had excellent competition in Texas Jack and my husband. They had shot Indians on the plains, they had ridden pony express, they had lain for days and nights when they did not know whether the next sun would see them crumpled in death, and they had managed to assimilate it all. But here was something new, something different. All the way from the wild, free West had they come, to be hustled and bustled about in a big city, there to learn that they were stars in something that had not even become permanent enough to be placed on paper. But Buntline was past paying any attention to them. Already his pen was scratching over the paper, while sheet after sheet piled up on the other side of the table. Now and then he would leap to his feet and rant up and down the room, shouting strange words and sentences at the top of his voice, then, bobbing into his chair again and grasping that pen, scribble harder than ever. One by one the clerks began to make their appearance, only to have reams of paper jabbed into their hands, and then be shunted into the next room with orders to copy as they never had copied before. Somewhat wildly my husband looked at Texas Jack, squirming about in his chair.

"Partner," he began, "I reckon we—"

"Shut up!" It was an order from the scribbling Buntline. Will slumped in his chair.

"I'm shut," he announced weakly.

The scribbling went on. At the end of four hours Buntline leaped to his feet and waved a handful of paper at the two flustered ones from the plains.

"Hurrah!" he shouted. "Hurrah for *The Scouts of the Plains*."

Texas Jack looked around hurriedly.

"Who're they?"

"*The Scouts of the Plains*? They're you. You're *The Scouts of the Plains*. That's the name of the play. Now, all you've got to do is to get your parts letter perfect."

"Get w-h-a-t?"

"Your parts—the lines that you're going to speak. That stuff I've been writing."

"All that?" Cody blinked. Texas Jack sank lower in his chair. "You mean we've got to learn what you've been scribbling there, so we can get up on the stage and spout it off?"

"Of course."

Cody reached for his hat and twisted it in his hands.

"Jack," he said at last, "I guess we're on the wrong trail. Maybe—maybe we're better at hunting Injuns!"

"But, boys—"

"I reckon I don't want to be an actor, after all." Texas Jack had risen, his long arms swinging at his sides. But Buntline was in front of them, pleading the fact that he already had paid out three hundred dollars, that they had made the trip from Fort McPherson just for this, that Will had sold off everything he possessed and that it wouldn't be fair, either to him or to themselves, to turn back now. Will scratched his head.

"Well," he announced at last, "I never went back on a friend. But this sure is pizen!"

"It sure is," agreed Texas Jack. "But give us those parts, or whatever you call 'em. We'll do our best. If I'd known all this, I'd never come on, honest I wouldn't. I thought all there was to playacting was to just get up there and say whatever popped into your head. And we've got to learn all this?"

He stared at his part. Cody was doing the same. Then they looked at each other.

"How long you calculate it'll take to learn it?" Jack asked of Will. My husband sighed mournfully.

"About six months."

"Same here. But—"

"Boys," Buntline was serious now, "either you've got to have both those parts committed to memory tomorrow morning or—well, we all lose. And just remember one thing, your reputation's at stake."

"Yeh." Texas Jack still was staring at that mass of paper in his hand. "And I'd rather be tied at the stake right now. But if I say I'll do a thing, I'll do 'er. Lock us up somewhere and we'll do our derndest!"

I know there were nights in Will Cody's life that were horrible nightmares from a standpoint of danger and privation. But I am just as sure that there never was such a night as the one when he tried to learn the first elements of being an actor. No one ever will know just what did happen in that room; from the outside it sounded like the mutterings of a den of wild animals. Now and then Will's voice would sound high and strident, then low and bellowing, with Texas Jack chiming in with a rumbling base. Every few minutes bellboys would rush up the hall with ice clinking in the pitchers, hand the refreshments through the door, then hurry away again, with a sort of dazed, non-understanding expression on their faces. And all the while, the rumbling of prairie thunder, the verbal flashes of lightning and crashing of mountainous torrents of speech would continue, while guests in the adjoining rooms made uncomplimentary remarks, and Ned Buntline, entering the "den" now and then, would stand a few moments to listen, then walk quietly away, somewhat like a man in a dream.

But nights must pass and that one faded away at last, to find Texas Jack and my husband on the dark stage of the theater, well-worn and wan and waiting for the next step in the new form of torture that had swooped upon them. The rehearsal was called, and Buntline, who already had engaged his company, hired a director, and looked after the printing and the distributing of dodgers, introduced the two stars to the rest of the company. One after another, and then—

"And this is Mademoiselle Morlacchi," he said as he introduced Texas Jack to a dark-eyed, dark-haired little woman.[1] "She is to dance just before the show, for a curtain raiser."

Texas Jack put out his hand in a hesitating, wavering way. His usually heavy, bass voice cracked and broke. There were more difficulties than ever now, for Jack had fallen in love, at sight!

Far in the rear of the stage, there was a third person who had watched the introduction and the little flash of mutual admiration that had passed between the two. Years before he had met Will on the Missouri and had come to admire him, with the result that he had requested and been given the management of the advertising part of the show: Major John M. Burke.[2] That morning Major Burke had met Morlacchi also—and he, too, had felt the flush of love.

And with this combination, the first rehearsal began. It was a wonderful thing, from the standpoint of a prairie stampede or a cattle roundup. But as a theatrical rehearsal, it was hardly a success. Jack and Will had learned their parts without regard to cues, entrances, or anything else that might interfere with free speech. The moment the director would call on one of them, he would begin speaking the whole of his part, line after line, with never a pause, never a stop for breath, booming at the top of his lungs, turning his back on the supposed audience, putting his hands in his pockets, and doing everything else in the calendar that no actor is supposed to do. Patiently the director led them around the stage, taught them the difference between the proscenium arch and the woodwings, pushed them off the stage and on the stage, forward and backward, only a minute later to see it all done wrong again. At last, almost desperate at having two to handle, he turned Texas Jack over to Mademoiselle Morlacchi, while he looked after my husband. And never did a pupil work harder than Texas Jack from that moment!

All day they rehearsed, and they were still studying their lines when the house began to fill that night. The mere mention of the fact that Buffalo Bill was to appear in a play had been enough. The house was crowded. Every well-known man with whom Will ever had hunted was there, while the galleries, balcony, and parquet were crowded with those who had read the stories of Buffalo Bill, as written by Ned Buntline. And, of course, Texas Jack and Will had to look out through the peephole. They turned to each other in dismay.

"I'm plumb scared to death!" Jack confessed.

"So'm I—" Then, desperately, "Jack—what do I say when I first come on the stage?"

Jack's jaw fell.

"Gosh," he exclaimed, "what do *I* say?"

They had forgotten their parts, forgotten them as completely as though they never had studied them. Wildly they rushed to the dressing rooms and began to cram again. The orchestra played the overture. The curtain went up, and then through the aisles and behind the wings went a stagehand, hurrying, excited—

"Where's Buffalo Bill?" he called, "where's Buffalo Bill?"

They dragged Will out of the dressing room, where, part in hand, he was struggling to reassemble those missing lines. Out on the stage they shoved him, where Buntline, playing the part of Gale Durg, who seemed to be some sort of a vague temperance character, obsessed with a mania for delivering lectures on the curse of drink, awaited him.

Once on the stage, Will just stood there, gawking. His lines had vanished again, his hands suddenly had assumed the imagined proportions of hams, and his feet had gained a weight that would surely have tripped him if he had taken another step. Gale Durg, the temperance advocate, moved close and whispered the cue line. It did no good. Will simply stood there, moving his lips in an aimless fashion, a dry gurgling sound coming from somewhere back in his throat. But that was all. Gale Durg, the destroyer of the Demon Rum, decided on desperate remedies.

"Hello, Cody!" he shouted. "Where have you been?"

Will blinked. Now he realized that he was on the stage and supposed to be saying something. Wildly he glanced about—and happened to see in one of the boxes a Mr. Milligan, popular in Chicago, who had recently been on a hunt with him.

"I've—I've been out on a hunt with Milligan," he announced.

"Ah?" Gale Durg, resorting to that method of "stalling" that has helped many an actor over a rough road, followed the lead. "Tell us about it."

Whereupon Will "told." On he rambled, with any wild story that came to his brain, on and on and on, while the prompter groaned in the wings and while the plot of the play vanished entirely. Finally someone backstage thought of Texas Jack and shoved him out into the glare of light. Then, one by one, the other players trooped on. And then—

The Indians! Chicago Indians from Clark Street and Dearborn and Madison, Indians who never had seen the land beyond the borders of Illinois, Indians painted and devilish and ready to be killed. It was the lifesaver. Out came Will's gun. Wildly he banged away about the stage; then, leaping here and there, he knocked down Indians until there were no more to knock. He was back home now, with Texas Jack at his side, pulling the trigger of his six-shooter until the stage was filled with smoke, and until the hammers only clicked on exploded cartridges. They yelled. They shouted. They roared and banged away at the hapless Illinois tribe, at last remembering vaguely that there was a heroine somewhere around the stage, and that they must save her. Whereupon they leaped forward, hurdled the bodies of the slain savages, grabbed the heroine around the waist, and dragged her offstage, while the curtain came down and the house roared its approval at the bloodthirstiest Indian fight in which either Will Cody or Texas Jack had ever participated.

The act was over. The next was devoted almost entirely to Gale Durg, while he died, making a speech on temperance almost as long as a political platform as he did so. By this time both Will and Jack had gained an opportunity to make another wild scramble for those parts, and the Indians had been rejuvenated sufficiently to allow them to be killed again. Therefore when the next act came, there was at least a semblance of the original lines of the play, to say nothing of another Indian massacre and the consequent rescue of the heroine, who had again happened along at just the wrong—or right—moment.

Finally, after two hours of torture for actors, Indians, and those two stars, the curtain came down for the last time. But the audience refused to leave. Louder and louder it applauded until, at last, white and excited, Will and Jack had to obey a curtain call. Their first appearance had been a wonderful success, perhaps all the more wonderful because of the fact that the play had been almost forgotten and those two plainsmen had gotten out there on the stage and given an exhibition of stage fright that no actor possibly could simulate. The audience had come to see Buffalo Bill and Texas Jack—and they had been entertained by the sight of two men who feared nothing, but who, at that moment, would have been afraid of their own shadows.

As for the newspapers, their criticisms were enough to make any play. If there is too much praise, or if there is not enough, it may be damning. But when a newspaper blooms forth in good-natured humor, it provokes curiosity! And certainly—but here is an example:

> There is a well-founded rumor that Ned Buntline, who played the part of Gale Durg in last night's performance, wrote the play in which Buffalo Bill and Texas Jack appeared, taking only four hours to complete the task. The question naturally arises: what was he doing all that time? As Gale Durg, he made some excellent speeches on temperance and was killed in the second act, it being very much regretted that he did not arrange his demise so that it could have occurred sooner. Buffalo Bill and Texas Jack are wonderful Indian killers. As an artistic success, "The Scouts of the Plains" can hardly be called a season's event, but for downright fun, Injun killing, red fire and rough and tumble, it is a wonder.

All of which was thoroughly agreed with by Will and Texas Jack. In fact, so much did Will coincide in the opinion that a week later, in St. Louis—

With Arta on my lap, I sat in the audience, watching the performance and waiting for Will to appear. At last, three or four Indians pranced across the stage, turned, waved their tomahawks, yelled something, and then fell dead, accompanied by the rattle-te-bang of a six-shooter. Out rushed Will, who assured himself that all three of the Indians were thoroughly dead, turned just in time to kill a couple more who had roamed on to the stage by accident, and then faced the audience.

I was sitting in about the third row, and Will saw me. He came forward, leaned over the gas footlights, and waved his arms.

"Oh, Mamma!" he shouted, "I'm a bad actor!"

The house roared. Will threw me a kiss and then leaned forward again, while the house stilled.

"Honest, Mamma," he shouted, "does this look as awful out there as it feels up here?"

And again the house chuckled and applauded. Someone called out the fact that I was Mrs. Buffalo Bill. High up in the gallery came a strident voice:

"Get up there on the stage! Let's take a look at you."

"Yeh!" It was Will's voice, chiming in. "Come on up, Mamma."

"Oh, Will!" I was blushing to the roots of my hair. "Stop!"

"Stop nothing. You can't be any worse scared than I am. Come on up."

Someone placed a chair in the orchestra pit. Hands reached out. I felt myself raised from my seat and boosted on to the stage, Arta after me. There in the glare of the footlights, my husband rumbling with laughter beside me, I felt that dryness, that horrible speechlessness that I knew Will had experienced that first night in Chicago—and for once it wasn't funny. Will pinched me on the arm.

"Now you can understand how hard your poor old husband has to work to make a living!" he shouted, and the audience applauded again.

I don't remember how long I had to stand there; it's all hazy and mist-like. After a long while, I remember sitting down front once again, while Will banged away at the Indians up on the stage. And after that, when I went to see my husband in his new role as an actor, I chose a seat in the farthest and darkest part of the house. But it did little good. For invariably Will would seek me out, and invariably he would call:

"Hello, Mamma. Oh, but I'm a bad actor!"

CHAPTER 12

The money was flowing in. Bad as the "stars" knew their play to be, it was what the public wanted, and that was all that counted. Week after week they played to houses that were packed to the roofs, while often the receipts would run close to $20,000 for the seven days. It was more money than any of us ever had dreamed of before. Unheard-of extravagances became ours. And Will, dear, generous soul that he was, believed that an inexhaustible supply of wealth had become his forever. One night—I believe it was in St. Louis—we entered a hotel, only to find that the rooms we occupied were on a noisy side of the house. Will complained. The manager bowed suavely.

"But you are liable to encounter noise anywhere in a hotel," came his counterargument. "For instance, I might move you to another part of the hotel and right in the next room would be someone who talked loudly or otherwise disturbed you. The only way you could have absolute peace would be to rent the whole floor and, of course, you don't want to do that—"

"Don't I?" Will reached for the roll of bills in his pocket. "How much is it?"

The manager figured. Then he smiled.

"Two hundred dollars would be a pretty stiff price to pay for peace and quiet."

"Paid!" Will had peeled the bills from his roll. "Now, let's see how quick you can make things comfortable for us. I've got a wife and babies and we're all tired!"

Never did anyone ever have such service. But it cost money. In fact, so much money that when the season was over, Will looked somewhat ruefully at his bank account. Instead of the hundred thousand dollars or so he had dreamed of possessing, the balance showed something less than $6,000. And Texas Jack's bankbook had suffered far more—for Texas Jack was in love.

Long ago poor Major Burke had given up all hope of ever winning the little dancer, and great big man that he was, he had confessed it. To me he had told his story, and to me he had unfolded his purpose in life.

"Mrs. Cody," he had said one night as we sat backstage watching the "performance" from the wings, "I have met a god and a goddess in my life. The god was Bill Cody. I came on him just at sunset one night, out on the Missouri, and the reflection of the light from the river was shining up straight into his face and lighting it up like some kind of an aura. He was on horseback, and I thought then that he was the handsomest, straightest, finest man that I ever had seen in my life. I still think so."

He was silent a moment, while some rampage of Indian killing happened out on the stage. Then he leaned closer.

"The goddess was Mademoiselle Morlacchi. But I can't have her, Mrs. Cody. I wouldn't be the man that I want to be if I tried. Jack's a better man—he's fought the West, and he's had far more hardships than I've ever seen and—and—he deserves his reward. I'll never love any other woman—but there's one thing I can do: I can turn all my affection from the goddess to the god, and so help me, I'll never fail from worshipping him!"

Many a year followed that, many a year of wandering, while Will went from country to country, from nation to nation, from state to state. There were fat times and there were lean, there were times when the storms gathered, and there were times when the sun shone; but always, in cloud or in sunshine, there was ever a shadow just behind him, following him with a wistful love that few men can ever display, Major John M. Burke. And when the time came that Will and I said goodbye forever, another man loosed his hold on the world. Throughout every newspaper office in the country, where John Burke had sat by the hour, never mentioning a word about himself but telling always of the prowess of his "god," there flashed the news that Major John M. Burke, the former representative of William Frederick Cody, had become dangerously ill. And six weeks later the faithful old hands were folded, the lips that had spoken hardly anything but the praises of Buffalo Bill for a half a century were still. Major Burke had died when Cody died; only his body lingered on for those six weeks, at last to loose its hold on the loving, faithful old spirit it bound and allow it to follow its master over the Great Divide.

But that is a matter of other years. We still were in the days of youth and of life. The West was calling to all of us, and back we bundled at the end of the season, once more to take up our home at the fort, while Jack and Will scouted through the summer months and made their plans for the coming season.

The stage had caught them now. This time they would not be such profligates. This time they would save—and more, they would be producers themselves. Hence the reason that they must work this summer and not make inroads upon that bank balance.

Already the play was being written, and a new star was to be added, Wild Bill Hickok. The summer passed and back we went to the East, while Texas Jack and Will began their play, and awaited Wild Bill. At last he came, to arrive one night while Will was on the stage, resplendent in the circle of the "limelight." Wild Bill, stumbling about in the darkness of the stage, looked out and gasped as he saw Cody.

"For the sake of Jehosophat!" he exclaimed, "what's that Bill Cody's got on him out there?"

"The clothes, you mean?" I asked. I was sitting in one of the entrances, Kit Carson on my lap. Long ago Kit had become a regular theatergoer; it was habit to take him to watch his father now. Wild Bill shook his head and waved his arms.

"No," he was growing more excited every minute, "that white stuff that's floating all around him."

I laughed.

"Why, Mr. Hickok," I explained, "that's limelight."

Wild Bill turned and grasped a stagehand by the arm. Then he dragged a gold piece from his pocket.

"Boy," he ordered, "run just as fast as your legs will carry you and get me five dollars' worth of that stuff. I want it smeared all over me!"

In fact, Bill needed a good many things smeared over him, for, while he might have been wonderful with a revolver, he was hardly meant for an actor. Like Jack and Will he had stage fright on his first performance, and, more than that, he never got over it.

"Ain't this foolish?" he exclaimed one night, after he had stuttered and stammered through his lines. "Ain't it now? What's the use of getting out there and making a show of yourself? I ain't going to do it!"

And there the theatrical career of William Hickok ended. He went away, back to his West, to his card games—and to his death. But the theatrical enterprises of Cody and Omohundro—that was Texas Jack's real name—went flourishing on.

Weird things were those plays. After the first season Will had purchased a house in Rochester, New York, where the children and I might live until he should come home from the road. Now and then we would join him for a while then return to the big, quiet house and its restfulness, where I might dream of the days of the West—and see in a vision the time when we would return there. For Will never looked upon his stage experience as anything but transitory.

Nevertheless, the public demanded him, and the public got him, in such wondrous pieces of dramatic art as *Life on the Border, Buffalo Bill at Bay, From Noose to Neck, Buffalo Bill's Pledge,* and other marvels of stagecraft. One of them I remember particularly, and the faded old manuscript lies before me as I write, *The Red Right Hand.*

Just what the Red Right Hand had to do with the play never was fully determined. However, a small detail like that made very little difference in those days. The thing that counted was action, and when the lines became dull, it was always possible for someone to pull out a revolver and start shooting. Even the manuscript provided for that. Just for instance, a few lines from its quietest act:

> *Hurry music. Shot is heard.* (I'm quoting now from the manuscript.) *Pearl enters, pursued by several Indians. She runs up on rock. Enter Indians, yelling. She fires one shot and an Indian falls. The balance of them yell and attempt to ascend the rock. She clubs them back with butt of rifle.*

Pearl—(*on rock*).... Back! Back! You red fiends!
Enter *Bill, hurriedly fires a few shots, and three or four Indians fall.*

Perhaps you'll notice how careless they were with Indians in those days. It didn't make much difference how many shots were fired; the number of Indians that toppled over was always more than the number of bullets that chased them to their deaths. But to that manuscript:

> ... *Red Hand enters hastily, follows off the retiring Indians and shoots once or twice and kills several Indians. Returns, sees Bill and raises rifle as if to shoot.*
> Bill—Hold on, Pard!
> Red Hand—(*Surprised*). What? Bill Cody?
> Bill—Red Hand? You here?
> Red Hand—Yes, Bill, and I'm glad to meet you. I heard you were to join the campaign, but had no idea that you had yet arrived. But it is always like you, Bill—sure to be near when danger threatens!

Can't you hear them, these two great-lunged men of the plains, roaring this at each other? Can't you imagine the gestures, the strutting, the pursing of lips as these scouts of the silent places, accustomed to the long, stealthy searches, the hours of waiting, the days of trailing, bellowed this travesty, while out over the footlights, a tenderfoot audience waited, gaping on every word, and assured itself that here was the true spirit of the West, the real manner in which the paleface and the Indian fought the great fight? But one cannot transport the prairie to the boarded stage and still keep within the mileage limits. And, besides, those audiences wanted their kind of thrills. They got them. Back to that manuscript:

> Bill—(*Takes his hand*). I always try to be, Red Hand, you bet! (*Looks up and sees Pearl, who has been listening.*) But say, look here, who is yon lovely creature that we have just rescued from those red fiends?
> Red Hand—By heavens! Bill, but she is beautiful. Yet I know not who she is.

Many a time I heard Texas Jack call a dance. Many a time I saw him swing off his horse, tired and dusty from miles in the saddle, worn from days and nights without sleep, when perhaps the lives of hundreds depended on his nerve, his skill with the rifle, his knowledge of the prairie. But I don't believe I ever heard him say, at any of those times: "Yet I know not who she is." Marvels indeed were those old-time "drameys," when the East, the West and the imagination of the Bowery dramatist all met in the same sentence. If I may return to the manuscript—

> Bill—(*To Pearl*). Fear not, fair girl. You are now safe with one who is ever ready to aid a friend, or risk his life in defense of a woman.
>
> Pearl—(*Comes down*). I knew not that the paleface hunters dare come into this unknown land of the Indian.
>
> Red Hand—Will you not let me see you to your cabin?
>
> Hermit—(*Suddenly appears on rock, shoots, and Red Hand falls. Rushes down with rifle in hand, sees Red Hand trying to gain his feet. Speaks*): Ha! My rifle failed me, but this will not! (*Draws large knife. Rushes toward Red Hand, and is just in the act of stabbing him when Bill rushes on him and, with knife in hand, confronts Hermit. Chord. Picture.*)
>
> Bill—Hello, Santa Claus!
>
> Hermit—(*Staggering back*). Buffalo Bill! Ha! Ha! Ha! Well met! I have sworn to kill you, and all your accursed race. Your hour has come! For this is your last!
>
> Bill—(*Calmly*). You don't say so?
>
> Hermit—By heaven I will keep my vow!
>
> *Music. Starts for Bill, who steps over Red Hand and faces him. They stare at each other and Hermit rushes on Bill. They cross knives. Pearl leaps into scene and grasps the wrist of Hermit.*
>
> Pearl—Father! Father! This must not be! (*Chord in 'G.' Picture.*)

That is sufficient. Perhaps now you can understand the plight of those two men of the West when first they gazed upon a "Western" play there in the hotel in Chicago, five days before their first performance.

Perhaps, too, you can understand why, in the agonized days of learning the new parts as the different plays came along, Will and Jack would stare at each other weakly then allow the manuscripts to slip aimlessly to the floor, as one or the other exclaimed:

"Gosh! We never talked like this!"

But there was the money, and there was that house in Rochester, and the big school that meant so much to Will because it meant so much also to the three children that he loved. And just how much he loved them! How much indeed—

It was late one night in April 1876. I had been sitting for hours, months it seemed, beside the crib of our little boy, tossing there in the parched agony of scarlet fever. Across the room lay Arta, crying and pettish from the same illness, and tucked away was Orra, also a victim. The world had grown black, and the darkness was descending all about me. Again and again I leaned forward, forcing back the sobs that I could scarcely restrain, trying to soothe the fevered little being, whispering over and over again:

"I've telegraphed, Honey. Daddy will be here tomorrow morning. He'll be here at nine o'clock, Honey. Go to sleep now; Daddy's coming, Daddy'll be here in the morning."

And in answer the little lips would murmur:

"Ten o'clock—ten o'clock."

"Nine o'clock, Honey. He'll be here at nine o'clock."

And again the answer would come:

"Ten o'clock. Ten o'clock!"

I knew what was happening far away, in Boston, where Buffalo Bill was showing that week, knew as well as though I were there, knew that out on the stage a man, his faced lined and old, was telling an audience that he could not go on with this mockery any longer, that tragedy had come to him and that he must obey its call. I knew from the time that I had sent the telegram calling him home that he would be able to catch the train that reached Rochester shortly before nine o'clock in the morning, and that by the time the clock struck, he would be in the house and beside his boy—the boy he had dreamed for, hoped for, lived and loved for. And if Kit could only live until then—it was my prayer! I knew that death was coming; I could tell it from the fear that clutched at my heart, the fear that tore its ragged claws into my very vitals. A mother knows—a mother can see in the eyes of the child she loves when the light is dimming; her own heart echoes the failing beats of the heart that is hers also. And if Kit could only live until morning—until nine o'clock! But faintly the baby lips answered:

"Ten o'clock—ten o'clock!"

The night dragged along on its weary path, while I sat there, counting the ticks of the old clock, sounding heavy and sonorous in the quiet room. Dawn came and the baby slept. The sun rose and he awakened, while I leaned over him, whispering:

"It'll not be long now, honey. Daddy's on the way. He'll be here at nine o'clock."

And once again the white lips that once had been so red and round and full, the drawn lips that once had laughed so prettily, parted with:

"Ten o'clock. Ten o'clock."

Eight o'clock. Eight-thirty. I waited for the whistle of the train, my heart pounding until it seemed that its every throb was a triphammer beating on my brain. The old, heavily ticking clock struck nine. The whistle had not sounded.

Again the minutes dragged on. Slower and slower and slower—a whistle, far away—a long, anxious wait and then the sound of hurried steps, the rushing form of a man who came into the room, his face white and drawn, his arms extended. As he knelt by the side of the baby we loved, the old clock on the wall struck ten! And almost with the last stroke, there faded the life from the pretty baby eyes, the little fingers twitched ever so slightly; there was a sigh, brief, soft and the choking sob of a great, strong man. Kit, our Kit, the baby for whom Will and I had dreamed—was dead.

We buried him where he wanted to lie, up in the big cemetery at the end of the street, where the trees flung wide their shade and where he had seen the flowers and the smooth mounds of green and where—with that childlike prognostication that all too often comes true—he had said he would like to be if he died. We buried him and said goodbye to him and then turned back to the big home, a tall, silent man, his lips pressed tight, his eyes narrowed and determined, and his great, strong arm about the wife who was not as strong as he, who grieved with all her heart yet was blessed with the surcease of tears.

Silently he walked about the house for a day or so, stopping to look at the bed where Kit had lain and died, then trying to smile for the sake of the baby and of the girl who lay fevered and ill. Telegrams came to him. He crushed them unread. Then—

"Mamma—" His voice had lost the old buoyant ring. "I can't go back to that—that mockery. It's always been a joke to me—those plays. And I can't joke now. I can't go on the stage and act—remembering—remembering—up there." He pointed hurriedly toward the cemetery. I put my arms about him.

"Will," I said, "it's spring. They're starting the expeditions now, back out home. It's your land out there. I'll stay here and wait, and hope. We've got enough money; we can live. I want you to go back out West again and ride and fight and—well, I know you won't forget."

"No," he answered, "I won't forget."

A day later, he went to rejoin the show again, but only to close its season and hurry home again. Within a week or so, we said goodbye at the station once more. Will was going back to the West, and I hoped that the West would give him again that old light in his eyes, that the fresh, clear air, the brilliant ruddiness of the sunshine, and the glare of the plains would take that pallor from his cheeks, that the excitement of the chase would once again return the great, happy booming that once had sounded in his voice. My trust in the West was fulfilled.

It was some time before I received a letter. Then I learned that Will was soon to take to the trail again, this time as the chief of scouts for General Sheridan. A letter that arrived shortly afterward told me, however, that he soon was to rejoin his old command, the Fifth Cavalry, under General Carr, and that a campaign was to start against the hostile Sioux. Again, a third letter told of a change in the command, this time the regiment being under General Wesley Merritt. Then silence.

A month passed while I nursed Arta and Orra back to health and strength. A second month and then the news flashed upon the world that Custer had been massacred, and that every Sioux in the Big Horn country had gone upon the warpath. Long before, Will had told me not to worry, and never to lose faith in his powers to defend himself. But now I was fighting against a new enemy—was Will again the old Will? Or had he allowed grief to weigh upon him until it had dulled his quickness of perception, his keenness of eye, his rapidity of touch upon the trigger?

Story after story came from the West of the horrors of that massacre, how the Indians had surged upon Custer and his command, surrounding him, annihilating the soldiery, fighting to the last minute, the last gasp of breath. News did not travel swiftly in those times; there was no casualty list forthcoming in a few days or weeks, such as one might expect now should a catastrophe of the same nature happen in this country. All that I knew was that Will was out in the West, that he was scouting for the gallant Fifth Cavalry, and that sometime, someplace, the Indians and that regiment would meet for revenge. And when they met would their fate be that of Custer?

The news came of another battle, and I gasped as I read the command. It was the Fifth Cavalry, hurrying to cut off the Dog Soldiers, as a number of renegade Sioux and Cheyenne were called. They had stopped the advance of eight hundred Indians just as they were seeking to turn into the heart of the Big Horn country and there join the hostile bands of Sitting Bull. I knew that Will had been in that battle, but that was all. Any knowledge of whether he was alive or dead—that was another matter. I found myself tormented with a new fear. It was I who had sent him into the West; it was I who had suggested that out there he might heal over the wounds that the death of Kit Carson had caused. It was I who—

There was a knock on the door, and I answered it, my heart pounding strangely. But it was only the expressman, with a small, square box. I looked at the label—all that it told me was that one of its shipping points had been Fort McPherson and that the consignor was William Frederick Cody. But that was enough. It told me also that Will was still alive, and apparently safe. For the shipping date was later than that of the Battle of the Warbonnet—such had been named the clash between the Dog Soldiers and the Fifth Cavalry—and that meant Will's safety, from that battle at least.[1]

Hurriedly I sought the hatchet and pried open the lid of the box. A terrific odor caught my nostrils. I reeled slightly then reached for the contents. Then I fainted. For I had brought from that box the raw, red scalp of an Indian!

Some way I managed to put the thing away from me when I recovered consciousness. Some way I managed to blind myself to the sight of it. But I couldn't wipe out the memory. And weeks later, when Will Cody rushed in the door, his voice thundering with at least a semblance of the olden days, I forgot myself long enough to kiss him and hug him again and again—then remembered that I was terribly angry.

"Will Cody!" I said. "What on earth did you send me that old scalp for! Aren't you ashamed of yourself? It nearly scared me to death!"

"No!" In his eyes was blank astonishment. "Why—why I thought you'd like that."

"Like it? Why, Will, I fainted!"

"Honest?" The knowledge that I was in the East now, gradually was beginning to break in on him. "Gosh, I never thought of that. I was so excited that I just said to myself that I'd send his scalp to Mamma and let her know just how fine a time I was having out there, because it was about the best fight I ever had and I knew that when you got my letter, you'd—"

"But I didn't get any letter."

"Not about Yellowhand?"[2]

"Who's Yellowhand?"

"Gosh!" Will leaned against the door and laughed. "What's the use of getting a reputation? Remember how I used to make fun of that playacting? Well, by golly, it turned out. I've had a duel!"

"With an Indian?"

"With an Injun—and I sent you his scalp, just for a keepsake, as it were. You see, General Merritt got an idea that maybe he might be able to cut off those Dog Soldiers. We marched all day and most of the night, and we prepared an ambush along Warbonnet Creek, just before the Dogs got there. Well, everything was fine. The Injuns showed up on the hill and we were just waiting to start popping away at 'em, when a wagon train showed up in the distance and some of the Injuns started after it. Well, then there wasn't much more chance to keep ourselves hid if we were going to save those wagons, so I took twelve or fifteen scouts out and drove off the Injuns that had started after the train. And about this time, out rode an old codger all decorated up and everything and began pounding his chest and riding around and cutting up fit to kill. I turned to Little Bat, our interpreter, and asked him what the old fogy was trying to do. Mamma, you ought to have seen him. He was riding up and down in front of the Injuns that were lined up on the hill, pounding himself on the chest and ranting around there like a crazy man. Little Bat listened to him a minute and then he told me that this was Yellowhand, who thought himself some heap big chief.

"'What's he want?' I says. 'Looks like he's got a pain or something.'

"'He says that before this battle starts he wants to fight Pahaska a duel.'

"Well, Mamma . . ." Will turned to me, for all the world like a small boy describing the catching of his big fish. "I couldn't take that, could I? I couldn't stand to have this old pelican riding around out there, making fun of me. So I just let out a yell and jabbed spurs into my horse. Out we shot from the lines and the minute I started after him, he started after me."

"And you shot him!" I was standing wide-eyed, Orra in my arms, Arta clinging excitedly to my skirts. Will waved his arms enthusiastically.

"That's just what I didn't do. Just when I started to pull that blamed old trigger, down went my horse's foot in a gopher hole. But the shot got his horse anyway. And when I got through rolling around on the ground, and wondering why that old codger didn't put a bullet through me, I looked up and saw him just coming out of a cloud of dust. That bullet had hit something anyway, and he didn't have any more horse than a rabbit. By gosh, Mamma, that was some fight!"

"And then what, Daddy?" Arta had gone to him and was tugging excitedly at his trouser leg. He laughed and, raising her in his arms, sat her on his shoulder.

"And then, what, honey?" he asked. "Well, then your daddy started running at old Yellowhand, and old Yellowhand started running at your daddy. The fall had knocked the guns out of the hands of both of us, and I knew it was going to be mighty touchy picking for your daddy if he ever slung his tomahawk at me. So I just kept dodging around as I went at him, so that he'd have a hard time hitting me, and pretty soon we were right at each other. Then—"

"Yes—"

"Well, then, I just jabbed my old bowie knife in his heart before he had time to get that tomahawk down on my head—and that's all there was to it."

"That's all?" The audience of the hero in his own kitchen was more than enthusiastic. Will grunted.

"Well, not exactly." He laughed. "I'd been ragin' around like a badger full of sand burrs about what they'd done to Custer. And when I saw old Yellowhand swallowing dust there, I just kept on working that bowie knife. And almost before I knew what I'd done, I'd 'lifted his hair' and was waving the scalp in the air.

"'First scalp for Custer!' I yelled, and then things sure did happen. All those Dog Soldiers made a rush at me, and all the Fifth Cavalry made a rush at the Dog Soldiers, and blame me if they didn't hit each other just about where I stood. I thought that fighting duels with Injuns was pretty good, but Mamma, it wasn't anything to what I'd gotten into from having a couple of armies running over me. I never saw so many horses' feet in my life. And there I was, just running around in circles." He laughed until the tears rolled down his cheeks. "Waving this old scalp and yelling 'first scalp for Custer' and trying to find someplace where somebody was shooting in my direction.

"Well, afterwhile things began to split up a bit, and I found a dead horse and laid down beside it. There was a dead soldier laying there too, so I got his gun and ammunition and began pumping away. Pretty soon the Injuns happened to remember that they had a pressing engagement over the hill, and about that time I got a new mount and managed to catch up with the general just as he was starting the pursuit. And how we did run those fellows!

"My, Mamma, but it was good!" Then he suddenly sobered. "We didn't do much laughing right then—we were too busy. There wasn't one of us that hadn't some friend with Custer. I'd known him, Mamma, and I'd always admired him—a lot. You know that. And we were going to get revenge. We sure got it.

"We chased those Injuns over the hill and thirty-five miles toward the Red Cloud Agency.[3] We drove 'em so hard that they lost horses, tepees, and everything else. Well, they got to the agency and went rarin' in and we went rarin' in right after 'em, and we didn't give a rap how many thousand Injuns there were around there. We were out for blood, and we didn't care what happened.

"But by the time we'd gotten to the agency proper, it was dark, and we couldn't tell what Injuns had been on the warpath and what hadn't. There were thousands of them around there, and we'd have licked every one of them if they'd ever showed anything that looked like a fight. But they didn't, Mamma, they were the meekest little lambs that you ever did see. And the first thing you know, out came an interpreter and asked me if I'd condescend to talk to old Cut-Nose."[4]

"'Who's he?' I asked.

"'Yellowhand's father,' the interpreter said. Well, Mamma, I kind of scratched my head. It's one thing to kill an old sonavagun in a duel and another to walk in and tell his pappy about it, but I took a chance. Know what he wanted? Wanted to know if I'd take four mules and some beads and stuff for that scalp and the warbonnet that I'd taken off of Yellowhand. And you can't guess what I told him!"

"What?"

"I said to him, just like this—" Will gestured scornfully. "That I wouldn't take forty mules for that scalp. I said to him that I wanted to send it to my sweetheart for a souvenir and then, just as soon as I got where I could box it up, I—"

"Sent it here—and I took one look at it and fainted. Will Cody . . ." But I smiled as I chided him. "Don't you ever send me another Indian scalp as long as you live."

Will chuckled rumblingly.

"I'll do better than that," he promised. "I'll never scalp another Injun!"

CHAPTER 13

Will's story was more than exciting—it was alluring, for it called up to me all the fascination of the West, the West that had gotten into my blood and never would leave. I wanted to go back there; I was tired of this existence in the East, and I, too, had my grief, which I desired to assuage in the bright, free sunshine of the West. I told my desires to Will.

"Mamma," he answered. "You're going to have your wish. This season—and then we'll have our home out there, where I can come in the summertime and just soak up the West until it's time to go back to the road again. Because, you know, they still seem to want me."

And, in fact, they were wanting him more than ever. With the beginning of the next road season, Will procured some real Indians from the Red Cloud Agency, among them some of the renegades that he had helped to chase after the killing of Yellowhand. With these appearing on the stage in a regular Indian war dance, the show business became more popular than ever, and the money rolled into the box office in a constantly increasing stream.

I traveled with Will nearly all that season, carrying our youngest baby with us, while Arta attended a seminary in Rochester. Then, in February, I said goodbye to the East and a glad "hello" to the West I loved.

It was a new West that I went to. Changes had come, even in the few years I had been away. The work of Will Cody and others of his kind had driven the Indians far from the settled lines of communication between the East and the far West, with the result that North Platte, Nebraska, near the Wyoming line, was a busy little place now, and growing constantly. It was there, on a farm that Will had purchased near town—he also had bought a tremendous ranch on Dismal River sixty miles away, in partnership with Major North, the former commander of the Pawnee scouts—that I was to make my home. And a far different home it was to be from the little log cabin in which we had lived at Fort McPherson.

We had money now, plenty of it. Never was there a losing day with the show in which Will was appearing. Never was there a time when records for attendance were not broken, while thousands who sought to see Will were turned away. The plays had become better now, and Will's acting had reached something that bore a semblance to a real stage presence. But let it be said, to his credit, that he never really became an actor in the true sense of the word. First and last he was a plainsman, with the plainsman's voice and the plainsman's bearing—and it was this that made him even more popular.

Yes, it was indeed a far different home. Furnishings came all the way from Chicago and New York. The lumber had been hauled across country, and there, out on the plains, we built a house that was little less than a mansion. And it was there that I greeted Will when he finished his season in May.

The summer months passed, while we rode the plains, made a trip through the tumbling hills to Dismal River, hunted and fished, and lived the true life of the West. Will had bought great herds of cattle, in partnership with Major North, and had caused them to be driven cross country from the eastern part of the state, while all about us ranchers were beginning to take up their claims and begin the life that Will had always dreamed of for the West. The untrammeled "Great American Desert" was beginning to fade forever. There was need of irrigation—and Will's money flowed freely into the projects. And where water flowed upon soil properly treated, there did the desert blossom. Again a dream that Buffalo Bill had cherished for years came into the being of reality.

A hazy, beautiful summer. Then Will went away, almost boyish in his reluctance to leave the West. But before he went—

"I've been thinking of something all this summer, Mamma," he told me, "something that will please you if I am able to work it out. I won't tell you what it is now—it will take a lot of planning and a lot of money. But it won't be this stage business; I'm sick of it!"

"And so am I!" I agreed. "I wish there was something else, Will—"

He laughed.

"That's what I'm trying to figure out!" he told me happily. "And someday I may be able to do it!"

It was years, however, before he succeeded, years in which I added to his ranch, and attended to the thousand and one details of farming life that must be looked after, while he was away on the stage; years in which a new daughter, Irma, came to us, and in which one went away. For Orra, the second of our children to be born in that little log cabin at Fort McPherson, died, to be taken back to Rochester and buried beside her little companion of those days of uncertainty, Kit Carson; years in which both Will and I tired more and more of the rough and tumble plays in which he toured the country. Then, at last, came the outline of the great scheme.

"I want to talk it all over with you first, Mamma," he said one night as we sat in the big living room of our North Platte home. "You're the first one I've told about it, and if you don't like it—"

"But you haven't told me yet, Will."

"That's right! Don't know just where to start. Well, the idea is this. All these people back East want to find out just what the West looks like. And you can't tell them on a stage. There ain't the room. So why not just take the West right to 'em?"

"How?" I was staring.

"On railroad trains!" Will was more than excited now. And so was I—but dubious.

"I don't understand. Do you mean to—"

"Take the prairies and the Injuns and everything else right to 'em. That's the idea! There ain't the room on a stage to do anything worth-while. But there would be on a big lot, where we could have horses and buffalo and the old Deadwood stagecoach and everything! How does it sound, Mamma?"

"Fine!" I was as enthusiastic as he. "And, Will, you can get that old Deadwood stagecoach too. I heard just the other day that it hadn't been used lately—you mean the one that was held up so many times?"

"That's the one. They've put a new one in its place, and they want to get rid of this old one. Seem to think it's unlucky or something of the kind. And, Mamma, we could have that run around the showgrounds and have the Injuns chase it, just like they really did chase it, then have the scouts and everybody come along and run the Injuns away. Wouldn't that be fun?"

"Oh, Will! And have real people in the stagecoach and let them shoot blanks at the Indians and—"

"Sure! Tell you what, Mamma, that'd be something they'd never seen before. That'd be showing 'em the West!"

So together we talked it all over, like two enthusiastic, happy children planning a "play-show" in the backyard. Then Will began to make his arrangements, first with Doctor Carver, who lived in the city and who had a number of trained horses; then with Merrill Keith, also of North Platte, who had tamed some buffalo and had them grazing around his house; with Buck Taylor, a cowboy; and with the various plainsmen about the adjacent country.[1] And finally, one day, we all went down to a large open space behind the railroad depot to hold the first rehearsal.

It wasn't exactly what could be called a performance. And it wasn't a rehearsal. Someone would run out a steer and Buck Taylor would lasso it, while Will and I sat on a pile of ties, lending our judicious wisdom to the arranging of the performance. Then the buffalo would be shunted in from the cattle yard, and Will would leap upon a horse and pursue them. After this would come his introduction and his greeting to the audience—of which I formed about 99 percent, and my baby, Irma, less than a year old, the rest. And invariably, when it was over, Will would turn to me and ask:

"How was that, Mamma?"

"I liked it, Will," I would answer. "But will you have to talk so loud?"

"Loud?" Then he would laugh. "Why, Mamma, they're making a canvas wall back East to go around this rigout that will be so long you can't see from one end to the other!"

Thus the practicing went on, while Will, in lieu of glass balls, would throw tin cans into the air and shoot at them, that he might see just how his "expert rifle shooting" would appear. One by one new ideas came, and gradually the show began to shape itself into the beginning of the tremendous affair that was to come in later years. The Pine Ridge Indian agency was not so far away, and Will went there, making his arrangements for the Indians who were to accompany the show to chase the old Deadwood stagecoach, do their war dances, and appear in the parades.[2] For Will and I had been reading up on circuses now and felt that we knew just what should be done.

But we didn't. We didn't know the first thing about it. Nor was it until Nate Salsbury, well versed in all the necessities of showmanship, came into the combination that the actual arrangements for the tour began to take shape.[3] And during this time—

Near us lived a little boy whom Will loved. Johnny Baker was his name, a grinning, amiable little fellow who worshipped the very ground that Will walked upon, and who loved nothing better than to sit on Will's knee in the long evenings and listen to the stories of the plains.[4] And when the "practicing" began down behind the depot, Johnny Baker would be sure to appear somewhere, watching wide-eyed, wondering, while the performance went through its various phases. And at last he summoned the courage to ask what was in his heart.

"Buffalo Bill," he said one day, "I wish I could go with you."

Will laughed.

"What would you do in a Wild West show, Johnny?"

But Johnny Baker had an answer:

"Well, I could black your boots and—and—make myself awful handy!"

So a new actor was signed up for the Buffalo Bill Wild West aggregation—Master John Baker. Will had taught him to shoot in the days in which he had played around our house—in fact, there never was a time when guns were not booming around there and Will was not shooting coins out of his children's fingers, while I stood on the veranda and gasped a remonstrance that the first thing he knew, he would have a fingerless family! All about the house were shells and shells and more shells, while every tree, every fence post, was at one time or another the resting place of some sort of a target. And when Johnny Baker joined the show, it was to shoot in the performance as a "Boy Wonder." And he lived up to his name, for there came the time when the "official announcer" would roar forth to the assembled throngs:

"And now-w-w-w-w, allow-w-w me to introduce to you, Johnny Baker, champion trick rifle shot of the world!"

Thus was another actor made and, for that matter, the whole thing was new to practically everyone who took a part. Not that they were doing a thing that was new to them in their rendition of the life on the plains—but doing it in a new atmosphere, and before an audience. Or at least, they were to do it before an audience, and constantly Will would shout to them as they practiced behind the depot:

"Now, boys, when we start this rigout just don't you pay any attention to the folks on the seats. Forget all about them. Just you don't know they're there and you won't get scared."

But, for that matter, it was to be a different thing from an appearance on the stage. There would be the big, wide lot in which to work, horses and solid ground and excitement. There would be no lines for the men of the saddle and the lariat—and practically every cowman who accompanied that exhibition could rope and tie a steer with his eyes shut—to say nothing of riding the wildest horse that ever ran—without half trying.

So, day after day and week after week, the rehearsals went on. Out from the East came the faithful Major Burke to ask for and receive the right to prepare the advance for the show, to look after the posting of the great bills that were being run off on the big presses in Chicago, and to "attend" to the newspapers. He came and he went again—the show was nearing its debut.

Finally, arrived the time when we all journeyed to Omaha, there to find great railroad cars that had been arranged for by Mr. Salsbury and painted with the name of Buffalo Bill. The long stretches of canvas had been put in place on the show lot and the seats erected. And it was there that the first performance of Buffalo Bill's Wild West saw the light of the show world.

And what a different thing it was from those foolish plays in which Will had been forced by public demand to appear! How clean, how sharp and bright, and how truly it depicted the West! Here was something that he could love and I could love—and we put into it everything that our hearts possessed. With the plays it had been a different matter; they were only a mockery, only—

"Why, gosh, Mamma," Will had said to me after the ending of one season, "I'd just like to know how many dramatic critics went crazy trying to figure out the plot of that thing. I appeared in it all season and I learned my lines, but I'm jiggered if I ever could find any head or tail of it. The only time that it got good was when the Injuns came on and got killed. And even that got tiresome!"

But with the Wild West show, it was different.

Here was riding, and here was roping; here the buffalo thundered along in their milling herd, while Will and the assembled cowboys circled them and displayed the manner in which the herds were hunted and the bison killed on the plains. Here was the old Deadwood stagecoach, and its story was one of realism. It was not merely a bit of "faking," or of stage scenery; it was the original stage, scarred by the bullets of Indians and highwaymen, its accoutrements rusted where it had lain by the side of the road for months at a time after some massacre, in which its horses had been killed and it abandoned. Here was Will, riding at a full gallop, his reins loose on his horse's neck, while, his rifle to his shoulder, he popped the glass balls that were thrown up ahead of him, never dreaming that he was working for a living—he was merely playing, playing just as he had played out on the broad expanses of the fields near our home in North Platte, where the ground was covered with the shells resultant from target shooting.

Here were the Indians, real Indians, who had come straight from the reservation and who had sufficient faith in the prowess of Pahaska to entrust themselves to him. An Indian is a chary creature. He reveres the man who can fight him and whip him—and for that reason, even the worst red-skinned enemy of Pahaska looked up to him as a worthy foe—and as a friend when the opportunity came to bury the hatchet.

So we were happy—for were we not still living in the West? Though we might travel to far parts of the world, here was the country we loved, still with us—the cowpunchers, the Indians, the plainsmen and scouts, the atmosphere and the life and the excitement.

Never was there a show that was more welcomed than Will's on that opening day in Omaha. And as for Chicago—

I can't remember the name of the place now. All I know is that it was indoors, with boxes for prominent persons, with a tanbark ring, and with poor old Major Burke running around like the proverbial beheaded chicken. For this was a big city, and here the test would come in earnest. And success meant worlds!

Our every cent was in that show now. It had cost thousands and thousands to purchase the equipment, to hire the actors, and to transport the big organization across the country. Other thousands were tied up in printing and the salaries of men going on in the advance to make the arrangements for the show's coming. And if we failed in Chicago, we knew that failure would follow us everywhere.

An anxious day of preparation. Then together Will and I, from one of the entrances, watched the filling of the seats. For a long time, it seemed that the great stretches of vacancy would never be eradicated, in spite of the crowds that were flooding in through the doorways. Then, at last, every seat was gone, every available bit of space taken, and the show began.

The first entrance brought applause. This grew to cheers and shouts. Throughout the long program the audience clapped and shouted its approval. Time after time Will was called forth, mounted on his big, sleek horse, to receive the approval of the tremendous crowds. There was no worriment after that—our fortunes were made.

Throughout the East went the show, and its fame went before it—to say nothing of Major Burke, traveling on and on, ever before, and talking constantly of just one being—William Frederick Cody. For Burke had transferred all the love that he had felt for Mademoiselle Morlacchi, his goddess, to Will, his god, and never was there a man more devoted.

Once upon a time—it was years later—in Portland, Oregon, a city editor leaned across his desk to his star reporter and handed him an assignment slip.

"Major Burke's over at the Multnomah," he ordered. "Go over and get an interview with him. What I want you to do . . ." And the city editor smiled. "Is to try to get him to talk about something else besides

Buffalo Bill. Try him on everything that you can think about that's foreign to Cody and see if you can't get him off the subject for once in his life. If you can do that, you've got a good story."

The reporter went on his mission. And when he came back two hours later, it was with a worn and wan expression.

"A fine thing you got me into!" he said jokingly. "I'm about half dead."

"Why?" The city editor's innocent look had a smile behind it.

"Why? Say, listen, I went over there to the Multomnah and got hold of Major Burke. I got him started on the Balkan situation, and during the first minute he mentioned at least ten times, ten different things that William Frederick Cody would do if he could only go over there and get into the scrap. Then I tried another tack and he was back at me on that. I changed to something else and he used the word 'Cody' on an average of once every five seconds. Then I made the mistake of mentioning something about the name of the hotel and the fact that it must be of Indian origin. That was my finish right there. Burke backed me up in a corner and told me Buffalo Bill's Indian fighting history from the cradle to the grave. I'm all worn out!"

And not once, during all of this, had Major Burke known the object of that visit. Nor did he feel that he was duty bound to mention Will's name—it was simply the blind adoration of a man who could think nothing else, dream nothing else, know nothing else, but Buffalo Bill.

Boys they were in their companionship, joking, laughing, bickering boys, always having some foolish disagreement, walking away from each other to pout a while, then finally to end up arm in arm, cemented by bonds that no quarrel ever could weaken. And only once did one of those quarrels ever amount to serious proportions, stormy as they might be.

It was in Italy, and Will had ordered certain preparations made at the docks. He arrived there to find that they had not been made and, what was more, that Major John M. Burke was among the missing. Will's arms went wide.

"Where's Old Scarface!" he shouted—a long, jagged scar on one side of Major Burke's cheek had given him the name. "Go out and find him. I want to know why he wasn't around here when this ship came in!"

Out went the emissaries, to search here and there, and at last to find Major John M. Burke, sweating and bedraggled in an Italian newspaper office. He had lost his interpreter, press time was coming, and John M. Burke was trying to tell the story of the coming of the Wild West show to an Italian editor who didn't understand a word of English. There they were, waving their arms at each other, both shouting at the top of their voices, and neither able to make the other understand. The searching party dragged the Major away and down to the docks. Will, his show delayed, the arrangements for its arrival lacking, took one look at the Major and waved his arms wildly.

"John Burke!" he shouted. "You're fired! Understand that? You're fired!"

"I understand," came the answer, as the advance man turned dolefully away. Five hours later, Mr. Salisbury, in London, received a telegram that read:

My scalp hangs in the tepee of Pahaska at the foot of Mount Vesuvius. Please send me money to take me back to the Land of the Free and the Home of the Brave.

But before Mr. Salisbury could even send a cable asking the cause of the disturbance, the world was smooth again, and the god and his admirer were arm in arm once more.

Far ahead of my story I have gone, it is true—but only by such an illustration could I convey the devotion of the man who traveled ahead of the show as it made its first trip through the country. The season ended and we went back to North Platte, there to plan and scheme again, and to dream of greater things for the coming season, things that would portray every feature of the winning of the West. That season came, and another after it. Then arrived the beginning of Will's trip of triumph.

We both had talked about it often and made our arrangements. I was to stay at home and look after the business of the ranch while Will was away. And he—he was going to a new adventure, Europe!

It was through Will's letters that I followed him on that trip, through the chartering of the Steamer Nebraska to carry his aggregation to

England, his arrival there, his opening performance, and then the visits of Gladstone, the Prince and Princess of Wales, and even Queen Victoria herself. And judging from those letters, there was enjoyment in every bit of it all.

"What do you think, Mamma," he wrote me once. "I've just held four kings! And I was the joker! It wasn't a card game, either. You remember the old stagecoach? Well, I got a request from the Prince of Wales to let him ride on the seat with me, while inside would be the kings of Denmark, Saxony, Greece, and Austria. Well, I didn't know just what to say for a moment. I was a little worried and yet I couldn't tell the Prince of Wales that I was afraid to haul around four kings with Indians shooting blanks around. So I just said I was as honored as all get-out, and we made the arrangements.

"And, Mamma, I just had to have my joke, so I went around and told the Indians to whoop it up as they never did before. We loaded all the kings in there and the prince got up on the seat with me, and then I just cut 'er loose. We sure did rock around that arena, with the Indians yelling and shooting behind us, fit to kill. And Mamma—I wouldn't say it out loud, but I'm pretty sure that before the ride was over, most of those kings were under the seat. It sure was fun.

"When the ride stopped, the Prince of Wales said to me that he bet this was the first time that I'd ever held four kings. I told him that I'd held four kings before, but this was the first time that I'd ever acted as the royal joker. Well, he laughed and laughed. Then he had to explain it to all those kings, each in his own language—and I felt kind of sorry for him.

"The prince gave me a souvenir, a sort of crest with diamonds all around it. It sure is pretty and I'm real proud of it."

Thus went Will's trip to England, and he came home a greater idol to the American small boy than ever. For three years his show did not move from Staten Island, and then it was only to return to Europe again, that he might repeat in France, Spain, Italy, and other countries what he had done in England, there to meet the rulers and potentates and receive from them gifts and souvenirs of their appreciation. Nor did the Pope refuse his presence when Will Cody went to pay his respects.

By this time, Will had become a true showman. Everything he saw, everywhere he went, he found something to intertwine with the thing that had become the realization of a great dream for him—his Wild West show. Witness:

"I've just come back from an interesting trip out to see the Coliseum," he wrote me once. "You know, that is the place where all the ancient Romans used to gather and stick their thumbs up or down when the gladiators came out to fight. That was where the lions used to eat up the Christians too, and all that sort of thing, and I thought it would be fine if I could take my Wild West show out there and give the performances inside the old place and really show these Romans how the Americans whoop it up. Well, I looked all over the place, but it's pretty well decayed. It's all falling to pieces, and it wouldn't do for a show at all. So I guess I'll have to give up the idea."

On and on the show went through Europe, and then it packed up for the winter at the little village of Benfield, in Alsace-Lorraine, while Will hurried back to this country for a rest until the season should open again. And hardly had he landed when there came the call for him—the old call of the West, of the saddle and the rifle. For the Indians had broken forth in their last campaign on the warpath.

CHAPTER 14

Far out into Nevada, lured by some mysterious message that no one ever could trace, emissaries of the Sioux Tribe had been lured to hear a greeting from a man who called himself God. Some innocent fool of a faker he was, who had even gone to the extent of piercing his hands, or burning them with acid, that they might simulate the scars on the hands of Jesus Christ. Somewhere he had learned a few of the tricks of electricity and had procured some electrical batteries and fireworks. And with these, he planned to delude the Indians.

Why? No one ever knew or ever will know. But the Indians went, selected from their various tribes, to hear his message, and then to hurry back to their camps again. Twisted and warped became that message. The Indians, fretting under government supervision and under a system of rations that was not always plentiful, leaped at anything that sounded to them like a prophecy of a return to the old days of the plains.

"Ghost shirts" made their appearance, cheap, cotton things, made by the Indians from pieces of sacking and splotched with ocher and red paint.[1] Here, there, everywhere, the story traveled that these shirts would be bulletproof, that the Sioux might again take to the warpath, and that this time, they need not fear the bullets of the palefaces. Throughout the Dakota countries, the tom-toms began to beat and the Indians to weave themselves in their weird dances about the campfires. Couriers hastened to Sitting Bull, requesting that he take part in the campaign. General Miles hurried from Chicago, and Will rushed toward Sitting Bull, that he might persuade the old warrior to remain on the path of peace. But before Will could reach him, Sitting Bull had been killed by some of his own people.

And then—Wounded Knee. The troops had been seeking to cut off the Indians under Big Foot from joining other forces that had reached the Bad Lands.[2] The Seventh Cavalry had surrounded them, and the order had gone forth that the Indians must surrender their arms. This they were doing when—

A shot! No one ever knew just from whence it came—whether from some soldier who had touched a trigger by accident, or from some Indian, crazed by the exhortations of the medicine men, dancing about, chanting, and playing on their bone pipes as they called for the Messiah to come to their aid. But the shot came, and with it, terror.

Indians and soldiers milled, the Indians fighting with their knives, the soldiers with their guns—even to the Hotchkiss cannon, which sent its great charges of shrapnel shrilling through the little valley of Wounded Knee Creek, killing braves and bucks, squaws and papooses indiscriminately. It was bitterly cold—here, there the Indians ran, seeking some escape; but there was none. When night came their bodies dotted the frozen valley, and the snow of a blizzard was beginning to kill those who had not died of their wounds.

It was to a scene like this that General Miles and Will Cody rode the next day.[3] With the first news of the conflict, they had ridden their hardest to reach the battlefield that they might quell the fight, but in vain. And now they looked upon only the slain, crumpled, frozen forms of those who had fallen. The last Indian uprising was at an end—now must come the real struggle, to so pacify the Indians, and to so convince them of the foolishness of their quest that never again would they seek to pit themselves against the overpowering elements of the American army. And it was through General Miles and Will Cody that this was accomplished.

A last great council was held. Haranguers told the stories of the Great White Chiefs. One by one General Miles made his promises for the future: that he would see that there was good treatment for the Indians—that the Indians must make good their promise to stay clear of the warpath and, to this purpose, furnish hostages whose lives would be forfeit should the promise fail. To this Pahaska added his promises and then—

"And if you follow the path of peace, I will try to be good to these braves that you hand into our keeping. I will take them over the great waters to strange countries. I will be kind to them."

And Will made good his promise, for when the peace pipe was smoked at last, Will left for Europe with a new assembly of Indians for his Wild West show, Kicking Bear, Lone Bear, No Neck, Yankton Carlie, Black Heart, Long Wolf, Scatter, Revenge, and the man upon whom all blame for the Indian uprising had been placed, Ta-ta-la Slotsla, Short Bull.[4] Nor was it until twenty years later that Will and I—or any white person, for that matter—were to hear the real, the pitiful story of Ta-ta-la Slotsla, and his journey to God that caused the deaths of so many of his tribesmen.

Times had changed. The West had grown from that brawny, brawling youngster that we had known in the younger days to a stalwart youth, with its great cities, with its tremendous ranches, its factories, and its industries. It was what Will had dreamed of back there in the old days when he was simply Will Cody and I his frightened young wife, making my first friendships with this wild, free West I really feared. Up in Wyoming, a town had spread itself near the canyon of the Shoshone, and its name was that of Cody. Down in Arizona were irrigation and mining projects that owed their births to Will. The thing that had been a desert once was blooming now. The Old West was nearly gone. And to Will there came an inspiration, that of sealing the picture while yet there was the chance, to do in film what he had done in his Wild West shows, and to make for posterity a thing that would live forever.

"I can get the capital!" he confided to me with a boyish enthusiasm that belied the sixty or more years that had come to him. "I can get the outfits and why, Mamma, wouldn't it be just the thing to go down into Dakota and put the last outbreak of the Sioux into motion pictures? I've written General Miles about it, and General Frank Baldwin down in Denver, and General Maus, and Lee, and all the others. They'll come. And then we'll send a copy of it to the government files for history."

"But Will . . ." I smiled as I used to smile in the old days. "How about the Indians?"

"They'll come. I'll just send out word that Pahaska wants them, and they'll come. Short Bull's still alive, and No Neck, and Woman's Dress, and a lot of the others. Just you wait and see. They'll come."

And so the preparations went forward, until at last we gathered in the little town of Pine Ridge, just at the edge of the Indian reservation. Twenty miles away was Wounded Knee, and there we went to camp until the time when the picture taking should begin.

Over the hills they came, in wagons, on horseback; from Manderson, from the far stretches of the Bad Lands, from the hills and the valleys, the old Indians who once had fought against Buffalo Bill. Withered were the faces of many of them now, old and aged the arms that once had swung a tomahawk. But with them also came their sons, the braves of today, strong and young. By the hundreds they gathered, each to come forward at the sight of the tall, straight man whose long hair now had turned from black to white, to take his hand and to exclaim:

"How kola! Waste Pahaska!"

"Waste Pahaska!" Good Pahaska, it meant, good Pahaska, who was their friend. Time had been when they had crept toward each other, each with his rifle poised for the first shot, but that was in the days of the past. He had been a good enemy then, an enemy who never took an unfair advantage, and an enemy who never showed fear. And that is the sort of an enemy the Indian reveres. Today, he was the same sort of a friend that he had been an enemy, and they obeyed his call like the call of some Great Master.

And so they camped, to dance at night in the cold moonlight, to sing the wailing songs of death in memory of the bucks and squaws, buried far up there in the long trench on the hill, the victims of Wounded Knee. Exactly where the tepees had sat on that red day of battle were the tepees stretched now; where the braves had sung their death song on that frigid afternoon in the '90s, now sang the survivors in the bleak days of autumn 1913. It all had its effect. Sons of braves who had fallen began to talk among themselves. Sons of squaws who had died, innocent victims of the battle, began to dream of a great scheme of revenge. Few were they in numbers, but their plan had the ramifications of wholesale death.

Out on the plains with us were six hundred members of the Twelfth Cavalry. From every costuming company in the East had the old uniforms been gathered, just such uniforms as were worn in the days when the soldiers were "boys in blue" and khaki was a thing unknown. Even to the old goloshes had the faith of costuming gone, and to the type of rifle carried by the soldiery, the 44.70. And therein lay danger!

Many a rifle had remained on the Indian reservation since that day at Wounded Knee. It had become, in fact, the standard rifle among the older Indian families, and ammunition—real ammunition was easily procured. When the time for the sham battle between the Indians and the soldiers would come to be placed in film as the cameras ground away, blanks were purposed, of course. But suppose—suppose that when those Indians started their mimic fight against the soldiery they gained a revenge for the defeat of Wounded Knee, and that the rifles they carried had in their barrels ammunition that was real, ammunition that was lead-tipped and deadly, while those of the soldiers contained only blanks!

It was a time of ferment. Back on the old battlefields again, the hearts and minds of the Indians were returning to other days. Old grudges, that long were forgotten, began to rise again. Councils were held—one afternoon the older Indians, not knowing of the plot that was beginning to teem in the brains of younger bucks, told their grievances before General Miles and Will, and received from them the promise that a report would be made at Washington. All through the camp were memories—every few minutes, some wailing squaw would make her way to the long trench atop the hill, there to stare down at the mound that contained the body of her loved ones, slain at Wounded Knee. Ceaselessly the death song shrilled through the chill air—the Indians were living again in the days when Big Foot led his band—and led it to death.

By night, atop the gray hills, circles formed, and dancing figures wailed here and there, while the tom-toms sounded and the guttural shout of the chieftains guided the dance. All about us were the reminders of a day that was gone—reminders that might bring death. And it was in the midst of this that Will got word of the plot.

Efforts had been made to buy cartridges in large numbers for the 44.70s. The requests had been refused. But whether the young Indians who sought to bring about a massacre had obtained them in other places—that was not known. Hurriedly Will assembled the chiefs, the old Indians whom he knew and whom he could trust. Quickly he told his story. Silently the old chiefs listened—old Woman's Dress, No Neck, Flatiron, and Short Bull. They grunted then paddled away. Shortly there came the call of the haranguer echoing through the Indian village:

"Enokone eupo! Enokone eupo!"

It was the call of assembly—my spelling, of course, is only phonetic. An hour more, and the old chiefs were again before their Great White Chief, their Pahaska. There would be no bullets in the guns when the white men met the Sioux before the Box with the One Eye. The matter had been settled. The young braves had seen the wrong. They would go—back whence they came. Pahaska need not fear for his paleface friends. The day of the warpath was over. And so it came about that Short Bull, charged for years with the fomenting of the war, came to be a peacemaker. And so it also came about that while there at Wounded Knee, back in the environment of the last Indian rebellion, he told his story for the first time, the story of a grieving, worn old man, wrongly accused, wrongfully treated, wrongfully used. For Ta-ta-la Slotsla, Short Bull, by his own story, was only a tool in the grip of Indian politics, a brave bringing the word of peace, only to find it transformed into the call of war.

It was in his little tent that he told us the story, to Theodore Wharton, the director of the history, to Mrs. Wharton, to Will, and to me.[5] A blizzard whirled and whined outside, while beside the little stove, a faded old man, a cheap overcoat wrapped close about him, huddled pitifully in his attempt at warmth. Beside him was his interpreter, Horn Cloud.[6] The marks of the warrior were absent from both of them now—no feathers or beads, no tomahawk or rifle. Short Bull, he who had been blamed for a war, was only a little, wizened, brokenhearted old man. There came a question, an interpretation, a flow of words from the old chief, a smile. The interpreter turned.

"He say you the first person who ever ask that," came the announcement. "He say to thank you—now he get to tell the truth."

Short Bull raised his arms. Long he spoke, then, in the voice of the interpreter, came his words:

"They say I am the man who brought war. No! I am the man who wanted peace. All these years I have waited—I have been Ta-ta-la Slotsla, the man forgotten by his people. They did not want me to tell because they knew that I would tell the truth. But the Long Sleep is coming. Ta-ta-la Slotsla will tell.

"My people were hungry in 1888 and in 1889. There was no wood to burn in the tepees and we shivered. On the Rosebud Agency, where I lived with my people, the squaw and the papoose cried for food, but it did not come. Then, all at once, we heard a message. The Messiah was coming back. The White Man had turned him out. The White Man did not love him anymore, and he was coming back to the Indian. There would be food and there would be fire for the tepees—the Messiah had said so.

"A brave rode to the Rosebud with a message from Red Cloud at the Pine Ridge Agency to choose a bravehearted man to go to the Messiah.[7] One chief was to go from each of the twelve tribes, and my people chose me. I obeyed. We met at the head of Wind River. Some of us rode. Some of us walked. It was many sleeps away, but we were going to the Messiah. He was at Pyramid Lake in Nevada, and he had sent for us.

"It was a long time before we got there. We knew where to go—the messages had told us. And one afternoon when we waited in front of the great rocks at Pyramid Lake, we looked up and he was there. He had come out of the air—we had not seen him before. Now, he was there and we kneeled down like we kneeled down when the missionaries prayed for us."

Horn Cloud, the interpreter, spread his hands. "I know about that," he said. "He hid behind big rocks, see—then jump out. They think he float through air."

But the story of Short Bull had begun again.

"It was at the setting of the sun, and the light caught on his robe, and it was all colors and blazed like gold and floated back to the west—"

"Changeable silk," I heard someone say softly. The story went on.

"He say for us to pray and be glad that we had met the Messiah. He say good times are coming for the Indian. He say when we go back to sing and dance, for the time would come when the Indian would not be poor. He say that White Man the Indian's friend. And when we look up, he was gone."

There was a moment of silence. I drew closer to Will at the shrill and the shriek of the blizzard without. Short Bull pulled the narrow collar of his old overcoat closer about his neck and spread his withered, scrawny old hands.

"There was a little house by the side of the lake and we slept in it," he went on, through his interpreter. "Then next day, a little white boy he come to us and he say his father want to see us in the willow patch—"

What fakery! Not contenting himself with imitating Jesus Christ, this being of Pyramid Lake had even given God a grandson! But evidently the Indians, dazed as they were by the supposed heavenly messages of this mysterious being, fired by the thought of happiness to come, did not stop to think of the inconsistency. The story was continued:

"We went to the willow patch. The Messiah was waiting—he had on a shirt with marks on it—like this." He lifted one of the "property" ghost shirts that were being used in the picture. "He show us his hands and there were marks in them where the White Man crucified him, and we say that the White Man turn him out but that he do not blame him. He say that the White Man had been bad to him, but that he was not angry. He say that the time has come when the White Man and the Indian shall be friends, and that we must go back and tell our people that they must live with the White Man in Peace.

"He says . . ." Ta-ta-la Slotsla was becoming vehement now. "That we must tell our people to stamp out all trouble. He say that our children must go to the White Man's school, and that by and by our children's children will grow to be the husbands and wives of the white woman and the White Man. Then there will be no White Man, no Indian; we will all be one. 'Do as I say,' he say, 'and on earth you will be together and in heaven you will be together. And then, there will be no nights, no sleeps, no hunger and no cold.' And we listened, and we were happy.

"He taught us to dance and he say for us to make ghost shirts like he wear and dance in them and praise the Messiah. He say for us to go home and spread the news that the Messiah had said for us to be at peace. And then he went away."

There was a long silence. When Short Bull's voice began again, it was strange and cold and hard.

"I went to my people. I told them what the Messiah had said, and they danced and were glad. Then Red Cloud, down at the Pine Ridge Agency, sent for me and I went, and American Horse and Fast Thunder and Red Cloud, they ask me what the Messiah had said, and I told them.[8] But they went out and told their people that I had said other things." His hands were clenched hard. "They say I tell them that the Messiah he tell me to get my people and drive the White Man back into the sea. They say I tell them that the Messiah promise to bring back the buffalo and the antelope if they drive the White Man away.

"I went back to my people, but they had heard what Red Cloud and American Horse and Fast Thunder had said. I begged them to shut their ears to the evil words of those who did not speak truth. But they were dancing now and building fires, and they would not listen to me.

"American Horse and Red Cloud and Fast Thunder sent me the ghost shirts to bless—and I blessed them. But when I sent them back, they told their people that I had made them bulletproof. They say that the Messiah he make me so I can stop my people from being hurt by the guns of the White Man. Then they send for me and tell me to come to Pine Ridge and fight the White Man. But I say 'No! I have seen the Messiah. I have seen the Man of God. I will live in peace. The Messiah he say to love the White Man and I will love him.'

"The Brule Sioux went through to the warpath and they tell me to come along. But I stay on the Rosebud. Old Two Strikes moved his camp from the Little White River toward the Pine Ridge Agency, but I stayed on the Rosebud. Then the young men ordered me to follow Two Strikes and I did.[9]

"They wanted cartridges, but I would not help get them. They say for me to fight the White Man, but I say 'No!'"

The little man had risen now and was pacing up and down. Over in the corner, his squaw was wailing. The thin hands of Ta-ta-la Slotsla rose high in the air.

"'No! No!' I tell them, 'No! I keep calling to you and you do not hear me! I try to tell you there shall be no war; you will not listen. You say the white soldiers will kill me? Then I will die—I will not fight back. Once I was a warrior, once I wore the shield and the war club and the war bonnet, but I have seen the Holy Man. Now there is peace; now there shall stay peace.'

"'You choose me as the bravehearted one to journey to the sunset to see the Messiah. I saw him and I brought you his message. You would not hear it. You changed it. Now—'" He spread his hands and bowed his black-haired head, in memory of a gesture of other days. "'I am silent.'"

The wind of the blizzard without had risen to a higher pitch, mingling with the wailing of the squaw in the corner. Short Bull folded his hands.

"The next day I saddled my horse. I rode away. I came to the pine hills and looked out into the distance. They were fighting the Battle of Wounded Knee. I went on. And yet they blame me for a war—my own people who had sent me to the sunset to talk to the Holy Man."

The old man was silent, huddling again by the side of the rickety little stove. The song of the squaw wavered and died away. She crept forward and took her place by the side of the man who was her brave, the man who had been blamed for a hundred deaths, yet who, in her eyes, at least, was ever blameless. And together we left them, the faithful old squaw and the brokenhearted, wizened old Indian who had seen and talked to God.

CHAPTER 15

And now, my story is ending. Indeed, the years of Will's show days were crammed with excitement, with many an accident in the long rushing journeys of the trains, many a "blowdown," and many a thrill. Yet, they were not the thrills that either of us had known in the old days—they were more of an echo, for the day of the old West that we had known in its raw, rough days was gone. Will had seen his desires fulfilled; he had watched the West grow until it was all that he had hoped for it—and saw in the future a greater dream of empire than even he had imagined back in the days of Hays City and our buffalo hunts. The paths that had been trodden by Indians were now the paths of industry. Automobiles shot here and there in perfect safety about the plains where the bison once had roamed, and where the danger of death had lain in every hill and valley and hummock.

Side by side, there were three of us who watched the years fade, and the sunset grow nearer—Will, dear faithful old Major Burke, and me. The season of 1916 ended and together Will and I came to Denver, where he planned to meet Johnny Baker, whose face now had begun to bear a few wrinkles in the place of the freckles that had shown there the day he asked Will to let him black his boots in the circus. The meeting was to make plans for a new show, for a greater show, for in spite of the various vicissitudes of the Wild West exhibition business, Will still believed in it. One thing had been borne to him, through the never-failing worship of youthful America, that he was an idol who never could be replaced, that as long as there were boys, and as long as those boys had red blood in their veins, they would thrill at the sight of him they loved and cheer the sounding reverberation of his great, booming voice as he whirled into the arena on his great white horse, came to a swinging stop before the grandstand, and raised his hand for the famous salute from the saddle.

Will had not aged, in spite of his years. He still was lithe and strong, still able to grip the ribs of his horse with strong, clinging knees, still able to raise his rifle and aim it with deadly effect. It had been only a year before that he had fought his way through the snows about our home at Cody and brought home a buck deer, felled with a shot from his rifle.

He had not aged, and his heart was young. But the years, in spite of the light weight they apparently made upon his shoulders, were fighting and fighting hard against the resolve that was in his mind, to live on and on, forever.

I went back to Cody, only to start at the sight of the editor of the little town paper bringing me the news that Will was seriously ill. But with his arrival there came a messenger from the telegraph station, with a telegram from Will.

"Don't believe exaggerated reports about my illness," it read. "They're trying to tell me I'm going to die. But I've still got my boots on, and they can't kill me, Mamma. They've tried it before."

I laughed as I read it. Time and again had the reports of his approaching death shot over the country—almost with every illness in his later years did the rumor go forth, and this telegram assured me that here was only another exaggerated report, only another wild rumor. But—

He wired me that he was going to Glenwood Springs, and that the waters there would help him.[1] At the depot in Denver, the reporters clustered about him, asking him about his illness. But he laughed at them and at the rumors. For was he not on his feet? Did he not have his boots on? Why, next season, he was going to start out with the biggest show that he ever had known—one that would make even his exhibition at the Chicago World's Fair seem diminutive. And how were we to know that already his mind was wandering, that the person who was speaking was not Will Cody, the strong, able-bodied man who had fought the plains, but only a shell, only a living thing that fought the approach of death even as he had fought the fight for the upbuilding of the West—fighting until the last atom of energy and reserve should be exhausted?

He did not know, those about him did not know, I did not know. But the news must come, and it hurried over the telegraph wires twenty-four hours later, a message from his physician:

"Colonel Cody is slowly but surely dying. There is no hope whatever for him. We are bringing him back to Denver."

It was there that I met him, a frail, white-faced man, the long white hair clinging about his temples, the lips thin and white and wan but a man, fighting to the end. He laughed at my tears, patted my cheek, and strove to assemble again the old, booming voice. But it was weak now and breaking.

"Don't worry, Mamma," he said time after time, "I'm going to be all right. The doctor says I'm going to die, does he? Well, I'm pretty much alive just now, ain't I. I've still got my boots on. I'll be all right."

But as the days passed, in spite of the fact that he still "kept his boots on," he began to realize. The last fight was ending—ending in spite of the fact that he was struggling against it with every fiber of his being. Long years in the past, up at Cody, he and I once had talked of death, as we looked out toward the varicolored mountains that hedged in our little town. And then he had told me of his desires—to be buried up there, where the last rays of the sun touched the hills at night, where the first glad glow sent its bright rays upward in the dawn. Then he had told me that he wanted to spend his last days in the little town he had founded, up there in his hotel, which bore his daughter's name.

Now, he was too weak. With every bit of strength he had, he struggled daily into his clothing that he might still strive on "with his boots on." His body was literally living off itself—yet he fought on; still he strove to laugh away our fears and joke about the inevitable.

"Not dead yet!" He would shake his long locks and raise his head. "No sirree, not dead yet! I'm a pretty much alive dead man, I am. I've still got my boots on!"

But—it was on the day before the end came—he very quietly viewed the subject in a different light.

"I want to be buried on top of Mount Lookout. It's right over Denver. You can look down into four states there. It's pretty up there. I want to be buried up there—instead of in Wyoming."

Then he swerved back to the old fight again. That night he played a game of solitaire and joked about what the doctors had said regarding his condition. He tried to bring a smile to our lips—we were all at the home of Mrs. Lou Decker, his sister—but the effort was feeble. Now and then he would turn anxiously, as though watching the door.

"I wish Johnny would come!" he said again and again—Johnny Baker, who was racing across country in the vain hope of being able to speak a goodbye to his "Guv'nor"; Johnny Baker, who, as a freckle-faced boy, had begged for a chance to black his boots; Johnny Baker, who loved him and who was beloved by him. Then he asked for Burke—but Burke was far away, too. The hours dragged on.

Ten o'clock came on the tenth of January, and with it unconsciousness. At twelve o'clock, the messages began to speed across the world. Buffalo Bill, my Will, was dead.

Out of a haze I remember the next few days, the long throngs of people stretching for blocks about the Colorado State House, where his body lay in state; the riderless white horse that once he had strode in his salute from the saddle, walking behind the flag-draped casket that carried his body; the tolling bells; the scurrying messenger boys, bringing condolences even from kings and presidents. Atop Mount Lookout, we kept his wish, far up toward the heavens, where below can be seen the stretches of the plains of Kansas and Nebraska, the hills of Colorado and the hummocks of Wyoming—his old roving places of other days. There we said goodbye, and now—

And now, up here in Cody, I face the sunset. My children are gone—Arta following an operation, Irma as a result of the epidemic, which claimed its toll even out here in the far West. I am alone, my life lived, my hands folded. I have seen them all go, one by one, according to the will of the Great Dictator; and it is hard to say the last goodbye and stay behind.

Yes, my life is lived, and out here in the West, where each evening brings a more wonderful, more beautiful blending at sunset, I watch the glorious colorings and feel a sense of satisfaction that it will not be long now until I see the fading of the sunset of my own little world, until the time shall come when I am with the children I loved, and the man I loved—on the Trail Beyond.

THE END

APPENDIX 1

The images included here capture Louisa Frederici Cody at different phases of her life from young womanhood to her final years. They suggest some of the ways she defined her life in relation to her husband and children and the settings of home and Wild West tour. A brief biographical sketch and portrait of Louisa Cody's cowriter, Courtney Ryley Cooper, is included.

Fig. 1. Portrait of Louisa Frederici Cody taken at age twenty-four, a year after her marriage. Buffalo Bill Center of the West, Cody, Wyoming. P.6.0907.

Fig. 2. Portrait of William F. Cody, Louisa F. Cody, and their daughter Arta Lucille Cody, ca. 1872. Buffalo Bill Center of the West, Cody, Wyoming. P.69.0239.

Fig. 3. Family portrait of William F. Cody, Louisa F. Cody, and their daughters Arta Lucille Cody and Orra Maude Cody, ca. 1883. Buffalo Bill Center of the West, Cody, Wyoming. P.6.0813.

Fig. 4. RIGHT: Seated portrait of Louisa F. Cody wearing a dark sequin and brocade dress and holding a feather fan, ca. 1885. Buffalo Bill Center of the West, Cody, Wyoming. P.69.0203.

Fig. 5. BELOW: William F. Cody and Louisa F. Cody seated in a spider phaeton carriage in front of a painted mountain scene, a Wild West backdrop in the show arena, ca. 1900. Buffalo Bill Center of the West, Cody, Wyoming. P.69.0195.01.

Fig. 6. A portrait of Louisa Cody, center, and her daughters Irma, left, and Arta, right, ca. 1900–1904. Buffalo Bill Center of the West, Cody, Wyoming. P.6.1664.

Fig. 7. LEFT: A portrait of Louisa Cody, 1915. Buffalo Bill Center of the West, Cody, Wyoming. P.69.0945.

Fig. 8. BELOW: William F. Cody and Louisa F. Cody, 1915. Buffalo Bill Center of the West, Cody, Wyoming. P.69.0916.

Fig. 9. Family portrait of grandchildren: Frederick Garlow Jr., standing on left, Jane Garlow, standing on right, and William Joseph "Bill Cody" Garlow, seated, with Louisa Cody, 1917. Buffalo Bill Center of the West, Cody, Wyoming. P.69.0198.

Fig. 10. Louisa F. Cody with Chief Red Wolf, ca. 1920. Buffalo Bill Center of the West, Cody, Wyoming. P.69.0202.

Fig. 11. Ranch house at Scout's Rest Ranch, North Platte, Nebraska. Louisa Cody's primary residence from 1886 until her death in 1921. Buffalo Bill Center of the West, Cody, Wyoming. P.6.0651.045.

APPENDIX 2

These excerpts from the 1904 divorce depositions expose the complex realities of the Codys' relationship in contrast to the one represented in Louisa's memoir. Their respective testimonies offer starkly differing visions of their shared past, while also indicating a motive for producing this posthumous account. As Sherry Smith suggests in the introduction to this edition, Louisa's memoir works to redeem Cody's reputation and, through him, her own, in the wake of the national scandal of the divorce trial. The details of that trial were spilled across the pages of countless newspapers from coast to coast. A sampling of newspaper coverage reflects the press's tendency to highlight some of the more sensational aspects of the testimony and demonstrates how the divorce attempt impacted the Codys' public image.

MRS. LOUISA CODY,
of lawful age, being by me first duly examined, cautioned and solemnly sworn, as hereinafter certified, deposeth and sayeth as follows, to-wit:

Direct Examination

BY J. J. HALLIGAN:

Q. Give your name to the reporter.
A. Louisa Cody.
Q. You are the defendant in this suit?
A. I am.
Q. Where were you married to the plaintiff, Mrs. Cody?
A. At St. Louis, at my father's house.
Q. In what year?

A. In 1866.

Q. How long had you resided in St. Louis at that time?

A. Since I was two years old.

Q. What was your occupation at the time of your marriage?

A. I was in a millinery store.

Q. What was your age at the time of your marriage?

A. I was twenty-two years old.

Q. How long did you remain in St. Louis after your marriage?

A. About one hour.

Q. And where did you go?

A. I went on a boat to Leavenworth city.

Q. What was the business of your husband, Colonel Cody?

A. He did not have any as I know of.

Q. What did you do when you went to Leavenworth?

A. We went to sister Eliza's house and after that went to Mrs. Goodman's house and stayed a while.

Q. How long did you remain in Leavenworth at that time?

A. I stayed there until my baby was born in 1866.

Q. That was your daughter Arta?

A. Arta.

Q. And what business did your husband follow during that time in Leavenworth?

A. He had a little one-room saloon, about the size of this, (indicating the room, in which witness is seated) after we lived there for a while.

Q. How long did he follow that business?

A. Not very long; he could not make it pay, and then he went to a tavern and he could not make that pay.

Q. Where did he go after that?

A. He got a wagon and a load of apples. He got some horses and a wagon, and then he went on the Kansas road, and went as far as Kansas City, Kansas.

Q. Was that the railroad known as the Kansas Pacific?

A. Yes, sir.

Q. Where did you go when he went up to Kansas City?

A. Before my baby was born, we rented two rooms. After he left there I went to sister Nellie's. The baby was six months old then.
Q. Where did you go then?
A. I went to Mother's and stayed there until he sent for me.
Q. Where did your mother live?
A. St. Louis: the house I was married in.
Q. What did you do during the time you were living in Leavenworth?
A. After I got back the second time, I was living with my sister Nellie. I did not have much to do; she helped me with the work and so she solicited some sewing for me, and I sewed there. He did not get home as quick as he ought.
Q. Was your husband at home when you left Leavenworth to go back to St. Louis?
A. No.
Q. When did you next see him?
A. When he came back the second time. He sent for me. I went out to his sister's, Mrs. Myers. He said I should come out to Salina, Kansas, to meet him.
Q. Do you mean he came back to St. Louis, or sent for you to come on to meet him?
A. Before that he came down to St. Louis to see me. He had his sister with him.
Q. When you left St. Louis on that occasion, he sent for you, did he?
A. Yes, sir.
Q. And where did you go?
A. I went to Salina, Kansas, to meet him. I was to meet a family by the name of Rose, and from there I went out to Fort Hayes.
Q. How long did you live at Fort Hayes?
A. I lived there about three months.
Q. What was your husband's business during the time you lived at Fort Hayes?
A. He was hauling wood and done a little of everything, I guess. He was not doing much on the railroad then.
Q. Did you start housekeeping when you lived at Fort Hayes?

A. No, we boarded.

Q. Where did you board?

A. We boarded at a house kept by a man named Perry. Dave Perry was the name. It was not the same Perry that lived here though.

Q. Where did you go when you left Fort Hayes?

A. I went home and stayed at Mother's and Father's.

Q. You went back to St. Louis again?

A. Yes, back to St. Louis again.

Q. How long did you stay there?

A. Two years.

Q. How many times during those two years did you see your husband?

A. About twice.

Q. How many children did you have at that time?

A. One, Arta.

Q. What did you do, if anything, during the two years you were with your mother in St. Louis toward keeping yourself?

A. I done sewing.

Q. Where did you go after you left St. Louis this second time?

A. Why, he was at Fort McPherson and we came out here.

Q. Did you ever live, that you remember of, at a place called Rome, a new city?

A. That was down in Hayes city, but I did not keep house there.

Q. How long did you live at Rome?

A. Three months. Rome was across the creek from Fort Hayes.

Q. When was it that you came to Fort McPherson?

A. That was after he came to Fort McPherson; he was scouting there with the army.

Q. When was it: in what year?

A. When Arta was three years old, and she was born in 1866.

Q. What was your husband's business when you lived at Fort McPherson?

A. Scouting.

Q. How many years did he follow the scouting business?

A. He was there—let's see—I had my three children then—about three years, something like that.

Q. Where was your second child born?
A. At Fort McPherson in a log cabin.
Q. In what year?
A. He was four years younger than Arta—Kit Carson. And she was born in 1866.
Q. How long had you been living at Fort McPherson when the second child was born?
A. Not so very long—about a year. I came there in the fall, and the next fall he was born.
Q. State what you did toward the support of the family while you lived at Fort McPherson.
A. I did not do anything to support the family. I took in sewing by his asking me to do some sewing. He asked me to do some sewing for Major Irwin's wife. He committed suicide and she wanted some black clothes made.
Q. State to what extent you did sewing while you lived at Fort McPherson?
A. I sewed there until my little boy was born.
Q. What did you do with the money that you received for the sewing?
A. I used some of it for the benefit of his sisters, as they helped with the work, and some I never received because he used it.
Q. How long did you live at Fort McPherson?
A. I lived there until—about three years.
Q. Where did you move from Fort McPherson?
A. We went to St. Louis first and from St. Louis to New York.
Q. And what was the occasion of your leaving Fort McPherson?
A. The Colonel got into the dramatic business.
Q. Where did you first go to live when you left Fort McPherson?
A. To St. Louis to my mother's.
Q. How long did you live at St. Louis?
A. We did not live there very long. He sent for me to come to New York.
Q. Where did you next start to housekeeping?
A. I went down to Westchester, Pennsylvania.

Q. And how long did you live in Westchester, Pennsylvania?
A. About nine months?
Q. Where was your husband during the time you were living at Westchester?
A. Traveling in his dramatic business.
Q. Where did you go to live after living at Westchester, Pennsylvania.?
A. Went to Rochester, New York.
Q. What was the occasion of going to Rochester, New York?
A. Because . . . Cody could come and visit me oftener. It was too far to Westchester, and it was too lonesome for me. He wanted me nearer him and so did I.
Q. How long did you live in Rochester?
A. Three years.
Q. What business did your husband follow during the time you lived at Rochester?
A. Dramatical business.
Q. Where did you go to live when you left Rochester?
A. I traveled a little while with him. I was about a year with him.
Q. How many children did you have when you lived in Rochester?
A. Three.
Q. Where was the third child born?
A. Down near Fort McPherson, in the same house the little boy was born in.
Q. Do you remember the year that your third child was born?
A. Twenty months after the little boy.
Q. You do not remember the year?
A. It was twenty months after.
Q. Did you lose any children in Rochester?
A. No, sir.
Q. Where did you next start housekeeping when you left Rochester?
A. In North Platte.
Q. About what time was it you started housekeeping in North Platte?
A. I do not exactly remember the year, but I have lived here twenty-seven years the last time. I cannot remember the dates.

Q. And where did you go to live when you came back?
A. Up here by the fairgrounds. No, I lived in the fort first. There used to be a fort here. I lived there a while until I got my house built.
Q. Had you and your husband purchased property prior to the time you came back.
A. He bought 160 acres just before I came back.
Q. And was that the place where you had your house erected?
A. Yes sir, right west of town here.
Q. How long did you live in that house?
A. Until it burned down.
Q. About how many years was that?
A. I don't remember now.
Q. About how long did you live on this place before yourself and husband purchased some other property?
A. A couple of years.
Q. About how many years after yourself and husband had been buying property out here—at what is known as the Cody ranch, that is—how long was it from the time you made the first purchase until the last, as near as you can remember?
A. I can't remember exactly. It is twenty-eight years since he made the first purchase, and then I bought different property myself, for him. I bought nearly all the property at the ranch; a little bit, Mr. Goodman bought.
Q. How many acres, do you know, there is now in what is known as Scout's Rest Ranch?
A. Over three thousand.
Q. When did you commence to live in the house where you now reside?
A. In 1893.
Q. And had your house up west of town burned down at that time?
A. Oh, yes; it burned down three years before.
Q. When did you commence living in the present residence in North Platte, with reference to the World's Fair at Chicago?
A. In the fall of 1893. (When he stopped from Chicago, he bought it that summer in 1893.) In November 1893.

Q. Was the property at the time it was bought in its present condition?
A. No, sir. It was not. I fixed it up a good deal myself. It was in a rough state. The house only was built.
Q. State what you had done to the property after it was purchased by yourself and husband?
A. Mr. Field built the barn, and I fixed up the grass and had the addition built to the house.
Q. Do you remember about what time the Colonel came home that fall?
A. In 1893, in the fall, in November.
Q. Was the property fixed up by the time he got home that time?
A. The barn was built, that was all. We had not got anything fixed in our house. It was all furnished when he bought it.
Q. In whose name was the house taken; who was it deeded to?
A. To me.
Q. And whose money bought it?
A. His money. He made a present to me of it. Mr. Boal bought it, and he made a present of it to me.
Q. Mr. Boal bought it for the Colonel?
A. Yes sir, from Mr. McKay.
Q. Have you lived there ever since?
A. Yes, sir.
Q. What kind of a house did you live in when you lived at Fort Hayes?
A. In tents.
Q. What kind of a house did you live in when you moved to Fort McPherson?
A. A log cabin.
Q. When your second child was born at Fort McPherson, state what Mrs. Walker did with reference to supplying it with clothes?
A. Why she gave me lots of little clothes. I did not have clothes enough for my baby. I was sewing for her at the time, and she gave me some.
Q. I will ask you to state how yourself and husband got along when you lived at Leavenworth?

A. I got along lovely with him. He did not live very long with me while we were there. We were very happy together.

Q. How did you get along when you lived at Rome—Fort Hayes?

A. We got along happily together, but he was not there very much.

Q. How did he treat you when you were living at those places?

A. He treated me lovely. I would not want a better man.

Q. State how you treated him.

A. I treated him the same as he treated me.

Q. State how he treated you while living at Fort McPherson?

A. He treated me all right. Once in a while he was cool to me, when his relations were around.

Q. Who lived with you at Fort McPherson?

A. Sister Nellie and sister May.

Q. When you speak of sister Nellie and sister May, do you refer to his sisters, or yours?

A. His.

Q. How long did they live with you at Fort McPherson?

A. Until they got married, a little before they got married.

Q. How long was that?

A. Well, one lived with me longer than the other. One and a half to two years somewhere along there.

Q. State what your treatment was of him, while you resided at Fort McPherson.

A. He was always kind to me.

Q. State what your treatment was of him while you resided at Fort McPherson.

A. I treated him as any lady should treat her husband.

Q. Did you have any quarrels during the time you lived at Fort McPherson?

A. No, I never had quarrels. That is a thing we never done in our lives, quarreled together.

Q. State what his habits were with reference to the use of intoxicating liquors during the time that you resided at Fort McPherson.

A. He drank a great deal and was away from home a good deal. I never knew where he went.

Q. State whether or not he used a considerable portion of his money in buying intoxicating liquors?
A. I never knew what he did with his money.
Q. State how yourself and husband got along when you moved to Rochester.
A. Very lovely; we got along nicely. He was always anxious to get home.
Q. State whether or not during the time you resided at Rochester, the Colonel would visit you as often as he could get away from his business?
A. Yes, he visited me as often as he could, and I visited him.
Q. State how often he visited you during the time you resided in Rochester.
A. Whenever he was close to Rochester, coming near home, he would run down and see me.
Q. State how he treated you during the time you lived in Rochester.
A. He treated me all right.
Q. State how he provided for you during the time you lived at Rochester.
A. He would send me so much money at a time, sometimes less and sometimes more.
Q. State how you treated him on his visits to you, when you lived at Rochester, during his visits.
A. I treated him as a wife should treat him. I was congenial with him and very happy.
Q. State what trouble, if any, you and Colonel Cody had during the time you lived in Rochester.
A. I never had any trouble with him, only his drinking.
Q. What were his habits with reference to the use of intoxicating liquors during the time you lived in Rochester?
A. He stayed in the saloons a good deal and got home late nights.
Q. Did you and he quarrel during the time you lived in Rochester?
A. No, sir.
Q. State what complaint he made to you during the time you resided in Rochester, and your treatment of him.

A. I never knew he made any complaint.

Q. How long was it after you left Rochester before you took up your residence at North Platte, Nebraska?

A. I was three years in Rochester.

Q. How long was it after you left Rochester before you began to reside at North Platte?

A. About one year.

Q. Did you accompany the Colonel on the road during the year between the time you left Rochester and the time you began to reside in North Platte?

A. Yes, I did.

Q. How many children did you have at that time?

A. Three children.

Q. State what trouble you had with your husband, if any, during this year that you traveled with him on the road?

A. I do not know that I had any trouble. I never knew it.

Q. State what complaints, if any, your husband made to you, during that time, of your treatment to him.

A. He never made any complaints to me.

Q. After you took up your residence at North Platte, Nebraska, how much of the year would your husband spend with you?

A. In the summertime—between the dramatical times.

Q. What business was he in at that time?

A. Dramatical business.

Q. And about how many months of each year would he be at home?

A. Two or three months—two months, sometimes three months.

Q. State what trouble, if any, you and he had during the time that you lived in this first house that you built, after returning to North Platte.

A. I never had any trouble . . . with him. He drank a good deal. That is about the most trouble we had.

Q. State what complaint, if any, he ever made to you about your treatment of him during that time.

A. He never made any complaint to me whatever.

Q. State what his treatment was of you at that time.

A. He was always very indulgent and tried to keep me as happy as possible.

Q. State how you treated him.

A. Just the same as he treated me. I was just as kind as I could be.

Q. About how long was it after you returned to North Platte until your husband went into the show business that is the Wild West Show?

A. That is twenty-two years ago last spring. Irma was born at that time. She was called the "Wild West baby." She was born in February, twenty-two years ago, and he started the show in May of that year.

Q. He started the Wild West business twenty-two years ago, did he?

A. Yes.

Q. Twenty-two years ago next May or last May?

A. This May, coming.

Q. Where was Irma born?

A. She was born in the house that burned down, in the west part of town.

Q. How many children have died?

A. Three at the present time.

Q. Where were you living when the first child died?

A. Rochester, New York.

Q. Which one died at that time?

A. Kit Carson, the boy, died of scarlet fever.

Q. Where were you living when the second death occurred among your children?

A. West of town here.

Q. After your husband went into the Wild West Show business, what part of the season would he be at home with you?

A. In the wintertime.

Q. About how many months in the year?

A. He would come home, then go back to New York, would go backwards and forwards all the time. Sometimes a week at a time and sometimes a month at a time. He was always going.

Q. About how long ago was it that you and he improved the farm, known as the "Scout's Rest Ranch," and put up buildings on it?

A. He had a small house on the ranch; it was only a small place then, you know. That was all until the Goodmans got there in the year he went to Europe. Then he put on more, put the addition on.

Q. Can you tell about how long ago it was?

A. About twenty-three years ago. The year he went to Europe, he commenced to improve that place.

Q. State what he did toward consulting with you about the purchase of the land he would make and the improvements on the place.

A. Before the Goodmans came there, I purchased a good deal of the land—was always very much interested in it. But when the Goodmans came there he took it away from me and would not consult with me about it, nor let me do anything.

Q. Mrs. Goodman is a sister of your husband, is she not?

A. Yes, sir.

Q. How long did they live on the ranch?

A. I don't know how long they lived on the ranch—could not tell you how long. They lived there part of the time, then they left and Mr. Cody gave it to my daughter to live on, Mrs. Boal. She was there a couple of years. Then the Goodmans came back again, and he turned it over to me.

Q. State whether or not, during the time that your husband was in the show or dramatic business, he would bring guests with him on his return to North Platte.

A. Always—most always. Very seldom he would come home without guests.

Q. State in what manner you treated the guests that he brought to your home.

A. I treated them the best I knew how. They seemed to be very well satisfied.

Q. State what preparation you would make, if any, for his homecoming, when you expected him.

A. I done everything to make it pleasant for his homecoming.

Q. State what acts of rudeness you ever committed toward any of his guests, at any time, that you know of.

A. I never was guilty of any rudeness.

Q. What was the custom of yourself and the Colonel about giving receptions, when he returned to his home after a season's work.

A. We always gave receptions together and made it as pleasant as possible.

Q. Who would be invited usually to those receptions?

A. The best people in town.

Q. State what you did, if anything, toward helping your husband entertain at those receptions.

A. I done everything I could to help him entertain and tried to make it as pleasant as possible.

Q. State what complaints, if any, your husband ever made to you about your conduct toward any of the guests that he brought to your home, at any time.

A. He never made any complaints to me whatever.

Q. State whether or not you attempted and tried to entertain his guests the best you knew how.

A. I done everything in my power to make it pleasant for him.

Q. State what were the Colonel's habits, with reference to using intoxicating liquors during the time that you have lived at North Platte, when he would come home from the show business.

A. He would drink and go downtown a great deal. He would come home very pleasant. He was always pleasant to me.

Q. State whether or not he ever abused you or complained to you of your conduct to him, in any way whatever, during the time you lived in North Platte.

A. He never abused me. He was always kind to me in every shape and form when I was by myself.

Q. Did he ever complain to you?

A. If I said anything to him about his drinking, he always pacified me and told me not to worry.

Q. I will ask you when you first heard that the Colonel claimed that you treated his guests with discourtesy?

A. When I went to California and came back. That was two years ago. The year Irma was married. She was married two years ago.
Q. How did you hear it at that time?
A. Through my daughter Arta.
Q. Had he complained to her about it?
A. Yes, sir.
Q. Had he ever complained to you at that time?
A. No, sir.
Q. And how long was that prior to the bringing of this suit?
A. That was the year we were in California, and then he did not bring the suit until just before Arta's death, and Arta is dead a year now.
Q. When were you in California?
A. The year Irma was married. I do not remember the year.
Q. Was it two years ago?
A. Yes. I can't remember dates; I have too much on my mind for that.
Q. I will ask you when the Colonel ceased to write to you?
A. Three years ago.
Q. What year was it in?
A. 1901.
Q. When was he here the last time?
A. Christmas, 1901.
Q. Had he written to you up to that time?
A. Yes.
Q. How frequently would you get letters from him up to that time?
A. Every week, every two weeks, and sometimes every day.
Q. Did you receive any letters from him after he left in 1901, Christmas 1901?
A. Yes sir, he wrote me a cross letter from Chicago. There was not much in it though.
Q. Did you receive any letters from him after that time?
A. No, sir.
Q. How frequently had you been receiving letters from him prior to Christmas, 1901?

A. Sometimes every day, sometimes every week, and sometimes every two weeks.

Q. I will ask you to state what complaint he made to you in his letters prior to Christmas 1901?

A. He never made any complaint prior to that.

Q. I will hand you defendant's Exhibits 20 and 21, which are attached to your husband's deposition, and will ask you if this is a letter you received from your husband?

A. That is the letters he wrote me.

Q. In what year did you receive them?

A. 1901.

Q. I will ask you if you saved all the letters your husband wrote you during the year 1901?

A. No, I did not.

Q. State how it was that you saved certain letters and did not save the others.

A. I saved them because of Mrs. Boyer acting the way she did on the ranch. To show them that he advised me to get them off.

Q. I will now hand you Exhibit 16 and ask you to state what it is.

A. That is a letter from the Colonel; that is his writing. He has wrote that with a stub pen.

Q. Is that your husband's writing on the envelope, Exhibit 16?

A. Yes that is his writing.

Q. When did you receive that, in what year?

A. In 1901.

Q. I will now hand you Exhibit 17, being a letter, and ask you to state whether or not that is the letter that came in the envelope Exhibit 16?

A. Yes, that is the same letter.

Q. I will now hand you Defendant's Exhibit 2 in your deposition, being Defendant's Exhibit 15, in your husband, Colonel Cody's, deposition, and ask you to state what that is.

A. That is a telegram from him. I received it here. I don't know whether he sent it or not. I know I received it.

Q. You received it on the day it is dated?

A. Yes, sir.

Q. I will ask you to state, Mrs. Cody, when you took up the management of the ranch?

A. The Colonel was at the ranch and came and told me that Mr. Goodman was going to leave and he did not know what to do, unless he put Boyer on the ranch, and that he was not a capable man to run the ranch, and he wanted me to see to it.

Q. The question is, Mrs. Cody, about what time was it?

A. It was in the fall, I think.

Q. Of what year?

A. I don't remember the year. It was when Mr. Goodman was to leave the ranch. He came to me and told me he was going to leave.

Q. What time was it with reference to the time that Mr. Boyer moved on the ranch, when you took the management of the ranch?

A. I do not remember dates of years.

Q. Was it about the time Mr. Boyer moved on the ranch that he turned the ranch over to you?

A. Mr. Boyer took the management—I took the management with Mr. Boyer just a little before she moved on the ranch, a couple of months.

Q. I will call your attention to Exhibits Number 2, 3, 4, 5, 6, 7, 8, 9, 10, 11, 12, 13, 14–17, 18, 19, 20 and 21, attached to your husband's deposition, and will ask you whether you received these exhibits through the United States mail, as letters from him?

A. Yes, I did.

Q. When you left Leavenworth, why did you go back to St. Louis?

A. Because the Colonel wrote me and told me to go.

Q. I will ask you how you conducted yourself toward the Colonel when you were traveling with him, while he was in the theatrical business?

A. I conducted myself as a wife and lady should.

Q. State what complaints, if any, he made to you about your conduct to him while you were traveling with him, when he was in the theatrical business.

A. He never made any complaints to me.

Q. State whether or not you ever drove your husband from home, or so conducted yourself toward him that he chose the saloon in preference to his home?

A. I never drove him from home.

Q. State what threats, if any, you ever made toward him or toward the children?

A. I never made any threats.

Q. State whether or not you, at any time, threatened to leave him?

A. No, I never threatened to leave him.

Q. State whether or not your husband ever complained to you that he left his home at North Platte because he could not have peace at home?

A. He never complained to me.

Q. I will ask you, Mrs. Cody, whether or not you have ever signed papers mortgaging property, for your husband to raise money?

A. I have.

Q. How many times have you signed mortgages on property for him?

A. Every year nearly.

Q. State how many times you refused to sign mortgages on property when he asked you?

A. I never refused to sign mortgages for him.

Q. You mean when he asked you?

A. Yes, when he asked me.

Q. State what you did toward procuring loans for him when he wanted to start out in his business?

A. Very often in the spring I borrowed money private for him, from private parties.

Q. I will ask you whether or not you said to Mrs. Bradford or to Dr. Powell, or anyone else, that you would bring the Codys so low that the dogs would not bark at them, or words to that effect?

A. I never did.

Q. State what you said with reference to bringing them so low that the dogs would not bark at them, or words to that effect, if anything?

A. I never said anything.

Q. Mrs. Cody, one Mrs. Boyer testified, in Cheyenne, that on various occasions you had given the Colonel dragon's blood to get control over him. State what the facts are with reference to that.

A. I do not know anything about that drug.

Q. State what you told Mrs. Boyer with reference to that, if anything.

A. I never told her anything.

Q. State whether or not you ever gave, at any time, your husband any kind of a drug for the purpose of making him sick?

A. Never.

Q. State what drugs you gave him, if any, for the purpose of making him sick or for the purpose of obtaining control over him.

A. I never gave him anything.

Q. State what you told Mrs. Boyer, if anything, about giving your husband a drug to make him weak so that you could get control over him and have him deed you his property?

A. I never told Mrs. Boyer anything.

Q. State what you told Mrs. Boyer, if anything, about the Colonel not providing for you properly.

A. I never told Mrs. Boyer anything.

Q. I will ask you to state, Mrs. Cody, what your habits are with reference to the use of vulgar, profane, obscene, and indecent language.

A. I don't know, my habits have always been very pure to me. I never use any of it.

Q. State whether or not you use such language.

A. Never.

Q. I will ask you, Mrs. Cody, what your habits are with reference to the use of intoxicating liquors?

A. I never use any.

Q. I will ask you to state what objections to Mr. Boyer you ever made to Mrs. Boyer.

A. I never made any objections.

Q. I will ask you to state what you did with reference to compelling Mrs. Boyer to discharge a girl who was working for her over there.

A. I never gave any objection to her having any girl. It was none of my business. She hired her own girls.

Q. Do you remember a girl over there by the name of Etchison, who was working for Mrs. Boyer?

A. Yes, I remember.

Q. State what objections, if any, you made to this girl.

A. I made no objection—I had nothing to do with her.

Q. State whether or not, at any time, you ever spit in this girl's baby's face.

A. I am human, not inhuman.

Q. Did you ever do such a thing?

A. No, sir.

Q. State what you ever did, if anything, to assist this girl and her child.

A. Mr. Boyer said it needed some clothes, and I gave the child some clothing.

Q. I will ask you to state if you remember the occasion on which yourself and husband attended a banquet at North Platte, given to him on his return from the World's Fair.

A. He went sober to that banquet.

Q. I asked you if you remembered that banquet?

A. Yes sir, I do.

Q. State what drug, if any, you gave him on that evening prior to the time you started for the banquet.

A. I never gave him anything.

Q. State what drug, if any, you placed in a bottle of liquor, from which he took a drink just prior to the time he started for the banquet.

A. I never put any drug in a bottle . . . he never took a drink of anything before he went to the banquet.

Q. State what you did, if anything, on that occasion, to have him in proper condition to go to the banquet.

A. My daughter, Miss Bentley, and Miss Farnesworth were with him all day long to keep him out of the saloon. And we gave him black coffee to keep him sober. And he was very proud to go sober to the banquet.

Q. State what his condition was at the time he went to the banquet.
A. He was sober when he went into the banquet.
Q. How near did you sit to him that evening at the banquet table?
A. I sat next to him, and my daughter Arta sat on the other side.
Q. I will ask you to state to what extent he partook of intoxicating liquors that evening at the banquet.
A. The chef waited on him, and I don't know how much he took.
Q. State what his condition became as the banquet progressed, with reference to intoxication.
A. He was very drunk, or something else was the matter with him. He was very sick or drunk.
Q. State to what extent his condition that evening was produced by any drug given to him by you.
A. I never gave him any drug.
Q. Do you remember one time when the Colonel was at home, when you gave him Garfield tea.
A. I gave it to him very often when it was necessary.
Q. Mrs. Boyer says that on one occasion when she was present at your house, that the Colonel was simply intoxicated and that you gave him Garfield tea and placed therein some drug, for the purpose of making him sick. State what the facts are with reference to that.
A. It is false. I never gave him any. It is a false report.
Q. State what the facts are with reference to your giving your husband certain household remedies to counteract the liquor he had been drinking.
A. I give him a good deal of black coffee. I give him some medicine I was taking. Called it female medicine, and he said that cured him.
Q. Who called it female medicine?
A. Cody did himself. He used to joke over it.
Q. State what the facts are with reference to your getting so intoxicated that Mrs. Boyer put you to bed.
A. I never remember the time of being intoxicated in my life.

Q. State what you said to Mrs. Boyer, if anything, about if her husband would leave her, you would keep him on the ranch.
A. I never said such a thing.
Q. State what the facts are, Mrs. Cody, with reference to keeping liquor in your house.
A. The Colonel brings liquor home and I keep it for him. Some of it is down in the cellar yet. I keep it locked up.
Q. Do you remember on one occasion, when you gave the Colonel some Garfield tea, that he fell over and you were required to put him to bed?
A. No sir, I never did.
Q. I will ask you if at any time during the time your husband was intoxicated, you said to him in the presence of Mrs. Boyer, or in anyone's presence, or to him when anyone else was present, "you are a drunken brute," or words to that effect.
A. I never did.
Q. State what you said to Mrs. Boyer, if anything, about stealing a bottle of whiskey in which you had put drugs to make your husband sick?
A. That is a false statement.
Q. Did you ever accuse Mrs. Boyer of stealing a bottle of whiskey?
A. I never did.
Q. Mrs. Boyer testified that it is your custom to take a drink of liquor the first thing in the morning when you get up. State what the facts are with reference to that.
A. I never took liquor of any kind or wines of any kind.
Q. State what you told Mrs. Boyer, during your acquaintance with her and during the year of the World's Fair, that you had gone down to Chicago and cleaned out the house, or words to that effect?
A. I never told Mrs. Boyer that nor . . . never made a confidant of her in any way.
Q. I will ask you if you know Mrs. C. P. Davis?
A. Yes, I know Mrs. C. P. Davis, but very slightly, only to speak to her.
Q. Was she at your house one time?

A. She sewed for two days at my house.

Q. I will ask you to state whether or not you complained to Mrs. Davis of your husband's infidelity, while she was at your house?

A. I never had any conversation with her.

Q. On that subject?

A. Not on that subject. I had very little conversation with her anyhow.

Q. I will ask you to state what you said to Mrs. Davis, if anything, about that you would have nothing to do with Colonel Cody when he came home?

A. Mrs. Davis was a strange woman to me, and I never said such a thing to her.

Q. I will ask you to state what the facts are with reference to that, as to whether or not yourself and husband slept and cohabited together, during the time he would be at home?

A. Always.

Q. You know, Mrs. Bradford, do you not, your husband's sister who resides in Denver?

A. Yes, sir.

Q. So you remember the date on which your daughter Arta died.

A. She died the thirty-first.

Q. Of what month?

A. January.

Q. What year?

A. 1904.

Q. And where were you when you heard of her death?

A. I was going on the train.

Q. Who was with you at that time?

A. Mrs. Bradford.

Q. What did you do when you heard of that fact?

A. We went right on, Mrs. Bradford and I, to Medicine Bow, and the Colonel telegraphed us to go back, and we went back to her house. He telegraphed to Hinckle for us to go back.

Q. And you returned to Mrs. Bradford's house in Denver?

A. She wanted me to stay there until we went to Omaha, and I did.

Q. When you were there did you receive a telegram from the Colonel with reference to a reconciliation?
A. No sir, I never received a telegram with reference to a reconciliation.
Q. Did Mrs. Bradford receive one that you know of.
A. She received a telegram that said that while he is on his sacred duties for me to be good to him, the same as though there was no trouble between us.
Q. Did the telegram that Mrs. Bradford received read about as follows: "May tell Lulu it is my desire, while attending to our sacred duties, to bury all personal difficulties. Brother."
A. It said that.
Q. Was there a telegram prepared in answer to that?
A. Yes, there was a telegram prepared in answer to that.
Q. I will ask you to state whether or not you were willing to have a temporary reconciliation with your husband?
A. Not for a while. It was forever or not at all.
Q. Who answered this telegram?
A. Mrs. Bradford.
Q. What did you tell her that she should answer?
A. I told her to answer that Arta—I cannot word it now, but I can word it.
Q. What did you instruct Mrs. Bradford to telegraph your husband with reference to this reconciliation?
A. I told her to tell him that he had broken Arta's heart by his false accusation. Not for a while only, it was to be forever or not at all.
Q. Was the telegram which you authorized Mrs. Bradford to send to this effect: "Aunt Lulu says you broke Arta's heart; suit entered under false accusation; never for only a while, forever or not at all."
A. That is just it.
Q. I will now hand you Defendant's Exhibit 3 and 4 and ask you to state what it is?
A. That is a letter from my daughter, before she died.
Q. When is the letter dated?

A. January 24, 1903.
Q. And when did you receive it prior to the time that you started to go to her? How many days before you started?
A. I think I started on this telegram—when I got a telegram from Mr. Thorpe that she was getting worse.
Q. How long did you get the letter before you started?
A. About three days. No, I did not get it three days before; it was just a short time. It takes three days to come from Spokane.
Q. Did you have this letter from your daughter at the time you authorized Mrs. Bradford to have this telegram sent to your husband?
A. I did. And Mrs. Bradford read it, too.
Q. You had the letter with you, did you?
A. Yes, sir.
Q. State whether or not you were thinking of the contents of that letter at the time you authorized Mrs. Bradford to send this telegram?
A. I was.
Q. State whether or not you ever dictated a telegram there at that time, to be sent to your husband, in the following language:
Q. "You are Arta's murderer; divorce entered under false accusations; forever or not at all."
A. Never. That is the only one I dictated.
Q. State whether or not you said, on that occasion, that your husband had murdered your daughter, or words to that effect?
A. Never.
Q. I will ask you to state what your desire was at that time with reference to a reconciliation with your husband?
A. I thought he would have reason enough to know that Arta's death was very hard to bear and he would be reconciled and withdraw his false accusation.
Q. Where did you and Mrs. Bradford meet your husband, with the remains?
A. At Omaha.
Q. Who was on the train; who composed the funeral party?

A. Dr. Thorpe, myself, Mrs. Bradford, the children, and the Colonel.

Q. Dr. Thorpe was your daughter's husband?

A. Yes.

Q. How long had she been married at the time of her death?

A. She was married on the first of January and died the thirty-first.

Q. State what your husband did toward greeting you when you met him at Omaha?

A. He passed right by me and did not notice me.

Q. I will ask you to state what you said to Mrs. Bradford, if anything, at her home in Denver, at the time you received this telegram, and was preparing this telegram, or at any other time, with reference to denouncing your husband, at the grave, as the murderer of your daughter?

A. I never said anything.

Q. State what you said with reference to creating a scene at the grave?

A. I never thought to make a scene, that was the least from my thoughts.

Q. Are you acquainted with Dr. Powell?

A. Yes, sir.

Q. Was he in the funeral party?

A. I do not know where he met us at all.

Q. Was he at Rochester?

A. Yes, sir.

Q. Did he come to your room, at Rochester, while you were at the hotel?

A. No sir, he never came.

Q. I will ask you to state whether or not Dr. Powell came to you in the hotel at Rochester and said to you that the Colonel desired a reconciliation, and that you replied, "I want nothing to do with him; he is rotten; I will have nothing to do with him. I will bring the Codys down so low that the dogs won't bark at them; and furthermore, I will denounce him at the grave as the murderer of my child," or words to that effect?

A. He never came to me, and I never had a conversation with him all the time I was there.

Q. I will ask you, Mrs. Cody, whether or not, when you were taking the carriages in Chicago, you heard your husband say to you, "Mamma, get into this carriage" or words to that effect?

A. He told them to put me in that carriage; someone, I do not know who it was. He did not address it to me at all.

Q. Did you get into the carriage, as directed?

A. Yes, sir.

Q. I will ask you to state whether or not, that you created a disturbance in the dining room of the Auditorium Annex at Chicago, with reference to the children of your daughter?

A. No, I did not make any disturbance with the children. The children are very peaceful, well-behaved children, both of them.

Q. State whether or not, at any time on that funeral trip, you shook your fist in Mrs. Bradford's face and told her that you would bring the Codys so low that the dogs would not bark at them?

Q. State what you told Miss Parker with reference to getting power over the Colonel, for the purpose of getting possession of his wealth, if anything?

A. She was only a child, and I never have any conversation with a child about anything like that, or anybody else.

Q. State what you told any person to that effect?

A. I never told any person anything.

Q. State whether or not you ever had any correspondence with a fortune teller in Battle Creek, Michigan?

A. No sir, I never had with a fortune teller, but I corresponded with Dr. Peebles at Battle Creek, Michigan.

Q. Is he the only person you corresponded with in Battle Creek, Michigan?

A. Yes, he is the only one.

Q. What other person did you have correspondence with besides Dr. Peebles?

A. Nobody at all.

Q. I will ask you whether or not you told this young lady you were consulting with fortune tellers?
A. No, sir.
Q. What are the facts with reference to your consultations with some clairvoyant or person in Denver?
A. Bradford and I used to go sometimes Sunday evenings to Professor Waldron's. Mrs. Bradford was the one that took me there. She said she was well acquainted with him, and we went there for amusement.
Q. State whether or not you ever received any letters from this man.
A. I have once or twice. I got Arta's and Irma's horoscope written there, which many other ladies have.
Q. State for what purpose you got it.
A. More for amusement than anything else. The Colonel read them himself.
Q. State whether or not you believe in the power of these people to foretell future events.
A. I do not believe in it but think it is lots of amusement sometimes.
Q. State whether or not you have regulated your conduct in any way by what this man told you?
A. No, sir. The Colonel knew it all the time.
Q. Was he home for Christmas?
A. Yes, sir.
Q. What present, if any, did he bring you on that occasion?
A. He gave me a little hand satchel, a beaded one, silver beads, with $50.00 in it.
Q. When did he leave on that occasion?
A. Christmas day.
Q. How many days was he at home?
A. About three days.
Q. Who went to the train with him when he went away?
A. We all did—Miss Colvin was there, myself and Irma, and I think Mrs. Goodman went, too.
Q. State how the Colonel bade you goodbye when he left?
A. He kissed me goodbye as usual.

Q. How did you bid him goodbye?
A. The same way, as we always have done.
Q. I will ask you to state, Mrs. Cody, what your feeling is at this time toward your husband?
A. The same as I have always felt to him.
Q. How is that?
A. He is the father of my children, and I love him, and I bore my troubles without any complaint.
Q. Do you love him at this time?
A. I do; he is the father of my children.
Q. I will ask you to state what your desire is at this time with reference to a reconciliation?
A. I would be willing to have a reconciliation on one condition.
Q. What is that?
A. That he clear me of trying to poison him as a false accusation.
Q. You think that he should retract his charge of attempted murder on your part?
A. I do.
Q. I will ask you to state, if your husband will retract the accusation that you tried to murder him, whether or not you are anxious for a reconciliation.
A. On that one condition.
Q. State how Colonel Cody addressed you when he spoke to you?
A. As "Mamma," most of the time.
Q. How did you address him when you spoke to him?
A. I said "Willie."
Q. How did you come to address him by that name?
A. He told me to call him Willie, as his mother used to do.
Q. I will ask you to state what you ever said to Mrs. Vroman about your husband being a drunken cowboy, or whether or not you ever called him that name in her presence?
A. I never said anything to Mrs. Vroman about Colonel Cody any time . . . did not associate with Mrs. Vroman as a neighbor.
Q. Did you ever call him by that name?
A. No, sir.

Q. State what you said to Mrs. Vroman, if anything, about getting a gold ring, in compliance with instructions from a gypsy.
A. What kind of a gold ring?
Q. A band ring?
A. I never owned one.
Q. State what you said to Mrs. Vroman about getting one?
A. I never said anything to her about it. As I say, I did not associate with her enough to talk to her.
Q. State what you said to Mrs. Vroman, if anything, about going down to New York, and that you were expecting to bring the Colonel home in a box?
A. I never had any conversation with her about it. I told her I was going to New York. She asked me for my cow and I let her take it.
Q. State what you said, if anything, to Mrs. Boyer about that you would rule or ruin your husband?
A. I never had no conversation with her with reference to that.
Q. Mrs. Vroman testified, in this case, that your daughter Irma came over to her house and acted as though she was under the influence of liquor. State what you know about that.
A. She testified falsely.
Q. State what complaints, if any, Mrs. Vroman made to you about the conduct of your daughter Irma at her place?
A. She never made any statement to me.
Q. State what she ever said to you, if anything, about Irma coming to her house and conducting herself improperly before her husband and her boys.
A. My daughter never acted improperly before anybody.
Q. I will ask you what Mrs. Vroman said to you?
A. She never said anything to me.
Q. I will ask you to state whether or not you remember a time when yourself and husband and Mr. and Mrs. Boyer went to a theater together?

A. I never was in company with Mrs. Boyer at any theater. She went by herself and we went by ourselves.

Q. State what disturbance, if any, was created in the theater at any time when you sat, with your husband, close to Mrs. Boyer and her husband.

A. I never knew of any.

Q. Do you remember going to a restaurant with your husband on one occasion, after the theater, and your husband ordered oysters for the party?

A. No, I do not remember. We always had our lunches at home.

Q. State what disturbance you created, if any, at that time, or at any other time, when in company with your husband at this restaurant?

A. I never had any.

Q. State what, if anything, you said to Mrs. Vroman about keeping your husband home from the wedding of Mr. and Mrs. Goodman's daughter, about the time of the wedding.

A. I had no conversation with Mrs. Vroman about it.

Q. What are the facts as to [why] your husband did not attend that wedding?

A. Because he was too drunk to go. I had called in Dr. Hingston—he almost had delirium tremens that night.

Q. When was Dr. Hingston called to attend your husband, with reference to the wedding?

A. He was called that day the wedding was and was with him three or four times that evening, because he was in a very critical condition.

Q. Are you acquainted with Dr. Thorpe who is now located at Burlington, Vermont?

A. Yes, he is my son-in-law.

Q. He was the husband of your deceased daughter Arta, was he?

A. Yes, sir.

Q. Did he accompany the funeral train to Rochester?

A. Yes, sir.

Q. State what conversation you had with Dr. Thorpe at Rochester, in the hotel there, with reference to a disturbance at the grave.

A. Doctor came to me and said, "Mother I hear there is going to be a disturbance at the grave." I says, "What do you mean?" He said, "I hear there is going to be a disturbance made at the grave." I tried to get him to tell what he meant but he would not. I said, "You need not worry, there will not be anything there." I said the Colonel would not make a disturbance. That is what I thought he meant.

Q. When did you first learn that there was someone who claimed that there would be a disturbance made at the grave?

A. When he came up and told me about it that time, that is all I know about it.

Q. Mrs. Cody, I will hand you Defendant's Exhibits 3 and 4, being the envelope and letter, heretofore testified to by you, and ask you to state whether or not that is the envelope in which the letter, Exhibit 4, was enclosed to you?

A. It is.

Q. Mrs. Cody, I call your attention to the date of the letter, January 24, 1903, and will ask you whether or not that is the correct date or not?

A. That is not the correct date. That was 1903 just because she made a mistake. She was sick and wrote it in a hurry. The letter will prove when it was written.

Q. I will ask you to state what year you received this letter in?

A. I received it in January 1904. She made that mistake quite often: putting 1903. She was sick and made that mistake quite often because it was so near the New Year.

Q. I hand you now Defendant's Exhibit 5, Mrs. Cody, and ask you to state what it is.

A. That is a pin or charm, given to him from Queen Victoria.

Q. Given to whom?

A. To Colonel Cody from Queen Victoria, and he brought it to me and gave it to me.

Q. How long have you had it?

A. Ever since he returned the last time from Europe.

Q. About how long is that?

A. He gave it to me the next day after he arrived home. I do not remember the year he came from Europe—I don't remember that.

Q. Whose picture is it, in the pendant.

A. Queen Victoria's.

Q. State to what extent you wore this piece of jewelry since you received it.

A. I wore it on certain occasions, when it was necessary. Not on every occasion, but on those where I wanted to dress up for.

Q. When was the last time you wore it?

A. At my daughter Irma's wedding.

Q. How long ago is that?

A. Two years ago, the twenty-eighth of February.

Q. State what you said to Mr. and Mrs. Boyer about your husband having lived five years longer than he ought to have lived?

A. I never said anything to them about it. I never said anything about it.

Cross Examination

BY MR. H. S. RIDGELY:

Q. When was you married to Colonel Cody?

A. In 1866.

Q. And where?

A. In my father's house in St. Louis.

Q. And where did you say you went right after your marriage?

A. I went on a boat up the river to Leavenworth.

Q. How long did you live in Leavenworth?

A. I lived there until my baby was born.

Q. About how long was that?

A. A year.

Q. Who did you live with there, if anyone?

A. With Mrs. Meyers sometimes, and sometimes with Mrs. Goodman.

Q. They were both sisters of Colonel Cody, were they?
A. Yes, sir.
Q. Married sisters?
A. Yes, sir.
Q. And you lived at their house?
A. Yes, sir.
Q. And they always treated you nicely?
A. They always acted to my face so.
Q. The facts are that they treated you nicely, Mrs. Cody?
A. I suppose they did when they were aways sometimes.
Q. Did Mrs. Goodman live in Leavenworth at that time?
A. She lived in the valley about five miles.
Q. About five miles from Leavenworth?
A. Yes, sir.
Q. What business did you say Colonel Cody went into shortly after you went up there?
A. He went into the saloon business.
Q. How long did he conduct the saloon?
A. A couple of months.
Q. It was satisfactory to you for him to be in the saloon business, was it not?
A. No, sir.
Q. You did not like for him to be in that business?
A. No.
Q. You and he had considerable trouble about him being in the saloon business, did you?
A. No sir, never had any trouble about it.
Q. But you objected to his being in the saloon business?
A. Yes, sir.
Q. And strenuously objected?
A. Not strenuously. I asked him to get out of it as I did not like it.
Q. You asked him to get out of it repeatedly?
A. No, sir.
Q. And continuously?
A. No sir, continually, I did not.

Q. During all the time he was running the saloon, you at different times requested him to get out of that business, and objected [to] his being in that business?
A. We had a conversation together about it. He was not making any money, and we talked about it and about his leaving the saloon business.
Q. Then the reason that you objected [to] his being in the saloon business was because he was not making money enough in that business.
A. Not altogether.
Q. That was one of the reasons?
A. Yes.
Q. Where did you live while he was running the saloon?
A. I lived at Mrs. Goodman's house partly, and then at some rooms there, and we boarded ourselves.
Q. And where did you go to live after your husband quit the saloon business?
A. Went up to Dr. Crook's house.
Q. How long did you live there?
A. A few months.
Q. And then what business did your husband go into, if any?
A. When he left the saloon?
Q. Yes.
A. He went into the hotel business.
Q. What hotel was that?
A. The Golden Rule House, he called it.
Q. That was simply a tavern, formerly owned by your husband's mother, was it not?
A. Yes, sir.
Q. How long did he operate that hotel?
A. A few months.
Q. What was the reason he quit operating that hotel?
A. He did not make any money, so we could not live there.
Q. You and Colonel Cody had some family trouble at the time you were living at that hotel?

A. No sir, we did not.

Q. You had some words there—while you were living at the Golden Rule House, did you not?

A. No, sir. I had my mother come and visit me there, and then she went home again.

Q. Your brother was there, too, was he not?

A. Yes sir, he was a little boy then. I was supposed to have visitors if I wanted them.

Q. Is it not true that Colonel Cody one day, while your mother was there, was singing a song that reflected on your mother, and you and he had some trouble about it?

A. No, sir.

Q. Where did you go after you left the tavern?

A. He took me down to Leavenworth and rented two rooms.

Q. And where did he go?

A. He got a wagon and some horses and went out west—he got them from his uncle, Joe Cody.

Q. And he sent your mother and brother back to St. Louis after he quit the hotel business?

A. No, sir. My mother was able to pay her own way. My father was able to give her the money to pay her way. Cody did not have any money then.

Q. Is it not true, Mrs. Cody, that you and Colonel Cody separated when you went out of the Golden Rule House?

A. No sir, it is not true.

Q. Is it not true that he took you to Leavenworth at your request and got you a home there and he went away on the plains?

A. He took me to what——I don't know whether you would call it a home. I had his sister Nellie with me. He could not make any money in Leavenworth, so he said, so he went out on the plains with a wagon and some apples and things to sell.

Q. And you requested his sister Nellie to live with you as your companion while he was gone. The sister who is now Mrs. Whetmore.

A. No sir, she was to live with me by his request.

Q. Was it not your request?

A. No, sir.

Q. Is it not true that Colonel Cody never took any apples out on the plains but fitted out a wagon, in which he took some potatoes and provisions and left for the frontier?

A. It is true he fitted out a wagon with provisions, but he told me he had apples and I took his word for it.

Q. You never seen the apples, did you?

A. No, sir.

Q. When did you next see your husband after he left for the west?

A. After the baby was born.

Q. Where did you see him?

A. In Leavenworth.

Q. He had returned?

A. Yes. He wrote—

Q. What did he write you?

A. He wrote for me to come to Leavenworth. He had sent me home in the meantime.

Q. He had sent you back to St. Louis?

A. Yes, sir.

Q. And he had furnished you the money to go back home on?

A. Yes, sir. And he sent his sister Nellie with me, too.

Q. You wanted her to go along with you, did you not?

A. He sent her. It was his wish.

Q. And you made no objection?

A. Of course not.

Q. While you was away this time, he sent you money to live on, did he not?

A. Very little—not enough for my support, altogether. My father supported me.

Q. Is it not true that at the time you lived in Leavenworth, that Mr. Cody, your husband, had Mr. Al Goodman, your brother-in-law, to provide for you and see that you had all the necessaries of life and your wants all satisfied?

A. No sir, he did not.

Q. Is it not true that Mr. Goodman brought you provisions?

A. He did sometimes but did not provide all the provisions.

Q. And other times Cody sent you money direct?

A. Yes, sometimes.

Q. When was it you went to Rome, Kansas?

A. My little girl was nine months old then.

Q. The Colonel wrote and told you that he had founded a town at the time?

A. Yes, sir.

Q. And that he named it Rome?

A. Yes, sir.

Q. And that he was worth a lot of money?

A. He never told me he was worth lots of money.

Q. He told you that he wanted you to come out to him?

A. He told me to come out, but he never had lots of money. He was working at grading.

Q. He had a town site there, did he not?

A. He supposed he had.

Q. But he did have, did he not?

A. He supposed he had.

Q. And you went down and found he had one, didn't you?

A. I found he had none.

Q. When you got there, he and a fellow by the name of Rose had a town laid out, and had sold a number of lots and had houses built in the town?

A. I did not see any houses built in the town. I saw a lot of tents, and I found that Rome had roamed away—had roamed to Hayes at that time.

Q. When you got there to Rome, your husband had a town laid out, and there were a number of people living in it?

A. He had a supposition of it laid out. When I got there, I seen no town, just tents.

Q. Did you expect to see, when you arrived, brick blocks?

A. No sir, I did not.

Q. And when you first went there, he told you he had a town there and showed it to you, and you believed it, and continued to believe it, until a man came along representing the K.P. R. and wanted them to divide up the interests in the town with him, and when they objected to do it, he founded another site and thus destroyed your husband's prospects for a town?

A. It was all supposition. He had no town.

Q. Is not what I stated in that question true?

A. No.

Q. Did not the fellow come there, representing the Kansas Pacific Railroad, and wanted them to divide up the interests of the town site, and when your husband refused, he founded another town and destroyed your husband's prospects of a town there?

A. He had only a supposition town, if he had a town. When he came down to meet me, the town had roamed off to Fort Hayes.

Q. But you found a town there when you got there?

A. No, sir.

Q. Did you not live in that town for a period of time, say three months?

A. I did not live in the town. I lived in a tent on the edge of the fort.

Q. Did you not live in a house with a tent at the back of it?

A. We had no house at all—had two tents.

Q. Is it not true that your husband, after he had been there for some time, had a contract with the K. P. Railroad to furnish them buffalo meat for contractors, and he went away on a hunt for two or three days, and when he returned he found the town had then moved away?

A. No, sir.

Q. And is it not true that when your husband returned from the buffalo hunt, he found you and his partners the only one[s] in the place where the town had been, and when he inquired what had become of it, you told him that a man by the name of Webb, who wanted an interest in his townsite, and who was a Kansas Pacific land man, . . . had started a new town about three miles away?

A. No, sir.

Q. Is it not true that when he came back there from that hunt, you criticized him and quarreled with him, because you thought that he had represented to you that he was worth a lot of money and that his money was in the town site and that the man Webb had killed all the prospects of the town.

A. No sir, he had no money to put in it and I knew it.

Q. Is it not true you and he had a quarrel about it?

A. No, sir.

Q. Is it not true that you demanded of him to be send back to St. Louis, at that time, to your parents?

A. Not while at Rome.

Q. Is it not true he sent you back from Rome?

A. No, sir.

Q. Where was it you demanded to be sent back to St. Louis to your parents?

A. I was sent back on his request.

Q. Where were you at the time you requested to be sent back?

A. I was at Fort Hayes, across the creek.

Q. And he sent you back, did he?

A. Yes, sir.

Q. And sent you money there after you got back?

A. He came back himself after I was there a couple of months. He did not have any money to send me.

Q. He was getting a salary from the Kansas Pacific Railroad, was he not?

A. No, sir.

Q. Did he not have a contract at that time to furnish buffalo meat for the government?

A. No, sir.

Q. You did not know he had such a contract?

A. No, sir.

Q. Is it not true that you knew he had one?

A. No, sir.

Q. Where did you go to from Rome?

A. Fort Hayes.

Q. Where did you go from Fort Hayes?

A. To St. Louis, to my home.

Q. Where did you go from St. Louis after you got back?

A. Fort McPherson.

Q. Returning to the time you were at Leavenworth, when your husband went out from Leavenworth to the west, did he not return to Leavenworth and visit you there?

A. Certainly.

Q. And you and he had a bad quarrel that time?

A. No sir, we never had a quarrel.

Q. And as a result of the quarrel there, you and he separated for good there at that time?

A. No, sir. We never separated and had no quarrel. It is a false statement.

Q. Do you remember meeting your husband in Leavenworth, Kansas, June 1868?

A. He came home after—in the summertime; I do not remember exactly what month—one time.

Q. Where were you living there in Leavenworth?

A. On Poughkeepsie Street.

Q. Did you not in 1868 have a family quarrel there, which resulted in your separation, and you separated for good at that time?

A. No, sir.

Q. Did you not agree at that time there that you were not suited for each other, and you went back to your home in St. Louis and he went on the plains again?

A. No, sir.

Q. Is it not true that you separated there and was apart for some time, and you went back to St. Louis and he again went to the plains?

A. No sir, we did not separate there.

Q. Is it not true that you did separate there and that his sisters, the ones whom you now complain of, made peace between you and brought you together?

A. No sir, that is false.

Q. That is not true?

A. No sir, that is not true. My husband went back to work, and I took sister Nellie and went home while he went back to his work.

Q. What work did your husband go back to?
A. Grading.
Q. Where?
A. At Hayes, Kansas.
Q. Is it not true that he was at that time employed in the United States Army?
A. It was after that he went in the army.
Q. That was in the year 1868?
A. I do not remember what year. I do not remember dates at all.
Q. Your husband was made chief of scouts in the U. S. Army by General Phillip H. Sheridan, in 1868, was he not?
A. I do not know anything about it. I only know what he wrote me.
Q. He wrote and told you he had been made such?
A. He said that. He was General Carr he told me. I got letters all the time from him. He said he could make more money in the army than on the railroad.
Q. Your husband had gone to Fort McPherson before you went there?
A. Yes sir, he went with the army.
Q. He was employed by the army when you came?
A. Yes, sir. And he sent for me.
Q. Who came to Fort McPherson with you?
A. Myself and baby. Cody met me in Omaha and brought me up himself.
Q. What year did you go to Fort McPherson in?
A. I could not tell. I do not remember dates; that is one thing I can't remember.
Q. Was it in 1869?
A. I can't remember dates.
Q. Your memory is not good on dates, then?
A. No.
Q. You had the same kind of a house there to live in that the other people lived in?
A. No, sir.
Q. You did not have as good a house as the rest of the people lived in?

A. The Colonel built his own house.

Q. But you had as good a house as the other people lived in at that time, didn't you?

A. Of course.

Q. It was as nicely furnished as the other houses at that time at the fort?

A. We did not have much furniture in those days.

Q. It was the best you could get, and your house was as well-furnished as the other houses in the fort, was it not?

A. Yes, we got commissary furniture, some of it—and some he bought himself.

Q. And Colonel Cody made arrangements with the commissary department for you to get your supplies there, did he not?

A. He attended to that himself, and I had nothing to do with it.

Q. His sister May, now Mrs. Bradford, lived there with you?

A. Yes, sir.

Q. Is it not true that the Colonel was out scouting a good deal, when he was there?

A. Yes, sir.

Q. And you and his sister May, when you needed anything from the commissary department, went and got it?

A. No sir, he supplied us every month himself.

Q. And he had arrangements made at the Suttler's stores there for you to get anything you wanted?

A. I do not know anything about it. I never run in debt. Do not make that a habit today.

Q. But you were always able to obtain from the Suttler's stores anything you wished?

A. I presume anything I needed. But there was a good many things I could not get.

Q. They kept calicos, ginghams, and woolen goods there, did they not?

A. Yes, but I did not choose to buy them, they were poor qualities.

Q. They kept them though?

A. Yes, but I did not choose to buy them.

Q. Yesterday, in your testimony, you stated that you and the Colonel got along well together when no one else was there; did you at any time fail to get along together when someone else was around?

A. We did not fail to get along, but he sometimes found fault with me, and I told him it was untrue, and he found it out himself in the end, that what they told him was not so.

Q. To whom do you have reference to?

A. His sister May used to talk about me to him very much, and when he found out the things she told was not true, he did not like it and sent her home.

Q. You and his sister May have been lifelong friends, have you not?

A. She always pretended to be.

Q. And you always treated her as such?

A. I did.

Q. Is it not true that while you were at Fort McPherson, Mrs. Cody, that you and the Colonel fell out, on one occasion, and you did not speak to him for three weeks?

A. No, sir. I am not one of the pouting kind.

Q. And is it not true that the only communication you had with your husband at that time there was through your daughter Arta?

A. No, sir. She was only a child, three years old at that time.

Q. He always treated you well at Fort McPherson?

A. Yes sir.

Q. And he has always treated you well?

A. Yes, he has always been good to me, especially when we were alone; better than at any other time.

Q. He was always good to you when other people were around, was he not?

A. He always pretended to be.

Q. But he always was, was he not?

A. I answered the question, did I not?

Q. You left Fort McPherson and went to live at Westchester, Pennsylvania?

A. No, sir.

Q. Where did you go?

A. He sent me home to my mother's in St. Louis.
Q. How long did you remain in St. Louis?
A. I lived there two or three months, until it got warm. Then he sent for me to come and visit him.
Q. When was it you went to live at Westchester, Pennsylvania?
A. That was when he was in the dramatic company.
Q. How long was it after you left Fort McPherson?
A. About a year.
Q. He had some relative down there, did he not?
A. Yes sir, he did.
Q. And the reason why you left there and went to Rochester was because you did not like his relatives, was it not?
A. No, sir.
Q. His relatives down there were Quakers?
A. Yes, sir.
Q. And you did not like the Quakers?
A. I had no objection to Quakers.
Q. When Colonel Cody was in the theatrical business, he always sent you money, and furnished it when you asked him for it, did he not?
A. He gave me money when he did not drink it all up and spend it.
Q. Did you say that you had hard work to get money out of him at times?
A. Yes, I did.
Q. The reason why was because at times he did not have any, was it not?
A. He made some nights over $1,000.00.
Q. But he had a large company and had to pay for their services, did he not?
A. When he made a thousand dollars, he could have paid the company and given me some, too.
Q. But he was at a large expense running his show business, was he not?
A. He made lots of money, and he could send me money as well as keep his company.
Q. You never wanted for money, did you?

A. Yes, I did, lots of times.

Q. I thought you said he always gave you all the money you wanted?

A. No, I said at times he gave me a good deal.

Q. You traveled with him on the road the year before you came to North Platte, with him with the show, did you not?

A. Yes, sir.

Q. You have been all over the United States with him and visited all the large cities?

A. No sir, I have not visited all the large cities.

Q. You have been in nearly all the large cities, though?

A. No sir, not all.

Q. And he always treated you nicely?

A. He was cool at times. When he was drinking he did not.

Q. You never objected to his drinking, did you?

A. Yes, I objected, as every wife should.

Q. You have mixed drinks yourself for him, here at North Platte?

A. No, sir.

Q. Mrs. Cody, you gave him liquor to drink, did you not?

A. Yes, I set out liquors to him, when he had company and wanted it, but I did not do it because I wanted to.

Q. You never made objections to it, did you?

A. Yes sir, I did. I always made objections. I made it in a kind way though.

Q. You and he separated in 1877, did you not?

A. I don't know whether I did or not in 1877.

Q. In 1876 then?

A. I don't know.

Q. But you and he separated in the '70s sometime.

A. We never separated.

Q. Now, I believe you said yesterday, Mrs. Cody, that you had never told Mrs. Boyer anything about obtaining any drug or what is known as dragon's blood from a gypsy?

A. I did not. It is a false statement.

Q. I believe you said you did not tell her anything of the kind?

A. No sir, I did not.

Q. I will ask you if you know Mrs. Canfield at Sheridan?
A. Yes, I do.
Q. I will ask you if it is not true that you told her that you obtained dragon's blood from a gypsy, with which you intended to get power over the Colonel.
A. No sir, I do not even know what dragon's blood is. Mrs. Pulver down here told me she made beef tea out of it.
Q. I believe you said yesterday that you were desirous at that time for a reconciliation with the Colonel?
A. On conditions.
Q. And that condition is that Colonel Cody make a retraction through the press of the charges made in this divorce suit?
A. Providing he does it in the right way.
Q. And in order for you now to accept a reconciliation from him, he has not only got to make a retraction through the papers of the charges he has made but has got to make the retraction as you dictate it.
A. As he knows it is false.
Q. That retraction on his part would have to be made a certain way?
A. As he knows it is false. He knows it is false.
Q. And before you become reconciled to Colonel Cody, you require him to make a retraction of the charges in his petition against you, and that he would have to make those charges in a certain way, to suit your pleasure, or you would not be reconciled to him?
A. He would not have to suit my pleasure but his own. He knows the charge is false from the bottom of his heart.
Q. Did I not understand you to say that in order for you to be reconciled to him, that he would have to make a retraction [in] the papers in a certain way?
A. Only on conditions.
Q. And before you would be reconciled to him, you would want a retraction made public?
A. Yes, sir. And he would have to make it to know from the bottom of his heart that it was false. He knows it is false and his conscience tells him so.

Q. You would require him to make a public statement through the public press, would you, before you would be reconciled to him, stating the charges he has made in his petition for divorce was false, from the bottom of his heart, and that he knew it was false from the bottom of his heart?

A. And to clear me of the name of would-be murderer. Yes, on the condition that he would clear my name of a would-be murderer.

Q. And those are the only circumstances under which you would consider a proposition of reconciliation?

A. I do not yet. That I will learn afterward.

Q. You would want him to do that first, and then you would consider the matter further?

A. It is his duty to do it.

Q. You would want him first to make a public retraction as above referred to, and then you would consider the matter further, as to further reconciliation?

A. Yes, I would. He never done it with his own free will either.

Q. Now, I believe you stated yesterday that, at the time he sent the telegram to Denver, through Mrs. Bradford, and to which you responded, "for all time, or not at all," that at that time you were willing to have become reconciled to Colonel Cody, your husband, if his telegram would have been for all time.

A. Yes, for I knew he would then correct the poison case. He would clear my name of would-be murderer.

In the District Court of Big Horn County, Wyoming

William F. Cody, Plaintiff,
   vs.
Louisa Cody, Defendant.

The following deposition was taken as per notice and stipulation, at Denver, Colorado, on March 23rd, 1904.

   William F. Cody, of lawful age, being first duly sworn by WILLIS F. WOLFE, a Notary Public in and for the City and County of Denver, Colorado, deposes and says:

Direct Examination

BY MR. H. S. RIDGELY:

Q. You are the plaintiff in this case, are you, Mr. Cody?
A. I am.
Q. You may state your name, age, and residence.
A. William F. Cody, fifty-eight years of age, residence Big Horn County, Wyoming.
Q. You are acquainted with the defendant, Louisa Cody, in this case, are you?
A. I am.
Q. What relation, if any, does she sustain to you?
A. My wife.
Q. When were you married?
A. Was married the sixth day of March 1866.
Q. And where were you married?
A. St. Louis, Missouri.
Q. What was your business at the time you were married?
A. Well, the last work I had been doing before I was married, I had been [a] stage[coach] driver.
Q. How long did you reside in St. Louis after your marriage?
A. I think about four hours. We went right aboard the steamboat, which pulled out that afternoon.
Q. And where did you go to at that time?
A. Leavenworth, Kansas.
Q. How long did you live at Leavenworth?
A. Oh, we were there three or four weeks perhaps. I rented a hotel five miles west of Leavenworth, and we moved out to this hotel, the Golden Rule House.
Q. How long did you conduct this hotel?
A. I think it was about four months.
Q. What was the cause, if any, that you went out of that hotel and quit the hotel business there?
A. Well, I seen that we were neither fitted for keeping a hotel, and Mrs. Cody's mother came to visit her, and shortly after her

coming there, I was humming a little song that the soldiers used to sing there about the Dutch, not thinking any that her mother was German, and it made Mrs. Cody angry and she give me a good deal of trouble about it. And her mother and her brother was there with her, and I seen it was no use of trying to live peaceably at home any longer and the best thing I could do was to quit the hotel and to get back on the plains at my old business.

Q. At whose request did you sell out the hotel and go back on the plains?

A. Well, I talked it over with my wife and she consented, we both consented that this would be the best to do, and her mother and brother could go back home to St. Louis. And she gave her consent provided that I would get her a house and furnish it in Leavenworth, which I did. She took up her residence in Leavenworth, Kansas, with a sister of mine, now Mrs. H. C. Wetmore, whom she wished as a companion as I was going away. She desired that.

Q. How long did you remain on the plains after your wife went to Leavenworth?

A. About nine or ten months when I returned to visit her, and during that time my daughter Arta had been born, during my absence.

Q. Who provided [for] and took care of your wife while you were on the plains?

A. I provided the money, and she took care of herself with the assistance of my sister.

Q. What was your occupation at that time on the plains?

A. Well, when I first went out, I was railroading and hunting, the first trip that I went out. This was during the winter of '66–'67. I was railroading and trading and hunting; I went out to make money, and I was just looking around for anything that would come along.

Q. The money that provided [for] her while you were away, was that sent by you to her?

A. Yes.

Q. In what manner did your wife treat you when you returned home to Leavenworth after the birth of your daughter Arta?

A. Well, for the first few days we got along very nicely, but, as I found out the summer before, our dispositions were not such as to get along well together, and I know the longer I stayed we were likely to grow into more trouble or something of that kind, you know. And so I concluded that I was going to return to the plains.

Q. What was her disposition toward you after you had been there a few days as to being congenial and compatible toward you?

A. Well, she didn't seem to get along well with my sister; there seemed to be some friction in the family, and she naturally complained of what appeared to me was fault-finding without a cause when I was doing the best I could, and general fault-finding; nothing that I could remember in particular, but general fault-finding. It kind o' grated on my nerves, and I pulled out to the plains again.

Q. What, if anything, did you do that gave her provocation to find fault with you at that time?

A. Well, I can't remember that I done anything in particular—well, I don't remember that I done anything in particular, except that it was the same old story that our dispositions weren't congenial. She was always wanting a home of her own, and of course I was young, I was only twenty-one, I married in my twentieth year, and I didn't know anything about business and I couldn't get a home in a minute. It is the same old story of family jars, that I had as well as others, only I thought I had it a little harder than others, and so I pulled out for the plains.

Q. How long were you on the plains after leaving at Leavenworth?

A. Well, the new railroad was building on the plains into the Buffalo country at that time, called Kansas & Pacific Railroad. I went to hunting buffalo for the contractors of said railroad, and I formed a partnership with a man by the name of William Rose. He had a good many teams and I had the influence to get the contracts, and we got a contract for grading a portion of the road; and on the line of our contract we discovered that we were right on the site of a splendid townsite proposition for a new town; and we concluded, he and I, that we would there and then lay out a townsite on our line where we were. This townsite was on Big Creek, Ellis County, Kansas. We had this townsite surveyed and platted, and I named the new town Rome; and we were selling lots quite rapidly, and we were giving lots away quite rapidly to get fellows to build there, too. In fact we had thirty houses in our town, small and large, and the prospect looked very fair for us; so much so that my partner and I begin to get the swelled head pretty well, and we thought we were going to be millionaires. And then I had a little house and a tent combined; it was about half house and half tent, but it was that home that she had been wanting, and I sent her money and told her to come right along on the next train and I would meet her at the end of the railroad; that I owned half the town and I owned $250,000.00. I met her and our little girl, our little girl Arta, she had Arta with her, at the end of the railroad, and from there I took them in wagons to the town of Rome, our home. Our town kept prospering until one day a man came there and looked it over, and I thought I was going to sell him quite a number of lots from the way he was looking the town over; but as I had to go out and kill some buffalo to get more meat for the contractors that afternoon, I turned him over to my partner, but he expressed a desire that he would like to kill a buffalo himself and I took him along with me, and he succeeded in killing a buffalo and was so delighted and seemed so happy over . . . killing a buffalo that I thought I would sell him a block when I got back that night. But he didn't say anything about buying any lots that night or the next morning, so I got my hunting outfit together as I had to go and kill some more buffalo, but before leaving he came up to me and he offered me one-twelfth interest in my own town. I thought he had gone daft, and I rode off and left him. I was gone two or three days on this hunt—three or four days, as I had to furnish meat for the contractors on ahead of the line where we were working. On my return, and when I came within sight of where the town of Rome had been when I left there, I discovered that most of the houses had pulled away or gone someplace or a cyclone had struck the town, and something was the matter, and when I got nearer I see people pulling down the houses, and I could see a string of teams moving lumber and everything away from the town; and when I rode in to where the town had been our little shack was still standing there; my partner and Mrs. Cody were there, and I naturally inquired what had taken place, what had happened. And they told me that that little gentleman that offered me the twelfth interest in the town was the gentleman who laid out the townsites for the railroad company and he wasn't crazy, but I would had better had accepted the twelfth interest; that he had gone two or three miles east of there and laid out a new town for the railroad company and had it to be generally known of the citizens of Rome that that was to be the railroad town and a division town of the railroad.

Q. What was your wife's conduct when you returned and found the town had moved away from you?

A. Well, she looked rather blue at me, and she said, "Where's that $250.000.00 that you are worth?" Well, I told her that I expected that it had gone off with the town—that I was busted: "That little fellow made Rome howl." She didn't like the country, and then she was dissatisfied with the country and didn't think I would make a success, and she wanted to go home to her parents, back to St. Louis. And shortly after that she did return to her parents back to St. Louis.

Q. What was her conduct toward you after she had expressed herself as being dissatisfied with the country?

A. Well, the way I took it, she seemed to think that—made little of my efforts to succeed in life, etc., or that I was a failure and something like that; and we had our little disagreements again. When everything was going all right and I was selling lots of lots, we seemed to get along pretty well; but when things were different and I wasn't getting along very well, things were the other way, and we could not get along so well; so I gave her money at her wish and sent her back to St. Louis so that I could get free-handed and try something else.

Q. Then her conduct toward you at that time was that she was dissatisfied with you also?

A. Yes, that was the impression.

Q. What was the year that you went to Fort McPherson, Colonel?

A. I went to McPherson in the spring of '69; I went there as guide and chief scout for the United States Army.

Q. Had you seen your wife prior to your going there?

A. Yes, I spent the winter of '67 and '68, after she returned to St. Louis, in hunting and scouting for the United States Army, and also I was United States detective for the United States Army, and during that winter I made quite a little money. And being desirous of seeing her and my child again, I had them to meet me at Leavenworth, Kansas, at [the home of] a married sister of mine, and I met her there sometime in June '68; and at this meeting we had a very serious time, so much so that when we separated from there—we separated at Leavenworth, she going back to St. Louis and I returned to the plains; at this meeting I didn't think that we would ever have another meeting; we had kind o' mutually agreed that we were not suited to each other; she was as glad to go back to her home as I was to go to the plains.

Q. What was the cause and who was to blame for the trouble that you had at Leavenworth in June '68?

A. Well, that would be a hard thing to answer.

Q. Was the trouble that you had brought about by acts of yours or by the acts of your wife?

A. Well, she was so dissatisfied and made it so uncomfortable for me that it was an impossibility for me—for us to be together, and I felt it better—the further apart we would be it would be better for us both.

Q. Was it her feeling and disposition at that time that when she came into your company and presence, she became dissatisfied?

A. Yes.

Q. When next did you meet your wife after leaving her at Leavenworth?

A. Well, I returned to the plains and scouted for the army until General Sheridan came and took command in person in the field. I had been carrying some long, dangerous dispatches for General Sheridan, and on my return to his headquarters he appointed me chief of scouts and guide for the army under his command, and I guided the army in the winter campaign of 1868 and '69; and after the winter expedition was over and the command returned to Fort Lyons to recuperate, I had made such a success and had been appointed to such a high position that I desired to see my wife and child again, thinking that she would be prouder of me now, as I had improved my position somewhat. And she might think better of me. And as the command was to remain at Fort Lyons several weeks to recuperate their stock and rest up the men and to reorganize for the summer campaign; I obtained leave of absence and went to St. Louis, Missouri, where she was at, to visit her, which I did for a few days. I disremember how many days, but a very few days as I had to return to my command to guide the expedition on another Indian raid.

Q. What was the treatment that your wife gave you on going to St. Louis on this visit?

A. We didn't have any trouble this time because I wasn't there long enough.

Q. When next did you see your wife?

A. During the summer—the command that I was with was ordered to the Department of the Platte, and our headquarters was established at Fort McPherson, Nebraska, and—as this was to be our headquarters for some time to come, and I [had] secured quarters, a house, or quarters, as we called it in those days, at this post—I sent for my wife and daughter and two sisters to come and make their home with me as I was then in a position to take care of them. My salary was not only a good one, from the United States government, but I had a share of all the captured stock—captured horses or captured property captured from the enemy.

Q. Did your wife come on to Fort McPherson to you?

A. Yes.

Q. How long did you remain at Fort McPherson with her?

A. About three years.

Q. What was her treatment toward you while you were at Fort McPherson?

A. Well, as I was kept so continually scouting and guiding the army, I was at home so little of the time, we didn't have much trouble when I was there and was gitting along fairly well. Whenever I seen a storm brewing if I was at the Fort, I would suggest a hunting party, and lots of the officers were so anxious to go hunting with me that I had no trouble in getting away from home whenever I chose.

Q. Were there many occasions when you were there that you devised means of getting away in order to keep from having trouble with her?

A. Oh, there were several times that I organized these hunts as I thought it would be better than to be around home.

Q. And these hunts that you organized, were they organized by reason of the fact of her conduct toward you?

A. Well, sometimes.

Q. Where did you go to after you left Fort McPherson?

A. In the fall of '72 I went to Chicago and there entered into the show business and went on the stage as an actor.

Q. How long were you in the theatrical business?

A. I was in the theatrical business about ten years—or, rather, ten seasons; we call it in the show business, we call them seasons.

Q. And where was your wife during the time that you were in the theatrical business?

A. Well, she occasionally would visit my company during our traveling tours and we—and in the summer of '73 we established a home at Westchester, Pennsylvania, and lived there—and she lived there when she wasn't visiting me with the show, and she got dissatisfied of Westchester and didn't like it there, and we selected Rochester for a new home—Rochester, New York.

Q. How long did you live at Rochester?

A. We moved to Rochester in '74 and lived in Rochester until the spring of '78 I think it was. I think it was '78.

Q. When you went into the theatrical business did you take your wife with you in '72?

A. She came on shortly after I organized the company—she and her father with her. I gave her father a position in the company.

Q. During the ten years that you were in the theatrical business, when she was with you, what was her conduct toward you?

A. It was very disagreeable at times as she insisted that I was making love to the girls on the stage, as I had to do. In one of the dramas, I had to make love to a girl on the stage, and she objected to the girl and she objected to my making love. In other words—I mean this stage love, you know—in other words, she was jealous of the women of the company. And she would find fault with one member of the company and another one and another one, and she kept me oftentimes very much riled up, or in other words very much confused, so that I didn't do my work or play my part as well as I could otherwise. In fact, it was a kind of a cat and dog's life all along the whole trail.

Q. You spent the vacation periods at your home with her, did you, in those ten years?

A. Well, you know, in the theatrical business, our seasons are in the winter; and in the summers, two of the summers I returned to the army. When I wasn't with the army or guiding a hunting expedition—in the summer of '73 I was on a hunting expedition; of course, I got pay for it—I was usually at home, wherever we were making our home.

Q. What was her conduct toward you during those ten years when you were at home with her?

A. Well, it was the same old story. Sometimes it would run smoothly for a while, and then something would come up and upset everything again and we would have our trouble.

Q. Was the trouble that you had during those ten years of your theatrical life occasioned by any act of yours?

A. I would say that it was not, if her disposition had been more in keeping with my own. Our dispositions were entirely different, that's what was the matter.

Q. What did you do after you went out of the theatrical business?

A. I went into what is known as the Wild West Show business.

Q. What year did you go into the Wild West Show business?

A. I went into the Wild West Show business in '83.

Q. Where was your wife living at that time?

A. When I went into the Wild West? North Platte, Nebraska.

Q. How long had she been living there at that time?

A. She went there in the spring of '78.

Q. What, if any, money did you give her at that time to buy property with?

A. Well, when she left the show, if I remember rightly, I gave her $3500.00, and kept sending her money as I made it—I don't remember the amounts.

Q. How long were you in the Wild West Show?

A. I started the Wild West Show in the spring of '83 and I'm still in it.

Q. And where has your wife lived since she moved to North Platte in '78.

A. She has called that her home ever since—North Platte, Nebraska. Of course, she didn't live right in the town but near there; the last few years in the town. The post office address was North Platte, has always been North Platte.

Q. What has been her conduct toward you when she has gone to visit you when you were on the road with the Wild West Show?

A. It has always been very depressing on me—to such an extent that not only myself but my partner were always glad when she was gone.

Q. Was her conduct that was so depressing on you occasioned by any act of yours?

A. No, I always tried to treat her as kindly and liberally as I could.

Q. What was her conduct toward you and your friends when you returned to your home at North Platte, Nebraska? I mean, during the years that you were in the Wild West Show business?
A. At times it was utterly unbearable, both to my friends and myself, to such an extent that both friends and myself have left the house.
Q. Was this conduct on her part toward you, during those years, occasioned by any act of yours toward her?
A. I am certain that it was not, if my home had been made a pleasant one for me. But my home was made disagreeable to such an extent that I am ashamed to say, but compelled to do so, that I chose the saloons and the wine cup at times in preference.
Q. What, if any, threats did she ever make toward you during the last years that you lived at North Platte?
A. Oh, she threatened me in many ways. She has threatened that she would fix me; she has threatened to leave me; she has threatened the children; and in fact, she did at one time leave.
Q. Were these threats that she made occasioned by any act of yours?
A. Not if she had been a woman with a reasonable disposition.
Q. When did you move from North Platte to Big Horn County, Wyoming?
A. I declared that was my home in '97, I should say, about '97.
Q. And you have made that county your home since that time?
A. I have called that my home. That is my home since, when I am at home.
Q. What was the reason, if any, that you left the home at North Platte, Nebraska?
A. As I had never had any peace up to this time during my married life, and I wanted to seek a place where I could have peace in my old age; and I went off up into that new, wild country to be away from trouble—domestic trouble.
Q. When was the last time that you were at North Platte?
A. You know that—honestly I can't just exactly remember, but about three years ago.
Q. What was your wife's conduct toward you at the time you were at North Platte, Nebraska, about three years ago?

A. Well, it was so disagreeable that I couldn't stand it any longer in many ways. There was no peace at home. I had deeded to her the very heart of our Scouts Rest Ranch there, which included most of the improvements on the ranch, and I had left on the ranch cattle and horses, carriages and wagons, farming implements, and after she had the deeds made for them, she, as what we would call it in Western expression, I was "counted out," and that didn't appear to me just right, and as she claimed them all and they were hers, I thought I had better go and seek me a home entirely away from her.

Q. During all the time of your married life with Mrs. Cody, Colonel, you may state what your conduct has been toward her as to your being kind and providing for her, and trying to get along and have a pleasant home?

A. I was universally kind to her, and I defy any man or woman to swear that they ever heard me speak an unkind word to her—a cross word. I do not believe in quarreling with either man or woman, and besides when I am drinking, I am the least quarrelsome. I will resent an insult quicker when I am sober that I will when I am drinking, because when I am drinking I have brains enough left to give the other fellow or woman the benefit of the doubt, for fear I may be mistaken. I have many faults and one of my greatest faults is my liberality. I am liberal with everyone and especially with my family and always have been. And I have always been in a position to give my wife and my family more money than most . . . men have. And I always look to the comfort and the support of my family first and above all things. I have had such a reputation of making so much money that they and the world at large think that I am made of money, and I have at times given money and went and borrowed money to give to my family when I actually didn't have it; but I didn't tell them that I was hard up . . . I have never let the world know that I was hard up when I have been hard up, because I don't believe that it is good policy to let the world know or let your family know when you are hard up; and I have kept it from them as much as I have from the outside world. And . . . never to my knowledge has my wife or my family asked me for money but what they got it. If I didn't have it, I would go and get it.

Q. Are you a drinking man, Colonel?

A. As a rule I am not. In the positions I have held since I was twenty years of age, I could not have held them had I been known as a drinking man. During my army life I held the position as guide of military expeditions composed of from one to seven thousand men, and the lives of those men depended on my clear brain to guide them safely through the unknown country in which we were passing; not only to guide them but to find water for them, not only for them but for our stock; and I say that no man, if he was known as a drinking man would have been entrusted with the lives of those men and animals, were he a drinking man. In my thirty years of the show business I have been the attraction, the star performer, and I think that the records will show that I have not missed to exceed ten performances in the thirty years. Had I been a drinking man I could not have done that.

Q. I will ask you, if you have drank anything during the last three years before going to North Platte, the last time you were there, when you were there and since that time.

A. With the exceptions of two occasions, one of which is when I broke my ankle in England last spring, and at one other time when I was very sick and weak with heart failure, stimulant was ordered by my physicians to take. With the exception of these two occasions, I haven't drank a drop of any kind of liquors or beer or wine.

Q. What has been your wife's conduct toward you in the transaction of your business in the way of turning your properties?

A. Most every businessman when he has his capital invested in real estate, at times it is necessary for him to carry on his other business, to mortgage such real estate; and several times I have been placed in that same position; and I have asked my wife to sign a mortgage with me, that I needed some ready cash; and she invariably refused, but I admit that on three or four occasions she did sign with me, but whenever she done so she would make a remark, similar to say, "Well, kiss it goodbye, that's gone." And finally she refused to sign her name to any piece of paper at all for me. I will admit that there is today a $2500.00 mortgage on some property that I could and would have paid long ago had she agreed to my selling some other property located in Minnesota, which is of no earthly use to her. But as she refused to sell that or sign any paper whatever for me, I let this $2500.00 mortgage remain as it stands today. I have other properties in real estate that I could handle today to advantage if she would sign the papers, but as she will not sign any papers, I find myself unable to conduct my affairs in a businesslike manner.

Q. What all property have you given her since your marriage?

A. I have given her about 800 acres of the Scouts Rest Ranch, which includes the Scouts Rest Ranch house, barns, granaries, outhouses, corrals, sheds, farming implements of all description, about a hundred head of horses, about a hundred head of cattle, several hundred pigs, and what is known as the Bowyer farm, with houses, stables, corrals, farming implements, horses, and cattle to run the farm. I have also given her the residence she lives in, one of the best in Western Nebraska, furnished; also carriages and horses and barn, and the real estate on which it is situated; also six dwelling houses in the town of North Platte, Nebraska, which are called tenement houses, houses that she rents; and eight town lots in the town of North Platte.

Q. About what time was it that you gave her this property, Colonel?

A. I gave this property to her at different times. I gave her the residence house in 1893 and the other property at different times since.

Q. Are you acquainted with the value of this property that you have given her?

A. Yes.

Q. You are acquainted and were acquainted at the time that you gave this property to her with the value of lands in Western Nebraska and the value of cattle and horses and the improvements?

A. Yes.

Q. What experience, if any, have you had in Western Nebraska in the buying and selling of land and the buying and selling of horses?

A. Well, I have had years of experience in it with both.

Q. You may state what the value of this property is that you gave her.

A. $125,000.00

Q. What, if any, money have you given her since your marriage?

A. I have given her money for the last thirty-eight years, and sometimes she would invest it, and sometimes she would use it as she pleased; I never cared. I have given her a hundred thousand dollars easy enough; counting us the different years that I know I have given her, that wouldn't touch it.

Q. What, if any, money have you given her in the way of paying her life insurance policies for her?

A. Well, I have kept my life insured for $25,000.00 for years in one company, $10,000.00 in another company, and $2000.00 in another company at the present time; and I have kept them up for years. Altogether my premium on my policies amounts to about $1600.00 a year, and even when I left home the last three years when I never expected to return, I have kept them paid up and not later than; just the other day I paid the one company—I paid to the National Life Insurance Company on January the eighteenth, 1904, $1470.00, and I have got another one coming due in April which I will pay. She is, Mrs. Cody is the beneficiary in the policies.

Q. What, if any, reconciliation did you attempt to effect with your wife since your estrangement during the first part of last February?

A. At my daughter's death, who died on January the thirty-first, 1904; I received the news on the first of February. I was traveling on the cars, but on the third of February, knowing that she and I would both accompany the remains to their last resting place at Rochester, New York, and with this great sorrow which seemed more than I could bear, and my heart felt very soft and tender toward all; I thought I would telegraph Mrs. Cody in a manner which might bring us together, as I wanted to see if her heart had softened any toward me and if this great sorrow yet might bring us closer together. And I sent my sister, Mrs. Bradford, a telegram: "Ask Lulu (that is my wife) that it is my wish that we bury our personal differences, while doing our sacred duty in burying our beloved child. Brother." When my sister showed her this telegram, she was at my sister's house here in Denver, my sister tells me that she went wild—went into one of her old-time tantrums, as they call it, and declared that she would not accept any terms, or words to that effect; and she wrote out herself several telegrams for my nephew, who was standing there, to take down to the telegraph office to send to me, and these telegrams were so abusive that my sister told her that those telegrams should not go out of her house. With that Mrs. Cody became so enraged that my sister thought that she was going to strike her. Mrs. Cody declared that the telegrams should go, if she had to take it to the office herself. My sister said that she would go to the telegraph office and denounce her, and she should not send them without she done it over her dead body, as they were cruel; they were unjust; that I had sent her a friendly telegram, one begging for peace, and the ones that she sent me were too outrageous to send. They finally compromised, however, on a telegram which was sent by the Western Union Telegraph Company and which I received at Billings, Montana, on February the third, 1904, in which she accuses me of being the murderer of my child.

Q. You may state, Colonel, if you have ever tried to be agreeable and compatible with your wife by urging her to go with you upon the road with the show, both in this country and in Europe.

A. I have.

Cross Examination by W. T. Wilcox:

Q. When Mrs. Cody was in Leavenworth the second year of your married life, did she live with your sister or your sister live with her?

A. In fact, at part of the time when she was keeping house in Leavenworth, in the spring of '67 or the spring of '68, she was living then with a married sister of mine, or visiting with her rather.

Q. I refer, Colonel, to the time that she went to Leavenworth after you abandoned the hotel.

A. Oh, that was in the fall of '66. Then my sister was living with her. I thought you said '67.

Q. And Mrs. Cody and your sister did not get along well together, did they, Colonel?

A. At times they did not.

Q. And she was wanting you to furnish a home of her own?

A. Yes.

Q. She was very anxious that you should establish a home so that you might live alone by yourselves?

A. No, in the fall of '66 when she went to housekeeping in Leavenworth, she wanted my sister to live with her as her companion and company as she knew that I was going to be away for the winter.

Q. But she was very anxious that you should have a home, was she not, Colonel, and that she could get to be by yourselves?

A. By ourselves?

Q. Yes.

A. No, she knew that I was going to be away.

Q. But she was very anxious that you should have a home, was she not, Colonel, as testified by you yesterday?

A. She was very anxious to have a home, but I wasn't, for I was on the plains, for my home was in the saddle. In other words, she would rather keep house than to board.

Q. And when you established with Mr. Rose the new town of Rome, one of the first things that you did was to establish a home, part house and part tent, and send for her, did you not, Colonel?

A. I did.

Q. How far was this town of Rome from the railroad?

A. About 90 miles from the end of the railroad where I met her.

Q. Describe the house that you moved into with your wife and baby at that time.

A. The house was a frame, but not large enough for all our wants, and we added to it a tent.

Q. About what was the size of the house part and what was the size of the tent part?

A. I think the house was about, the frame part of it was about twenty-by-thirty, and the tent was about twelve-by-fourteen.

Q. You say, Colonel, that when you returned from the hunting expedition, and found that the railroad company's townsite man had succeeded in getting the most of the town of Rome moved away, that Mrs. Cody looked very blue. You felt pretty blue yourself at that time, didn't you, Colonel?

A. No. I never feel blue. When I have any losses, I just make up my mind to let the past be gone and forget the past and build up the future. I passed it off as a huge joke and said we will make it some other place. I was young then. I didn't care for such misfortunes, and I don't at the present day.

Q. But you did not think it strange that Mrs. Cody felt blue when she saw all your bright prospects vanish at that time, did you?

A. I don't know as I thought anything about it at all. I thought she ought to take the world as I took it.

Q. She, realizing that her ability to make you happy in the little home that you had established [would not come to pass, that] would naturally make her feel blue, would it not?

A. I don't know as it would or not. I couldn't answer as to what she thought. I didn't waste five minutes' thought on it; I just went to looking 'round what next I could get at and try and retrieve our losses. And I told her that I would take her to the Hotel Perry, that was the hotel that had been in the town of Rome, and as soon as we could get the hotel opened for guests, we could go over and board there at the hotel, which we did. You know he had moved the hotel over to this new town—Rome was an old give-out town by this time.

Q. In a very short time Mrs. Cody went to St. Louis after that, did she, Colonel?

A. A few weeks after that.

Q. And that was the judgment of both you and her that it was the best thing to do at that time.

A. Well, she said she wished to go back to her parents at St. Louis and I consented and she went to St. Louis.

Q. And you left that place to seek a new employment, did you?

A. I remained right there at Hays, hunting buffalo for meat, which I sold, and scouting and United States detective for the United States Army.

Q. Now when you were doing well and prospering, you and Mrs. Cody were happier than you were when things were the other way, as testified by you yesterday?

A. Yes, sir. I think all people are that way.

Q. While you and Mrs. Cody at that time occasionally had your little differences, they were not serious at that time, were they?

A. No, not particularly so.

Q. Most of us have our little family differences at times, don't we, Colonel?

A. Well, I don't know about that. I have led such a busy life that I can't keep track of the other people's troubles; I have enough of my own.

Q. Now, after Mrs. Cody went to St. Louis to her father's at this time, you met her next at your sister's in Leavenworth, the next June, did you?

A. Yes, I think it was about June, yes.

Q. You going down to Leavenworth and she coming up from St. Louis to Leavenworth?

A. Yes.

Q. Now, was your meeting at that time at the same sister's?

A. No, not at the same sister's. It was at another sister's.

Q. Which of your sisters was it that you met her at that time?

A. I met her at my sister Eliza's. She was married to a man by the name of Myers. My sister was married and keeping house in Leavenworth.

Q. How long did you visit each other at that time?

A. I think it was in the neighborhood of ten days or two weeks.

Q. Now you said yesterday that when you parted at that time, Mrs. Cody was as glad to go back to her father's in St. Louis as you was to go again out upon the plains, did you not, Colonel?

A. I believe I did, yes. Or at least I meant that I was as glad to have her go back there.

Q. Were you drinking at this time, Colonel?

A. No, sir.

Q. You were not drinking liquor any at that time?

A. Not at that time.

Q. What period in your married life was it when Mrs. Cody first complained of your drinking?

A. Not until the later years, because when I was a young man I didn't drink enough liquor of any description to injure me in any way or to interfere with my business.

Q. Can you tell us, Colonel, about the period in your life when Mrs. Cody did complain of that fact?

A. I think it was after we had moved to North Platte, and in fact she never complained so much about my drinking at any time, because she said I was better natured when I was drinking than when I wasn't.

Q. When you say North Platte, Colonel, do you mean North Platte or Fort McPherson?

A. No, North Platte.

Q. The next time that you saw Mrs. Cody after she left Leavenworth for St. Louis and you left for the plains, you took a trip to St. Louis the next spring to see her, did you, Colonel?

A. Yes. The spring of '69.

Q. And you had no trouble at that meeting?

A. Nothing very serious, for I was only there but a very few days—I forget just the number of days—because I had to get back to the command.

Q. And it was during this summer that you visited her at St. Louis that you sent for her and two of your sisters to come and make their home at Fort McPherson in Lincoln County, Nebraska?

A. Yes.

Q. Which of your sisters, was it, Mr. Cody?

A. I forget whether they both came there at the same time, or whether one came on and the other followed; but they both came there, to Fort McPherson, Nebraska, my sister Nellie and sister Mary.

Q. Was either of them the same sister that you have referred to as living in Fort Leavenworth and keeping house there?

A. One of these was the one that went to live with her as a single girl when she first kept house, but neither of them was the married one.

Q. Will you briefly describe the house or home which was occupied by yourself and family during the three years that you lived at Fort McPherson?

A. It was a log house, comfortable log house, with three rooms and a kitchen.

Q. And you and Mrs. Cody got along very well you say during the time you were at McPherson?

A. Well, at times we got along pretty well.

Q. You had no serious trouble at that time?

A. Nothing particularly serious. I was away from home a great deal of the time, scouting for and guiding the army.

Q. You sent into the show business in '72, did you?

A. I did. In the fall of '72.

Q. And Mrs. Cody for a while continued to live at North Platte, did she?

A. Only for a few weeks.

Q. And then where did she take up her abode?

A. She didn't take up her home, but she joined me in St. Louis, Missouri, where I was giving performances, and she traveled with me the better part of the winter with my dramatic company in different towns which I visited.

Q. How many small children did Mrs. Cody have at that time?

A. I think we had three children: Arta, Orra and Kitty.

Q. Where and at what time were the two younger children mentioned by you born?

A. I think they were both born at Fort McPherson, Nebraska.

Q. And was it while Mrs. Cody was with you during the time you have just testified to that she became jealous of you and thought that you were making love to some of the girls?

A. That was the beginning of her jealousy; that was when I got in the show business.

Q. Then it was during this time that she first complained of that fact, was it, Colonel?

A. Yes.

Q. Who were the girls that she was jealous of?

A. Oh, no one in particular. The whole bunch, I think.

Q. And was there no one in particular about that time that she was jealous of?

A. Not to my knowledge.

Q. Was she very troublesome with her accusations at that time?

A. No, not particularly troublesome. But her quietness sometimes was more aggravating than if she had come out and made a good fight.

Q. Then you moved to Westchester about that time, did you?

A. In the spring of '73.

Q. And Mrs. Cody was quite closely confined to the home there with the children, was she?

A. Well, part of the time, when I was in New York making arrangements for my next season's tour, she was with me, and back and forth to New York and Philadelphia. She wasn't at home all the time, only when I was there; as my relatives who lived at Westchester, Pennsylvania, were on the Quaker order and she didn't like their quiet ways, and she was not friendly with them, and that made it rather disagreeable for me because they were very pleasant people, only on the Quaker order, and I told her to keep quiet and make it as pleasant as possible, and when I started out on my next season's tour, we would try and find a new home where there wouldn't be so many Quakers.

Q. And it was about this time that you moved down to Rochester, was it?

A. No. In September we started the show again, and I think she remained with the show until we got to the town of Rochester; and she seemed to like that town of Rochester, and it was hard for her to travel around with the small children—we decided that there would be the best place to take up our residence, as the town was centrally located and I would be more apt to be at Rochester that I would be in most any other town.

Q. And how long did you continue the home in Rochester?

A. About three years and a half.

Q. And during all of that time you were on the road during the show season, were you?

A. In the summer of '74 I went back to the army and guided what was known as the Big Horn Expedition in the Big Horn Basin Countries and Big Horn Mountains.

Q. Well, the balance of the time that you lived in Rochester, what did you do?

A. In the winters I was on the road giving exhibitions. Sometimes she would come on to visit me, and sometimes she would go back to Rochester, where our oldest little girl was going then to school.

Q. Was it while you were living in Rochester that you lost one or more of the children?

A. Yes, we lost our little son in Rochester.

Q. Do you remember his age at the time of his death?

A. He was five years and six months old when he died. He was five years, six months, and twenty-two days, if I remember rightly.

Q. You stated in your answer yesterday that if Mrs. Cody's disposition had been more in keeping with yours, you would have got along more pleasantly. That would be true, would it not, Colonel, if your disposition had been more in keeping with hers?

A. I think if my disposition had been more like hers, it would have been worse than a keg of dynamite going off.

Q. You don't think she was always entirely to blame, do you, Colonel?

A. Well, I wouldn't say as to that.

Q. The $3500.00 which you state that you gave Mrs. Cody in the spring of '78 was invested in a home in North Platte, or near North Platte, was it not?

A. Yes.

Q. And it was the home that was occupied by you and Mrs. Cody until the fire of about ten years ago, when it was destroyed?

A. Yes, in about 1893. We occupied it when I was at home. No, it was in '92. Well, it was in the winter of '91 or '92.

Q. You state that Mrs. Cody visited you at times when you were on the road with the Wild West Show, and you were glad when she left. Can you tell us any particular thing that she did or that she complained of that caused you to rejoice when she left?

A. No, I can't remember anything particular, but she was complaining so often about one thing and another thing and different things that would naturally come up that it kept me disturbed and made me nervous, and I was doing a very particular act in the way of shooting that when I would get excited and nervous over these family jars, I wasn't in a fit condition to do justice to my performance.

Q. Mrs. Cody never complained, did she, Colonel, that you did not treat her liberally?

A. Yes, she did complain of that on many occasions. She would see the vast crowds of people flocking to the show, and she would imagine that I made a great deal more money than I told her that I was making. She could not realize the enormous expense that I was under; and often during rainstorms and bad weather our business was bad, yet our expenses were just the same; and she complained that I was extravagant or I would spend my money—instead of give it to her or keeping it for our old age or something.

Q. Mrs. Cody has always been a very saving and economical woman, hasn't she, Colonel Cody?

A. Yes. I give her credit for that. But I have often, not only one year, but many different years, I have sent her large sums of money and when I got home, when I would git home, and I would ask her what had become of the money, the different moneys that I had sent her, she would refuse and in fact never gave me an account of where the money went to, and this would bring on another scene, and I would quit the proposition; I wouldn't say no more about it. I would rather not go into details of where the money went than to have trouble.

Q. Was Mrs. Cody ever a lady who spent money foolishly upon dress, or did she have any expensive habits?

A. No, she was not an extravagant woman; neither did she spend much money on dress or jewelry in any way; and that was the reason why I couldn't account [for] where the money had gone to. If she had been an expensive or extravagant woman, why I might have guessed where the money had gone to; but as she hadn't spent it on herself, I couldn't imagine what had become of the money. And I thought at the time, and I still think, that she must have money at her command in some place that I don't know anything about.

Q. She had to look after the expense of your daughters, who were young ladies, and that was quite a burden, wasn't it, Colonel?

A. She did in a partial way; but I generally furnished my daughters when they got a little older, as they did when they began to bud out as young women . . . And they relied on getting money—coming to me for money instead of their mother. I don't remember of her buying any valuables—garments for either of them.

Q. You being away from home so much of the time, the responsibility and care of your daughters was largely left to Mrs. Cody, was it not?

A. Yes, when they were at home, but as my daughters got able to go to school, they were either away at boarding schools or . . . they were visiting with me. My eldest daughter was visiting with me not only in England, in different portions of England, but she was on the continent of Europe, and during the winter of '87 and '88 she kept house for me in England.

Q. Mrs. Cody made a good mother to your daughters, did she not, Colonel?

A. I think she could have been a much better mother in many respects; although I think she loved her children, she was irritable and cross and peevish with them at many times when it was uncalled for. She would threaten to leave them and make all kinds of dire threats to the children when it was utterly unnecessary.

Q. She raised your two daughters that you have always been proud of, didn't she, Colonel?

A. I think I had about as much to do with raising those daughters and training their minds in a good way as she did. And what I objected to the most when I would put them at boarding school and pay for their schooling, she did not allow them to remain there as she should have done; particularly with my daughter Irma, who would have had a much better education now than she has if she had been allowed to remain in such schools as I placed her in.

Q. You stated yesterday, Colonel, that Mrs. Cody's conduct toward you and your friends when you returned home to North Platte during the years of the Wild West Show business was unbearable to such an extent that your friends and self left the house. Will you please give the names of the friends who left the house by reason of the acts of Mrs. Cody?

A. There was so many of them that I could not recall the names, but some of them will be present at the trial to testify to this question.

Q. Can you name a single person that by reason of Mrs. Cody's conduct was compelled to leave your home during that period?

A. There were several of them, but I don't care to mention their names because they will be present at the trial to answer this question.

Q. Do you refuse, Colonel, at this time, to give the name of a single person who was compelled to leave your home, as testified to by you yesterday, by reason of the conduct of Mrs. Cody?

A. I do for the reason that I see by one of the today's papers, newspapers, that they have in some way got ahold of what this testimony is that I am now giving and I do not—will not—give out any names in answer to this question as these friends of mine who are to be witnesses in this case would not like to have their names mentioned as present.

Q. You understand do you not, Colonel, that all proceedings with reference to matters in court and trials are public, and that Mrs. Cody, the defendant in this suit, has a right to know in order to be prepared to meet the issues in this case, the names and address of the parties that are expected to testify against her character and her conduct as charged in your petition under your oath, in order that she may meet the issues in this case?

A. I do and my answer to that is that I am not trying this case in the newspapers, but I propose to have this case tried in court. I do not know who her witnesses are to be, nor neither do I ask to know, nor neither do I propose to give my witnesses' names away at the present.

Q. Mrs. Cody has made no charges against you up to this time, Colonel. Are you not willing that the woman who has been your wife for thirty-eight years shall know the names of the persons whom you expect to testify with reference to her conduct upon which you are trying to procure a divorce in this case?

A. I have already stated my answer.

Q. Do you know that all of the parties whom you claim were compelled to leave your home by reason of the conduct of Mrs. Cody will be present as witnesses on the trial?

A. Not all of them, but some of them.

Q. Will you then give us the names of those who will not be present at the trial?

A. I will not, as I do not know just who and how many of them I will have at the trial as yet.

Q. Will you tell us, Colonel, how many persons were compelled to leave your home in North Platte as testified by you yesterday by reason of the conduct of Mrs. Cody?

A. Well, the period extended over some ten or twelve years' time, and I couldn't tell how many they were.

Q. Will you tell us about how many?

A. That I couldn't tell either. I couldn't say about how many, because they were at different times. Sometimes they were in small parties and sometimes singly.

Q. Will you tell us what the business was or occupation of those parties who were compelled to leave your home by reason of the conduct of Mrs. Cody?

A. Some of them were there to see me on business; some were there as our guests; some of them were there by my invitation.

Q. Will you tell us the year that parties were there to see you on business and were compelled to leave the house by reason of the conduct of Mrs. Cody?

A. Well it was during all the years from '78 up to '90.

Q. Where did it occur, at which of the different homes that you have had there at North Platte?

A. It occurred at both of the homes that we had there at North Platte.

Q. What was the reason given by Mrs. Cody for requiring these parties to leave the house?

A. Her main reason, as a rule, was because she didn't like them, and she would be angry and say that she wouldn't have them around the house, they couldn't come in her house, they couldn't stay in the house, that that was her house.

Q. Were any of them residents of Lincoln County, Nebraska?

A. Some of them were.

Q. Did she object to these parties by reason of their habits?

A. She objected to some people, and she didn't know what their habits were, just because she happened to be angry and she just wouldn't have them.

Q. Did she object to any by reason of the fact that they were drinking and intoxicated?

A. Not that I remember of. Because I would be the first one to resent anyone in my house that was drunk or disorderly or disrespectful, disrespectful to my wife or my children.

Q. Will you tell us the manner in which she excluded them from the house?

A. In different ways, by her actions.

Q. Will you describe her actions?

A. Well her actions were so different on different occasions that it would be impossible to do it.

Q. Can you describe any of her actions on any of the occasions?

A. More that being rude to them and lettin' them know that they were not wanted at the house or in the house, making different remarks in regard to it to such an extent that the parties would leave. It would humiliate me, and on several occasions I left with them and tried to smooth it in ways—saying, well Mrs. Cody is not feeling very well today, or something, anything to smooth it over.

Q. Will you tell us what she said that was rude or what she did that was rude?

A. A woman has many ways of showing when she is displeased and so many different ways, it is hard to remember them.

Q. Can you remember any of them at this time?

A. I do not. I cannot recall at this time just what the words were she used.

Q. Can you give us the substance of the words that she used?

A. Oh, they were in so many different ways that I can't just remember the words and sometimes—Of course, sometimes a man's actions sometimes speaks louder than words to company in the house that their presence is not required.

Q. Can you describe her manner at any time which spoke louder than words?

A. You know about as well as I do, I guess. I guess you have seen the manner yourself.

Q. Did Mrs. Cody use physical force upon any occasion?

A. Not actual physical force, but threats.

Q. Do you remember the threats?

A. Boiling hot water was one of the threats that she generally used, run them out by pouring hot water on them, scalding them. Boiling hot water used to be one of her favorite weapons—threats.

Q. Do you remember the names of any persons that she threatened to run out with boiling hot water?

A. If I do, I will not give their names at the present time.

Q. You stated yesterday, Colonel, that Mrs. Cody had threatened you. Will you state when that occurred?

A. At different times during the years between—during the last ten or twelve years we have lived at the Platte.

Q. Will you give the language?

A. Well, in different ways and threats: that she would "fix me," so that I couldn't go to Europe in fact, or on different things that I would propose to do.

Q. Give her language as close as you can.

A. I have given it there in that answer.

Q. Did she use any other language that you now remember except what you have given in the answer above?

A. Oh, there were so many occasions of those threats and what she would do, that they got to be such an old story that I can't remember the exact language on any special occasion.

Q. Did you think she was serious on those occasions, Colonel?

A. I certainly did to such an extent that I was at times actually afraid to eat or drink anything in the house.

Q. Can you give the years when you were afraid to eat and drink in the house?

A. Well those would be along in '97 and '98 and '99, more particularly those years, and I was warned by the servants of the house and by friends and relatives to be very careful of what I ate or drank that she gave me, as she had threatened to them what she was going to do.

Q. What is the name of the servants who warned you?

A. The servants and the people who were at work for us at the time and my friends and relatives will be at the trial, some of them will, and they will testify in court.

Q. Do you refuse at this time to give the names of any of the parties who warned you as you have testified to above?

A. I do, as I have before stated my reasons.

Q. In your petition filed in this case, which is sworn to by you, you allege that Mrs. Louisa Cody, the defendant, attempted to poison you. Will you tell us the date that that occurred?

A. That was in the fall of 1900.

Q. Do you remember the date?

A. I do not remember the date; it was in November or the early part of December of 1900.

Q. Was it before you took your wife and Irma and went to New York that fall?
A. If it was in 1900, the year we went to New York to visit Irma, it was before we went to New York.
Q. Was it the same fall that Irma attended the Leiter Ball?
A. Well, if it was that winter that Irma attended the Leiter Ball, it was before.
Q. Where did it occur, Colonel, the attempted poisoning?
A. At our home at North Platte, Nebraska.
Q. Who was present at the home at that time?
A. I hardly think there was anyone at home besides our servants at that time—yes, her father was in the house.
Q. Who were the servants?
A. I just can't call their names now, who were the servants just at that time.
Q. How do you know that Mrs. Cody attempted to poison you?
A. I was warned by parties to be particularly careful at that time, and I went home and I was very ill. I had eaten not very much, but I had drank some coffee and I was taken very ill and I went upstairs to my room and went to bed. After I was in bed she came to my room with a water glass about two-thirds full of a reddish kind of a mixture for me to take. I told her to set it down on a chair by the side of the bed and I would take it when I felt a little better. She went to her room as I supposed—to her own room to go to bed as I supposed, and when she was gone I got up and hid this mixture, whatever it might have been, under the stand, with the intention that I would take it the next day and keep it and have it analyzed. Afterward I went to sleep, and the next morning when I went to look for this mixture I could not find it.
Q. Did you ever see it after that?
A. Never could find it, never seen it.
Q. Do you know what it consisted of?
A. I do not. I was alarmed by having been warned that I would be given something that would "knock me out," that was what they called it.

Q. Then you don't know whether it was claret, lemonade, or what it was?

A. I know that it was neither claret nor lemonade, because it was a kind of a reddish-looking thick mixture.

Q. You say you were not feeling well that day?

A. I was not.

Q. What was the nature of your illness?

A. Well, I had been over to the ranch. I had been working and counting cattle and horses; I had been working and tired out, overworked, had caught a fearful cold and—

Q. Then it wasn't what was in the glass that made you sick, because you didn't take that.

A. I didn't take that, because I had been warned not to take anything that looked suspicious. In fact, I had been warned not to take anything.

Q. The facts are, Colonel, you were eating and drinking and sleeping right along there, weren't you, Colonel?

A. Well, I was only there for a few days. I was up at the ranch part of the time, and I was at the house part of the time.

Q. And after this you continued to stay there, and eat and drink and sleep?

A. No, I went away.

Q. And took Mrs. Cody with you down to New York?

A. No, not at that time.

Q. How long was it after that when you took Mrs. Cody to New York.

A. I think it was two or three weeks. I think that was in November, and I think when we went to New York, if I remember rightly now, I think it was just before Christmas. I had promised to take her down, the holidays, I think it was the Christmas times, to spend the holidays in New York with our daughter Irma, who would have a Christmas vacation. And I went back and took her to New York. And while in New York we stopped at the Waldorf-Astoria. The Hoffman House was my old home while I am in New York, but as I wanted to give my daughter a good time and I knew she would have quite a number of school visitors, young ladies, school visitors to visit her; although the Hoffman House in my opinion is as good a hotel as the Waldorf-Astoria, but it is not so much of a ladies' house as the Waldorf, and I thought the Waldorf—thought she would enjoy the Waldorf better than the Hoffman, so we stopped at the Waldorf.

Q. How long were you in New York with Mrs. Cody at this time before you returned home?

A. I should say about ten days or two weeks, whatever Irma's vacation was. I don't know just exactly how long they do have a vacation. I should say about ten days.

Q. And then where did you go when you returned from New York?

A. If I remember rightly, she went back to North Platte and I went to Big Horn County, Wyoming.

Q. Was that the winter, Colonel, that you had Mrs. Cody up in Big Horn County for several weeks?

A. I don't remember of Mrs. Cody being up in Big Horn County with me in the winter. I invited her to go, and had all arrangements made for her to go, but she didn't go.

Q. You told us last night that upon your return from New York, you thought you went to Big Horn County, Wyoming. When did you next return to North Platte?

A. It was sometime in the month of February 1901.

Q. And how long did you stay there at that time?

A. About two days. If my memory serves me right, about two days.

Q. And when did you next return to North Platte?

A. I haven't been there since, for the reason that I went to North Platte on this visit, or rather a business trip to invoice the properties that I owned there. Mrs. Cody and myself drove out to the Scouts Rest Ranch in a buggy, and I was inquiring of our foreman in regard to the cattle and the horses, the amount of grain and hay that we had on hand, and everything pertaining to what was on the ranch, and in what condition it was, and I also made some suggestions in regard to how the cattle and horses ought to be handled. When Mrs. Cody spoke up in his presence and says, "I am the boss of this ranch and you'll take your orders from me." As I did not want a scene there to contradict her, when she got through with giving her orders, we drove back to our residence in the town of North Platte, and as I knew that the way the situation stood then, as she claimed the ranch as her own, also the town property was her own, as I had deeded it all to her, I did not argue the point with her, but quietly packed my trunk, gathering up a few of my personal effects which were my own, such as my personal clothing—I left all the rest, and left her and that house forever, and I haven't been back since.

Q. That was in February of 1901, was it?

A. Yes, sir.

Q. Who was the foreman that this conversation was before?

A. I can't remember his name. He was a man that she had employed there.

Q. Did you have correspondence with Mrs. Cody after that?

A. Not to my knowledge—I don't think that I have ever written her a word personally.

Q. Did you ever write her any letters after that?

A. I can't remember, but I think not. If I did do so, it escaped my memory.

Q. Can you give us the date in February?

A. I cannot. I can't remember those dates that way. Coming and going as I am, I can't remember dates.

Q. Now is it not a fact, Colonel, that you visited Mrs. Cody and was with her for a number of days, living and cohabiting together, in December of 1901?

A. What's the word *cohabit*, living as man and wife?

Q. Sleeping, yes.

A. Well, we have not. We haven't for years.

Q. What do you say as to visiting Mrs. Cody for a number of days in December 1901 at her home in North Platte, Nebraska?

A. I don't remember of being there in December 1901.

Q. Your memory as to matters that have occurred of recent years is somewhat defective, is it not, Colonel?

A. Yes sir, my brain has been so overloaded with business and the troubles that I am not good on remembering the dates of the last few years.

Q. And at this time you have no remembrance whatever of visiting Mrs. Cody at North Platte in December of 1901?

A. I have not.

Q. Do you remember, Colonel, of meeting with a little party of gentlemen in North Platte on Christmas Day at high noon, twelve o'clock, in which a number of toasts were proposed and drank, and that I myself proposed a toast to you in honor of you, and that this was on December the twenty-fifth, 1901, in North Platte, Nebraska?

A. It seems to me I remember of the occasion you allude to, but I cannot remember the year.

Q. And don't you remember that on the afternoon of that day, on an afternoon train, you left North Platte and came to Denver, Colorado?

A. I cannot remember the circumstances. I am moving too much. I am different from a man who spends his life always in one town. My business and my life compels me to move so often and so quickly that I cannot remember the dates and times of when these moves take place.

Q. And don't you remember, Colonel, that you was at our home in North Platte for a number of days in December and that you and Mrs. Cody were upon very pleasant and friendly relations; that you visited different business houses with her, talked over and discussed the ranch business; that you were in Major Walker's insurance office and talked about the insurance upon the properties there; that you were at the ranch with Mrs. Cody a number of different times; and that when you left on the twenty-fifth day of December for Denver you invited Mrs. Cody to accompany you; and that the only reason that she did not was because she was not very well herself and her father was there at her home and was sick or not strong, and he being an old gentleman about ninety years of old, she did not think that she had better leave him and come with you on your trip to Denver?

A. I will say that whenever I was in company or before strangers with my wife, no matter what troubles was racking my heart, I never made it apparent to strangers that there were any differences at all between us, and I treated her with kindness and with respect at all times. As far as this meeting and this party that you speak of, I do not remember. And I may still be mistaken in the exact year, whether it was December—whether it was Christmas 1900 or 1901 or February 1900 or 1901 that I last visited North Platte. I am not positive on those years, and I will not state whether it was 1900 or 1901, but it was one of the two.

Q. Are you positive upon this point, and that is, that at the time you thought Mrs. Cody had a poisonous drink, which you did not taste, was before you took the trip with her to New York?

A. It was—to visit our daughter, you mean?

Q. Yes.

A. Yes. It was. And the reason why I went back and took Mrs. Cody on the trip to New York: I had promised my daughter Irma to bring Mrs. Cody to New York and come with her so that we might spend our holidays vacation with her, my daughter.

Q. If you were at North Platte the last time in December 1901, had you been in constant correspondence with Mrs. Cody during the entire season prior to that date?

A. If I am mistaken in the year and it was not until December 1901 that I visited North Platte, then I would have been in correspondence with Mrs. Cody. But, if it was in February 1900 that I last visited there, instead of 1901, then I was not in correspondence. But I cannot make it clear in my mind whether it was February 1900 or February 1901 that I was last there.

Q. If the time that you say Mrs. Cody had a poisonous drink in a glass was in November or December 1900, and you visited her again for a number of days in December 1901, then you were in correspondence with her for about a year after the poisonous drink . . . you think was offered to you, were you not?

A. If it was 1901 that I last visited North Platte instead of 1900, then probably I did.

Q. You stated last evening that you had been warned by relatives to be careful what you ate and drank prepared by Mrs. Cody. Do you remember about the time that the relatives so warned you?

A. I was warned for the last years—the last few years at different times, and from these warnings I was in a continual state of fear of my life.

Q. Were those warnings from relatives who were upon friendly terms or who had been on unfriendly terms with Mrs. Cody for many years?

A. They were on comparatively friendly terms, as she frequently visited at their house and houses, although I will admit that I don't believe that there was very much love between either of them. But the relatives were not the only ones who warned me. But I was warned by people who were not related as well.

Q. Do you know whether or not there was any foundation for their warning you, or whether they had a motive in so warning you other than the protection of your health?

A. Some of the friends who warned me had no personal motive whatever, more than for the protection of my health. They had heard Mrs. Cody say what she was going to do to me, and on those grounds they thought that it was right that they should warn me.

Q. You do not know of your own personal knowledge that they had heard Mrs. Cody say anything with reference to that, do you, or are you taking their word for it?

A. I am only—I only acted on what they told me, and I am giving their word for what they told me. I consider that when a person is warned by relatives and also warned by outsiders who did not have a motive, it was well for me to heed and believe what they said, as I felt confident in my own mind that they would not have warned me of these threats of Mrs. Cody had they not heard her make them.

Q. Who were the relatives, Colonel, that so warned you?

A. I have declined to answer this question before, and I now positively decline to answer it.

Q. Who were the friends who so warned you, Colonel?

A. I decline to make their names known at the present time.

Q. About how many years ago were you first warned by your relatives?

A. As near as my memory serves me, it was about six years ago.

Q. And about how many years ago was it that you were first warned by friends?

A. I should say about five years ago.

Q. Will you give us the residence of the relative that warned you?

A. I will not.

Q. Will you give us the residence of the friends who warned you?

A. I will not.

Q. Have you testified to the only time that you thought Mrs. Cody attempted to poison you?

A. No. I have at different times—I cannot state the dates—that she has given me things to take, and after taking them I have been sick and complained of the things she had given me to take, as I said that they had made me sick or, in other words, they positively did not agree with me.

Q. Can you give about the dates and place?

A. No, but this occurred mostly in the last four to five and six years ago—three to six years ago.

Q. Can you be any more definite with reference to the time and place and the circumstances connected with it?

A. I cannot more than that it was at North Platte, Nebraska.

Q. Why, Colonel, so you object to giving me the names of the relatives who so warned you, that Mrs. Cody at her trial may be prepared to show whether or not the parties were enemies or friends of hers?

A. For the same reason as that I have given my reasons before.

Q. You desire, do you not Colonel, that Mrs. Cody shall have a fair opportunity to defend herself against the serious charges, which, if true, are a crime against law, that you have made against her?

A. I am perfectly willing for her to have a fair trial.

Q. I will say to you, Colonel, as counsel for Mrs. Cody, that it is absolutely necessary that Mrs. Cody shall have the names of the parties whom you say were compelled to leave the house by reason of her acts, and the names of the parties whom you say warned you, in order for her to have an opportunity to meet the charges which you have made against her. And that she has a legal right to know the names, at this time, of these parties. Being advised of these facts, do you still refuse to give the names of these parties at this time?

A. I do.

Q. You gave as your reason last evening for not divulging the names of the parties who were excluded from your home by the acts of Mrs. Cody, that it was on account of something printed in the papers of Denver, I understood you to say, upon yesterday. Will you give me the name of the paper in which the objectionable article was published?

A. The different papers of Denver hinted at the article, or at the proceedings of this testimony, in different ways, and it's not necessary for me to mention any paper in particular at the present time, for the simple reason that since this trouble or this suit was instituted, it has been my utmost desire to keep this family trouble of ours out of the newspapers; and from the very beginning of this suit, I have positively refused to give any information to the newspapers; and all the newspaper notoriety that this case has had up to date, none of it has been given by me; and I don't propose to mention any one paper that will or could be brought up and that it could be said that I was the instigator of gaining any notoriety through the public press. I refuse to give the name of any one paper. For my part, I am not trying this case in the newspapers, but I am trying to have it tried by an impartial court. I have nothing to say or nothing to give out for publication at this present time.

Q. You knew, Colonel, when you filed your petition in the court of Big Horn County, making serious charges against Mrs. Cody, that the petition became a public document and was liable to be published in the papers, did you not?

A. I was afraid and feared that it would, as I am a public man; the newspapers are always anxious to get anything regarding any public man, but I took every step and every means in my power to keep this family trouble out of the public press, and I was not the first one to start it in the public press.

Q. You were interviewed by the four principal dailies in this city, nearly a column's interview, the day that you arrived to give your testimony in this case, were you not, Colonel?

A. I was not interviewed by the four daily papers of this city on the day of my arrival. I felt that they would be hunting for me, and I was told that they were hunting for me to interview, and I avoided them in every possible manner that I could, from being interviewed. I read [an] article, however, that purported to have come from me that I had nothing to do with.

Q. Were you interviewed by representatives of either of the dailies the day you arrived, Colonel?

A. A man came up and spoke to me who claimed to be a reporter of the *Post*, and some other paper—I don't know which one. In fact, there was one or two reporters got ahold of me in the mysterious way they have of doing things, but I told them as little as I possibly could. I told them that, with all due courtesy to the press, that this was a family matter, that I had nothing to say against any woman, and especially my wife, and that it was my desire and my wish that they would say as little about it as possible.

Q. You have alleged in your petition under oath, filed in this case, that the defendant, Mrs. Cody, refused to allow you to bring your friends and guests to your home. Will you give me the names of the friends and guests which Mrs. Cody refused to allow you to bring to your home?

A. I will not.

Q. Will you state the manner in which she refused to allow you to bring friends and guests to your home?

A. Well, there were so many different ways and so many different times, and she put it in so many different kind of words, calling my friends, those that she didn't want me to bring to our home, calling them all manner of names, which she had no reason or cause to call them, that it would be impossible to state all the objections that she had.

Q. Can you be more definite, Colonel, in your answer to that question?

A. This is as definite as I can make it.

Q. Do you expect to be present at the trial of this case in Big Horn County?

A. Much as I would like to be, it is positively beyond my power to be present, as I am under contract and under heavy penalty to open my Wild West Exhibition in England on April the twenty-fifth, 1904. At Stoke on Trent. The dates are arranged. A portion of my company are already there; others will be sailing for England in a very few days. I have to be at Stoke-on-Trent by the fifteenth of April to organize my company and rehearse it for the opening on the twenty-fifth of April, the date on which we given our first public exhibition. Were it possible, I would certainly be at the trial in person.

Q. You testified yesterday, Colonel, that the weapon which your wife used in running people out was scalding hot water. Will you tell us whom she ever ran out by pouring scalding hot water on them?

A. I don't think I said that she ever poured scalding hot water on them, but I said that was one of her favorite weapons of threats, was hot water.

Q. Did she ever to your knowledge run any of the guests out of the house with boiling hot water?

A. She did not, as I remember of. If she did, she done it when I was not present.

Q. Then you do not want to be understood as saying that Mrs. Cody ever scalded any of your guests with boiling hot water?

A. No, I did not say that she did. I said that she only threatened.

Q. Now, Colonel, whom did she threaten with boiling hot water?

A. Threatened so many—that was one of her favorite threats.

Q. Can you name one person of your guests or acquaintances that she threatened to scald with boiling hot water if they did not leave the home?

A. I decline to mention any names.

Q. Could you mention any names if you so desired?

A. I might do so.

Q. Do you now remember any person that she run out of the home by threatening to scald them with boiling hot water?

A. Well, in that I decline to answer.

Q. You stated in your direct examination that you were not a drinking man. Is it not a fact, Colonel, that at periods during your life during the past twenty years you have drank to excess and intoxication at a good many different times?

A. I have drank at different times in the past twenty years, but never drank enough to injure me constitutionally or to interfere with my business or to interfere with my taking care of my family.

Q. Your periods of drinking were principally during your vacations when you were at home, were they not, Colonel?

A. I drank more, perhaps, when I did not have actual business to attend to and I wanted a recreation than when I did when I was attending to business.

Q. And during your vacations when at home and at your drinking periods, is when you have had more or less friction with Mrs. Cody?

A. Well, I've drank quite often at home when my home would become unpleasant to me, and I would have some trouble with my wife, and at such times I drank more or less.

Q. Isn't it a fact, Colonel, that on a number of occasions during the past fifteen or twenty years you have frequently returned home from your show season in an intoxicated condition?

A. I don't doubt but I have on a few occasions, because I felt that my long season was over, the strain of business was off, and like a great many others I sought a little recreation and a little pleasure from my labors.

Q. And haven't you frequently remarked, Colonel, that you could recuperate and rest better during your vacations when you were having a period of intoxication than you could any other way?

A. I have remarked that in drinking, when I was drinking, that it had a tendency to relieve my brain of the heavy strain that had been placed upon it, and by taking stimulants at different times, I forgot my labors and work and I could rest up my brain by throwing off the thoughts of work and labor for the time being. But I never drank in my life to such an extent that I couldn't quit at any time I would set. I never drank so much that whiskey got me so in its power but what I could quit it whenever I chose to. In other words, I was master of the situation. And taking it altogether, in the last twenty years, I have drank less than thousands of men who are not called drinkers at all.

Q. And your drinking at times has been a bother by Mrs. Cody and your daughter Irma, has it not?

A. It has been objected to by Mrs. Cody but never by my daughter Irma.

Q. And has not Mrs. Cody during your drinking periods complained that certain of your companions and friends had a bad influence over you, and that if it were not for your liberality and big heartedness with your friends, you would not drink to excess as you did on some occasions?

A. I don't know as she ever complained that any friends or any particular men had a bad influence over me at all.

Q. And did not Mrs. Cody, through your daughter Irma, at one time request a man . . . generally known as Pony Bob to leave North Platte for the reason that while there, by reason of his influence, you were in an intoxicated condition?

A. If she or my daughter ever requested Pony Bob to leave there for these reasons, it was done unbeknownst to my knowledge, as I considered and still consider Pony Bob a gentleman and a true friend, and [he] would be the last one to advise or ask me to take a drink if he thought it was going to be injurious to me in any way, shape, or form.

Q. Where is Pony Bob at the present time?

A. When I came through Chicago about four weeks ago, he was at the Auditorium Annex Hotel, Chicago.

Q. Is it not a fact that for a number of springs before you left your home at North Platte, that Mrs. Cody, the defendant in this suit, mortgaged the property which you had described as hers in your direct examination, in order to provide you with money with which to open the show season?

A. On two occasions, I think it was, I found it necessary to raise some cash, as many other men have had to do, to continue the business, and as the property every dollar of it was bought by myself and paid for out of my own earnings, I thought it no more than right, nor no more than a business proposition, that I should be entitled to raise some money on my own property if I chose to; and on two occasions, I think, or it might have been three, as there is a law in the state for the wife to sign a mortgage on real estate, I asked her to do so; and it was very hard work to get her consent to do so. She always objected to it, and said that I would speculate, that I would lose the money or I would not be able to pay the mortgage off and we would lose the property; and it was always one of those things that I dreaded to do to ever ask my wife to assist me in any way in raising money to carry on my business, and whenever she would sign a mortgage of this description, she would make the remark: "Well, I'm signing my death warrant, and I kiss it goodbye."

Q. While you say, Colonel, that you earned the money and the property was yours, during the time that you were earning this money, Mrs. Cody was bearing and raising children for you, was she not?

A. Yes.

Q. And during your married life, has she not borne you four children?

A. Yes.

Q. I understood you to give, Colonel, as one of your reasons for the bringing of this divorce suit, that Mrs. Cody was unwilling to join with you in deeds and mortgages, as you may desire; are you not willing to dismiss this divorce proceeding?

A. These were only one of the reasons which you speak of that induced me to bring this suit for divorce, but there are other and greater reasons why I am suing for a divorce.

Q. Then your greater reasons are something besides the interfering with your business transactions?

A. Yes, sir.

Q. How long, Colonel, has your extreme desire to get a divorce from the wife of your youth and the mother of your children taken possession of you?

A. For many years, I have known that sooner or later divorce proceedings would take place, but I postponed it until my children were grown and married and had homes of their own.

Q. Has the same grounds for divorce which you now have existed for a number of years?

A. The main grounds has existed for years; that is, the grounds of incompatibility of temper.

Q. You stated in your examination that on the third of February you sent a telegram to Mrs. Cody looking toward an amicable adjustment of your differences. Did you mean by that, that you were then contemplating, if Mrs. Cody was of the same spirit, to abandon the suit which you had commenced against her for divorce?

A. My main desire in sending that telegram was that we should bury all our personal differences for the time being while we were attending to our sorrowful, sad duties of burying our beloved child; and I did not know what it might lead up to. I felt that it would give me a chance to once more see her and notice her and see if this great sorrow had softened her in any way. I would like to see and be close to her again to find out if it might not be possible that all could be forgotten and a reconciliation might take place, whereby, through the death of our beloved child, it might be the bringing of us again together. But when she telegraphed me back that I was the death of our daughter and she would have no—bury no differences, I know that same old spirit still had life and had force as I had known for thirty-eight years, and I knew that there was no more chance, no more hope for me to expect a little peace in my old age than I had ever had. And I knew that I was going to be placed in a most trying position, that is, that she would not speak, as she had refused . . . in this telegram, and moreover she had made threats that she would create a scene over the dead body of our child, such a scene as no one had yet ever looked upon, or words to that effect; and hearing of this threat, I telegraphed to St. Paul, Minnesota, for Dr. Powell, my foster brother, to join me at Chicago as I needed his strong brotherly support. When he came, I told him of the threats that Mrs. Cody made; I told him of the telegram which I had sent her and of her answer, that I had no idea what she intended to do, but I wished him to be as close to her as possible at every moment of the time in which he could be, so that if she threatened to take my life, he would be near at hand. I telegraphed for Johnnie Baker, my foster son, to meet us at Rochester, New York, which he did. I gave him the same instructions as I did Dr. Powell. On the morning before the funeral took place, she told Dr. Powell that she was going to make a scene over the dead body of her child, that she was going to denounce me, that she was going to get even with me, and made threats of different descriptions; and during the funeral service and also at the cemetery, Dr. Powell was on one side of her and Johnnie Baker on the other, watching every movement that she made. None of us knew in what manner or form she might attempt to carry out her threats. It is true we did not speak on the trip. I seen that every attention and every comfort was given her. I had her the state rooms in the Pullman car, I had her carriages, I superintended all the directions for transportation to and from the funeral, the arranging for the funeral services; I ordered the largest flower piece that could be arranged; I gave the florists carte blanche to get up the largest and finest that they could; and on this floral tribute to our daughter, I had on this both of our names placed. I paid all the expenses while at Rochester, got her transportation and her state room back . . . home again. And so we parted.

Q. Did you hear Mrs. Cody make any threats upon that occasion?

A. No, I did not personally, because I did not come within hearing of her, but I have witnesses who will appear at this trial who did, and I will produce the telegram, or the copy of the telegram, sworn to by the operator.

Q. Have you a copy of the telegram with you at this time?

A. I have not.

Q. Are you sure that language of that telegram as you gave it in your direct examination is the exact words of that telegram?

A. That was the exact words—as near as I could remember the words, but that was the substance.

Q. Was not the substance and the language of that telegram that Mrs. Cody did not desire a reconciliation upon the funeral occasion but that she desired it for all time?

A. I just can't remember every word of that telegram, but a copy of it will be produced under oath from the operator at the trial.

Q. It is a fact, is it not, Colonel, that Mrs. Cody met you and [the] funeral train at Omaha when neither Dr. Powell nor Johnnie Baker was present? That she offered no demonstrations of any kind, and while you spoke to all of your friends and acquaintances that were there at that time, you never gave your wife of thirty-eight years, and the mother of the dead child, a look of recognition?

A. The train that I was on when it arrived in Omaha, it was a through train for Chicago, was met there by Mr. McCune, one of my agents, whom I had telegraphed to meet Mrs. Cody and my sister and the grandchildren and do everything possible for them until the train I was on with the remains and my son-in-law Dr. Thorpe arrived. When the train which I was on pulled into the depot at Omaha, Mrs. Cody, my sister, and the grandchildren, with Mr. McCune, who was looking out for them, took them immediately into the Pullman. She passed by, nearby where I was. I looked toward her. My sister and the little grandchildren ran up to me and kissed me, and while I was embracing them, Mrs. Cody passed into the Pullman. By this time quite a number of the most prominent men of Omaha had came down to the depot to pay their respects. Among them was a delegation from the Elks Lodge, from No. 39 Lodge of Elks in Omaha, bearing a beautiful floral piece to be placed on the casket, [which] . . . was placed on the casket in the car. I spoke and shook hands with my friends, thanking them for their kind thoughtfulness, for coming down [on] such a stormy, cold day to pay their respects; also I thanked the Brother

Elks, and also had them to extend my thanks to the Lodge for their beautiful flowers, and by this time the train was ready to start, which we did.

Q. And was it not her custom when you were home on these vacations to try and invite a few friends to meet you frequently and often at your home; she tried to make your vacations when you were home as pleasant and agreeable as she could?

A. It was not a custom, but she did, at times, invite friends to the house, but not as frequently as I would have liked. She could be pleasant when she chose to be.

Q. And when you left the home at North Platte the last time, did you not leave on friendly and agreeable relations with Mrs. Cody and her friends?

A. No, not on friendly terms heart to heart between her and I, because she knew that I was displeased at being turned down at the ranch; but I used the same tactics as I always have done through life to try and conceal any words or troubles by putting on a smiling face outwardly while my heart might be aching inside. This I have to do in my business as a showman. No matter how bad the business is, we have learned that our capital and stock is a smiling countenance and a buoyant spirit.

NY *Sun*

Buffalo Bill Seeks Divorce | Charges That His Wife Tried to Kill Him in 1900. And Says That Their Relations Are Intolerable—She Denies His Allegation and Believes That He Desires to Marry a Younger Wife—Will Resist the Suit.

Denver, Col., March 11—Col. William F. Cody, "Buffalo Bill," the scout, hunter and hero of the frontier tales, has brought suit for divorce from his wife, with whom he has lived for thirty-eight years.

He charges that she tried to poison him in December 1900, that their relations are intolerable and she is incompatible. Mrs. Cody, who is a Catholic, will resist the suit. The action was begun in Wyoming several weeks ago, but the papers were suppressed until today.

Mrs. Cody, who is wealthy and has a large farm in North Platte, Neb., denied the charge of attempted poisoning named in the divorce complaint. She said:

"I suppose Will wants a young wife, one who will bear him an heir, for our boys are all dead. I know there is a young woman whom he has been taking around the country for several years, and who, I understand, is now in Washington.

"Whether he expects to marry her, I do not know, but I do know that he can't cast me off. I shall fight to protect my name. He shall not have a divorce.

"I have often asked him to take me to England, but he always had some excuse for not doing so; either he could not afford it or he considered it unwise for both of us to endanger our lives on the water, as we had so many interests that some one must look after.

"But he usually could afford to take some other woman. One of his trips was pretty expensive, however. It cost $50,000 to get out of his entanglement.

"Will is one of the kindest and most generous men I ever knew. When he was sober he was always considerate and gentle. If I had him to myself now, there would be no trouble. His environments have caused him to put this upon me. It is not like him to do such a thing."

Quincy Daily Journal

Buffalo Bill is Seeking a Divorce | Wants to Get Rid of Old Wife Who Has Been His Helpmeet for the Eight Years, to Marry, She Says, a Younger Woman. | He Charges That She Tried to Poison Him and Wouldn't Entertain His Friends—His Charges, His Wife Says, are Untrue and Absurd.

NORTH PLATTE, Neb., March 12—Col. William F. Cody would divorce the woman, who for thirty-eight years has borne his name and has been his devoted helpmate and has given him five children. Mrs. Cody was in her girlhood a belle in St. Louis.

Col. Cody filed suit in Wyoming two months ago but has carefully suppressed the process. He charges his wife with an attempt to poison him. The second ground on which he desires separation is the averment that marital relation[s] [have] been made intolerable to ** n by his wife's refusal to entertain his friends at his former home in North Platte.

"My friends tell me," said Mrs. Cody, who reluctantly spoke of the subject, "that he wants a young wife, one who will bear him an heir, for our boys are all dead.

"He can't cast me off like one of whom he has tired. I will fight to protect my name. He shall not have a divorce."

Mrs. Cody's contest ** be solely in self-defense; she will not ask for a divorce herself.

Suit is a Surprise

Except to a few intimate friends, the news of the Cody divorce suit will come as a startling surprise. It will cause astonishment abroad as well as in America, for Col. Cody's reputation is international.

While his wife has not participated in his world-wide car** remaining at home to care for their investments, while he has traveled around the globe, it has been generally proposed that their relations were pleasant. Even in this city, which has been the family home for more than thirty years, and where the wife has **aded almost continuously, the announcement created surprise.

The romance of the dashing young army scout and the handsome St. Louis girl begun at the close of the civil war, long since disappeared but to outward appearances they had merely settled down to the commonplace relation of mutual esteem which comes in the latter years of many married couples.

"Will is reckless with money," said the faithful wife, "and that I could best help him by nursing our investments. He realized this himself, for whenever he turned over money to me to buy property, he said: 'You hang on to this, lovey, we may need it someday. If I ever come to you to mortgage ** don't you do it."

Mrs. Cody is a Roman Catholic, and on that account would not apply for a divorce.

Relatives Responsible

"I would not do f** anyway," she said today. "I would not please the people who are putting him up to this business. One of the ** e is his sister, whose husband runs the Wyoming ranch and lives off the colonel. She is not satisfied with what she is getting, and thinks that if she could be rid of me she would get more. She has done her worst to separate us, and at last she has talked him into it.

"The charges he makes are absurd and he cannot substantiate them. I suppose he imagined that I would let the matter go without contest, but I will not rest under such injustice. If necessary, in order to defend myself, I will tell the court of all the indignities which I have patiently suffered for years."

Regarding the charges of attempted poisoning, Mrs. Cody said:

"I can't imagine how he conceived that story. There is not the semblance of foundation for it. Moreover, he says that it occurred in North Platte. As a matter of fact, on the day he names, we were visiting in Rochester, N.Y., where our children are buried.

"Regarding that charge that I have refused to entertain his friends, I will admit that on some occasions I have done so. But it was always under circumstances that would compel any self-respecting wife to enter protest. I have always been glad to entertain his guests when they were respectable people or behaved themselves decently. But I have at times objected to the character of some of the persons he has brought here and to the conduct of others who were respectable as far as their reputation and standing were concerned. Why, I have had these rooms piled with drunken men stretched out on the floor.

"I never protested to my husband while an orgie was in progress, but remonstrated when he became sober."

Always Remained at Home

In all his trips abroad Col. Cody has never taken his wife.

"I have often asked him to take me to England," Mrs. Cody said, "but he always had some excuse for not doing so; either he could not afford it or he considered it unwise for both of us to endanger our lives on the water, as we had so many interests that someone must look after."

There is little rancor in Mrs. Cody's attitude toward her husband.

"Will is one of the kindest and most generous men I ever knew," she said. "When [he] was sober he was always considerate and gentle. If I had him to myself now, there would be no trouble. His environments have caused him to put this upon me. It is not like him to do such a thing."

The people of the city are loyal to Mrs. Cody. Their devotion was evidenced Wednesday night, when [a] prairie fire swept down on their ranch, four miles west of town. Fully 400 persons rushed out to the plain, and [for] four hours [they] fought to save the buildings from the flames, which were fanned by furious winds.

An old friend of the family, who has known the Codys ever since they came here in 1869, said concerning the divorce:

"It is the meanest act of Bill Cody's life. I doubt if he will ever dare show up."

APPENDIX 3

Courtney Ryley Cooper (1886–1940)

On September 29, 1940, renowned western and crime novelist Courtney Ryley Cooper, wearing only his pajamas, committed suicide by hanging himself from the water pipe in a closet in his room at the Weylin Hotel in Manhattan.[1] "In my clothes is $43 in cash. I think my bill is about $32. Give the hotel $32," read a note he left behind. Thus ended the life of one of Buffalo Bill's forgotten press agents.

Courtney Ryley Cooper began working with William F. "Buffalo Bill" Cody after Buffalo Bill's Wild West and Pawnee Bills Far East were forced into receivership. Buffalo Bill became a headline for the Sells-Floto Circus as a press agent, where he met Cooper, who described his brief connection to Cody in his 1923 memoir *Under the Big Top*. Although this period marked a low in Buffalo Bill's performing career, it allowed Cooper to broaden his writing into western history.

Cooper was born on October 31, 1886, in Kansas City, Missouri, to Baltimore T. Cooper (1847–1898) and Catherine Grenalds Cooper (1850–1934). Cooper was the youngest of his immediate family, composed of him and his sisters, Lillian Manahan (1870–1932), Eula Swanson (1875–1907), and Genevieve Smith (1878–1954). At sixteen, Cooper ran away from home and became a circus clown. Throughout his writing career, Cooper peppered his vast literary output with works that reflected his love of circuses: *Under the Big Top* (1923), *With the Circus* (1924), *Lions 'n' Tigers 'n' Everything* (1924), *The Jungle Behind Bars* (1924), *Circus Day* (1931), and *The Boss Elephant* (1934).

Cooper began working as a reporter for the *Kansas City Star*, the newspaper that also launched Ernest Hemingway's writing career. Cooper became one of the *Star*'s leading reporters and served as a contributing reporter to the *New York World* and the *Chicago Tribune*.

In 1913 Cooper began writing for the *Denver Post*, then owned by the entrepreneurs Harry H. Tammen and Frederick G. Bonfils, who transformed the *Post* into a prime example of yellow journalism. Cooper began working for the *Denver Post* the same year Bonfills and Tammen placed Buffalo Bill's Wild West and Pawnee Bill's Far East into receivership. The bankruptcy settlement forced Buffalo Bill to become the star attraction for the Sells-Floto Circus, also owned by Bonfils and Tammen.

Relegated to riding into the arena and waving to the crowds, per the settlement, Buffalo Bill worked with Cooper to generate publicity for the Sells-Floto Circus. In his book *Under the Big Top*, Cooper praised "Buffalo Bill" as "the man in whom my sun and endeavor rose and set." Cooper noted that as a press agent, he arranged a parade of Buffalo Bill's Rough Riders to salute the mayor of Chicago, who was unfortunately out of town and missed the honor. He also drafted a cablegram to the king of England in Buffalo Bill's name, offering to fight in the Great War on behalf of the British. In describing these successes and his humble appearance, Cooper noted, "A bald, long-nosed press agent was behind it."

Cooper briefly suspended his career as a press agent to join the United States Marines upon America's entry into the "Great War" in Europe. Per his obituary, Cooper collected historical information documenting the experience of the U.S. Marine Corps during their deployment to France. This experience was detailed in his edited works published in 1919: *Dear Folks at Home: The Glorious Story of the United States Marines in France as Told by Their Letters from the Battlefield*, compiled by Kemper F. Cowing, and his novelization of *The Eagle's Eye: A True Story of the Imperial German Government's Spies and Intrigues in America* by William J. Flynn, retired chief of the U.S. Secret Service.

After the war Cooper incorporated his experiences in Colorado and his past relationship with Buffalo Bill to publish several nonfictional and fictional books on the American West and two western legends: Annie Oakley and Buffalo Bill. In 1919 Cooper collaborated with Buffalo Bill's widow, Louisa Frederici Cody, in publishing *Memories of Buffalo Bill*, a biography that offered a wife's perspective of the famed scout and showman. Despite the renowned conflicts and estrangement of the Codys throughout their marriage, Cooper and Louisa's work presented a heroic account of Buffalo Bill, skipping over the infamous divorce proceedings, Cody's reported infidelities, and other marital problems.

Despite focusing on the famed Buffalo Bill narrative from his widow Louisa's view, the work quickly went out of print. However, Louisa was pleased with the resulting book and wrote to the *Ladies Home Journal* that, after reading the first three chapters, she found this "version of my autobiography [. . .] correct and according to information he received while here [in Cody, Wyoming]." Although his collaboration with Louisa Cody established him as a western author, Cooper later described Louisa's character negatively. In an undated Buffalo Bill movie pitch to agent George T. Bye, Cooper described Louisa as "a dumb, yet worshipful woman who lost her husband almost the day she married him, fought vainly and desperately all her life to regain and hold him—and did not get him until Death was literally creeping in the door to take him from her forever."

Cooper continued publishing various fictional books about Buffalo Bill, including *Oklahoma*, which he dedicated to Buffalo Bill's business colleague Major Gordon W. "Pawnee Bill" Lillie (1926), and *The Last Frontier*, which appeared in 1923, providing readers with a dramatic adventure featuring Buffalo Bill. The latter first appeared on film and provided illustrations from the "photoplay" of the book. In addition to contributing to radio shows and writing various articles, Cooper authored the following western novels: *The Cross-Cut* (1921), *The White Desert* (1922), *and End of Steel* (1931). In 1926 he published *High Country: The Rockies Yesterday and To-day*, which offered readers a history and geographical description of the Rocky Mountains.

Through another "Buffalo Bill's Wild West" connection, Cooper published his most recognized work, *Annie Oakley: Woman at Arms*. In a letter to his editor, Mr. Green, Cooper noted that he attempted to use Oakley's brief autobiography to finish the work, but much of the writing was his. "Had I known the condition of the diary and its lack of information," Cooper wrote, "many things in the diary, I found to be wrong: memory had played its tricks." To enhance the work, Cooper asserted, "I have tried to make it more than a picture of Annie Oakley from my knowledge of Buffalo Bill . . . I was able to give a true picture of the times in which this woman lived, and of her surroundings in the Bill show, without which, I do not believe that the Annie Oakley story would have amounted to much." Despite these challenges and Cooper's heavy hand in writing the book, his biography of Annie Oakley is considered by many to be her autobiography. *Annie Oakley* was Cooper's most successful work and has been reprinted in various editions.

Shortly before his death, Cooper became friends with J. Edgar Hoover and shifted his genre to crime stories and the early exploits of the Federal Bureau of Investigation. His collection of crime books included *Ten Thousand Public Enemies* (1935), *Marijuana: Assassin of Youth* (1937), *Designs in Scarlet* (1939), and *Here's to Crime* (1941). Upon news of his death, Cooper's widow, Genevieve R. Furey, intimated to the press that her late husband "had been morose over alleged snubs he had received in Washington when he sought to inform officials of German activities he said he detected in Mexico." She also noted he shared his concerns with J. Edgar Hoover, but the FBI publicly denied hearing such reports from Cooper.

Was Cooper on the trail of another extraordinary, adventuresome story, regarding German spy activity as World War II spread? Or did the author become entrapped within his own dramatic mind, resulting in a tragic end to his productive writing career? A few days after his passing, the *Casper Tribune-Herald* reported Cooper planned to visit the Valley Ranch in the late fall season, then owned by Larry Larom and located near Buffalo Bill's famous TE Ranch. If Cooper had survived to make this trek to Wyoming, reconnecting with the American West and rejuvenating his past connections with Buffalo Bill, would he have forgone taking his own life and continued adding to his abundant stories? Even with this tragic end to his own life, in addition to being Buffalo Bill's press agent, Courtney Ryley Cooper firmly established himself as raconteur extraordinaire.

Fig. 12. Courtney Ryley Cooper. Courtney Ryley Cooper Papers, American Heritage Center at the University of Wyoming.

NOTES

Introduction

1. Louisa Frederici Cody and Courtney Ryley Cooper, *Memories of Buffalo Bill* (New York: D. Appleton Company, 1919).
2. Louis Warren, *Buffalo Bill's America: William Cody and the Wild West Show* (New York: Alfred A. Knopf, 2005), 44.
3. Cody, *Memories of Buffalo Bill*, 4.
4. Joy Kassen, *Buffalo Bill's Wild West: Celebrity, Memory, and Popular History* (New York: Hill and Wang, 2001), 136.
5. Warren, *Buffalo Bill's America*, 49–55.
6. Warren, *Buffalo Bill's America*, 55–58, 108, 114–15.
7. Warren, *Buffalo Bill's America*, 157.
8. Warren, *Buffalo Bill's America*, 232–33.
9. Kassen, *Buffalo Bill's Wild West*, 139–141.
10. Kassen, *Buffalo Bill's Wild West*, 157.
11. Glenda Riley, *Divorce: An American Tradition* (New York: Oxford University Press, 1991), 1–8, 85–87, 124, 135–37.
12. Appendix 2, 248
13. Appendix 2, 253
14. Appendix 2, 290
15. Appendix 2, 279
16. J. J. Halligan, "Direct Examination," unabridged edition, codyarchive.org, 2025.
17. Appendix 2, 207
18. Appendix 2, 225
19. Warren, *Buffalo Bill's America*, 503.
20. Warren, *Buffalo Bill's America*, 502.
21. Warren, *Buffalo Bill's America*, 503–11.
22. Warren, *Buffalo Bill's America*, 513.

23. "Opinion of the Court," Sheridan County, Wyoming, March 8, 1905, copy provided by Buffalo Bill Historical Center.

24. "Opinion of the Court," Sheridan County, Wyoming, March 8, 1905, copy provided by Buffalo Bill Historical Center.

25. Courtney Ryley Cooper, *Under the Big Top* (Boston: Little, Brown and Company, 1923), 22, 24.

26. Shirley Leckie, *Elizabeth Bacon Custer and the Making of a Myth* (Norman: University of Oklahoma Press, 1993). For another example of two army wives who wrote memoirs to answer their husbands' critics, see Shannon Smith, *Give Me Eighty Men: Women and the Myth of the Fetterman Fight* (Lincoln: University of Nebraska Press, 2008). Neither Margaret nor Frances Carrington were widows when they wrote their defenses of Colonel Henry B. Carrington's reputation; Margaret predeceased her husband. He eventually married Frances, whose husband, George Grummond, had died in the Fetterman Fight, another army disaster in the American West.

27. Quoted in Kassen, *Buffalo Bill's Wild West*, 140–41.

28. Kassen, *Buffalo Bill's Wild West*, 141.

29. Cooper, *Under the Big Top*, 46.

30. A.L.A. catalog, 1926, Century Past: Free Online Library, accessed January 19, 2022, www.http:/centurypast.org/librarybioindex/library-biographies-1/.

31. E.S.W., review of *Memories of Buffalo Bill*, by Louisa Frederici Cody, *Mississippi Valley Historical Review* 7, no. 3 (December 1920): 284–86, https://www.jstor.org/stable/1891231.

32. It is important to note that while the Nineteenth Amendment, ratified in 1920, ostensibly enfranchised all woman citizens, women of color—particularly African American, Native American, and Mexican American women—were denied the vote until many decades later.

33. Cody, *Memories of Buffalo Bill*, 19–20.

34. Cody, *Memories of Buffalo Bill*, 88–89.

35. Cody, *Memories of Buffalo Bill*, 94.

36. Cody, *Memories of Buffalo Bill*, 64.

37. Cody, *Memories of Buffalo Bill*, 73.

38. Cody, *Memories of Buffalo Bill*, 133.

Chapter 1

1. John Francis Frederici, 1818–1905.

2. Elizabeth Frederici, 1846–1937.

3. Samuel Cody, 1841–1853.

4. Isaac Cody, 1811–1857, Martha Cody (half-sister), 1835–1858, Julia Cody, 1843–1928, Laura Ella (called Helen and Nellie) Cody, 1850–1911, and Charles Cody, 1855–1865.

5. Established in 1827, by Colonel Henry H. Leavenworth, to supply and protect westbound migrants, Leavenworth became the Kansas Territory's first incorporated community in 1855.

6. The Kickapoo Agency was a reservation under the management of the Bureau of Indian Affairs in the Department of the Interior.

7. Mary Ann Laycock Cody, 1827–1863.

8. The Kansas-Nebraska Act of 1854 created two new territories and applied the principle of popular sovereignty by allowing settlers to determine the status of slavery in each territory. This act repealed provisions of the 1820 Missouri Compromise.

9. The Free State men opposed the expansion of slavery into the western territories.

10. Russell and Majors was named for business partners Alexander Majors and William Hepburn Russell. This firm, also led by William B. Waddell, handled most of the government-contracted freight to military forts in the West in the 1850s and '60s.

11. In what became known as the Utah War, then-colonel Albert Sydney Johnston (1803–1862) was charged by President James Buchanan with leading U.S. troops to establish federal control over Mormon settlers in the Utah region. The conflict lasted from May 1857 until July 1858.

12. Located in present-day Nebraska, Fort Kearny was established in 1848 as a supply depot for travelers bound for California and the Pacific Northwest.

13. James Butler Hickok (1837–1876). Hickok would also achieve notoriety as a frontiersman. Like Cody, he would work as an army scout, a lawman, and, briefly, a stage actor.

14. The Pony Express mail service, formed by the freighting company Russell, Majors, and Waddell, continued in operation from April 1860 to October 1861. A horseback relay system carried mail between St. Joseph, Missouri, and Sacramento, California. Riders exchanged horses every 10 to 15 miles over a 75-to-100-mile route. The ten days required to cover 1,800 miles was expedient at the time but rendered obsolete by the advent of the telegraph.

Chapter 2

1. Construction of the Kansas Pacific Railroad began as part of a federal contract with Union Pacific to connect St. Joseph, Missouri, to Denver.

Chapter 3

1. George Armstrong Custer (1839–1876). A lieutenant colonel during the Civil War, he achieved lasting notoriety for his death and defeat at the Battle of Little Bighorn in 1876.
2. Arta Lucille Cody Thorp, 1866–1904.
3. Designed by Joseph Murphy, these four-wheeled covered wagons were commonly employed in nineteenth-century western migration.
4. George Augustus Armes (1844–1919) served with General Winfield Scott Hancock during the Civil War. He published a memoir in 1900 that included an account of Cody killing a buffalo; it was titled *Ups and Downs of an Army Officer*.

Chapter 4

1. John Burwell "Texas Jack" Omohundro (1846–1880) was originally from Virginia but made his way west after the Civil War. He first went to work in Texas but came north to Kansas with a trail drive and eventually found work as a scout at Fort McPherson.

Chapter 5

1. William Averill Comstock (1842–1868), a.k.a "Medicine Bill," was the grandnephew of James Fenimore Cooper. According to Cody's sister, Helen Cody Wetmore, among the stakes in the Buffalo killing contest was the right to use the nickname "Buffalo Bill." See Helen Cody Wetmore, *Last of the Great Scouts: The Life Story of Col. William F. Cody, "Buffalo Bill"* (Chicago: Duluth Press, ca. 1899; Project Gutenberg, 2006), https://www.gutenberg.org/files/1248/1248-h/1248-h.htm.

Chapter 7

1. General Philip Henry Sheridan (1831–1888). Eventual commanding general of the U.S. Army, Sheridan was commanding officer of the Department of the Missouri when he met Cody.
2. Santanta (ca. 1819–1878), also known as Set'tainte (White Bear), was a Kiowa war chief who helped negotiate the Medicine Lodge Treaty in 1867 and became known as the "Orator of the Plains."
3. General Eugene Asa Carr (1830–1910) obtained the rank of Union brigadier general during the Civil War. He was active in the Plains Indians Wars in the 1860s and 1870s, leading campaigns against the Sioux including the Bighorn and Yellowstone campaign in 1876. Endorsements like this one played a vital role in Cody's path to celebrity. He would draw upon testimonials from figures such as Generals Carr and Sheridan repeatedly throughout his show career to authenticate his frontier persona.

4. The Battle of Summit Springs brought an end to the Dog Soldiers' influence among the Cheyenne. The Cheyenne were subsequently moved to Lakota reservation land in the Dakota Territory.

5. Tall Bull (1830–1869), a chief of the Cheyenne Dog Soldiers, was killed during the Battle of Summit Springs.

Chapter 8

1. Windham Wyndham-Quin (1841–1926), the fourth Earl of Dunraven, would later acquire land in Colorado and attempt to set up a game preserve. In 1925 he published an account of his hunting experiences titled *Hunting in the Yellowstone* or *On the Trail of the Wapiti with Texas Jack in the Land of Geysers*. Lady Dunraven was Florence Kerr, second daughter of Lord Charles Kerr.

2. Chief No Neck (Tahu Wanica, ca. 1850–1886), was a Hunkpapa Sioux who married an Oglala Sioux woman. No Neck became an Indian scout with the U.S. Ninth Cavalry and was chief of Indian police at Pine Ridge Agency, where he was known as a peacemaker during the second Ghost Dance movement of 1890. Red Cloud (1820–1909) was an Oglala leader and war chief who led a successful resistance against the U.S. Army in 1866. Sitting Bull (ca. 1831–1890) was a Lakota chief and the most well-known Native American to participate in Buffalo Bill's Wild West. He gained renown during the Great Sioux War of 1876–77 when he led his Hunkpapa band in multiple battles, including Little Bighorn.

Chapter 10

1. Ned Buntline was the pseudonym of the dime novelist Edward Zane Carroll Judson (1813–1886). The title "colonel" came from his term of service with the Union Army during the Civil War. In addition to a prolific writing career, Judson was an editor, temperance lecturer (although he drank heavily himself), and political activist (most notably for the nativist Know-Nothing Party). He would introduce Buffalo Bill to a national audience with *Buffalo Bill, the King of the Border Men*, a serialized story in the *New York Weekly*, published in 1869.

2. Grand Duke Alexei Alexandrovich (1850–1908), the fourth son of Tsar Alexander II, toured the United States for three months, from November 1871 to February 1872. His travels took him from Boston to New Orleans with the American press covering every stage of the journey.

Chapter 11

1. Giuseppina Antonia Morlacchi (1836–1886) was an Italian American dancer and actress. In 1872 she performed in the western drama *Scouts of the Prairie* with William Cody and Texas Jack Omohundro, whom she later married.

2. John M. Burke (d. 1917), also known as "Arizona John." He would work as a press agent with the Buffalo Bill Combination and Buffalo Bill's Wild West for over thirty years. He is credited with playing a major role in Buffalo Bill's celebrity through his manipulation of the press and his use of innovative marketing techniques.

Chapter 12

1. In July 1876 Cody was involved in a skirmish at War Bonnet Creek in which he killed a Cheyenne named Yellow Hair. Cody used the incident to associate his own public persona with that of the newly martyred George Armstrong Custer.

2. A Cheyenne subchief. "Yellow Hand" was a mistranslation; his actual name was "Yellow Hair."

3. The Red Cloud Agency was a reservation for Oglala Sioux, Northern Cheyenne, and Arapahoe in the 1870s Wyoming Territory.

4. Cut-Nose (Marpiya Okinajin, or He Who Stands on A Cloud) was hanged in Mankato, Minnesota, in 1862 as part of a mass execution of thirty-eight Dakota warriors for their involvement in attacks on white settlers during the Dakota Uprising.

Chapter 13

1. William Frank "Doc" Carver (1851–1927) was working as a dentist in Fort McPherson when he met Cody. He moved to North Platte and developed his skills as a marksman, later becoming a full-time performer. In 1883 he would partner with Cody in his first attempt at the exhibition business. The "Wild West: Hon. W. F. Cody and Dr. W. F. Carver's Rocky Mountain and Prairie Exhibition" would last only one season before the two men parted ways, eventually becoming bitter rivals. William Levi "Buck" Taylor (1857–1924), billed as the "King of the Cowboys," was a featured performer in the Wild West beginning with its first season. At six feet five inches in height, Taylor made a striking figure. His performance centered on horsemanship skills such as picking objects off the ground on horseback at a full gallop.

2. Pine Ridge Agency, an Oglala Lakota Indian Reservation located in southwestern South Dakota.

3. Nate Salsbury (1846–1902) was a theatrical manager and performer who formed his own company, Salsbury's Troubadours, in 1874. He produced comic burlesques with considerable success in the United States, Britain, and Australia for a decade before joining Cody as managing partner of Buffalo Bill's Wild West in 1884.

4. Lewis H. Baker (1869–1931), better known as Johnny Baker, was for many years a fixture in William F. Cody's personal and professional life. As a young

boy in North Platte, Nebraska, Baker idolized Cody, who came to look upon Baker as a foster son. Baker accompanied Cody's Wild West on tour from its inception and was a regular cast member by 1885. Originally billed as the "Cow-Boy Kid," Baker often competed with Annie Oakley in trick shooting contests, among other roles.

Chapter 14

1. Worn by members of the Ghost Dance religion, these clothing items were believed to hold spiritual power.

2. Involving as many as three hundred shooting victims among the gathered Lakota people, the Wounded Knee Massacre was the deadliest mass shooting in American history. Approximately sixty-four U.S. Cavalry troops were killed or wounded. Big Foot, Si Thanka, was also known as Spotted Elk (ca. 1820/25–1890). As a leader of the Miniconjou Sioux, he was known as an effective negotiator, but he was among those killed by the U.S. Seventh Cavalry at Wounded Knee.

3. Nelson Appleton Miles (1839–1925) was a Union brigadier general during the Civil War and was subsequently involved in most of the major campaigns in the Plains Indians Wars.

4. Kicking Bear, Mato Wanartaka (1846–1904), was a first cousin to Crazy Horse. With Kicking Bear's marriage to Chief Big Foot's daughter Woodpecker Woman, Kicking Bear became a band chief of the Minneconjou Sioux and fought for the Lakota Nation during major battles, including the Rosebud and the Battle of Little Bighorn. He was later imprisoned for his involvement in the Ghost Dance movement and subsequently released to join the European tour of Buffalo Bill's Wild West for the season of 1891–92. William Black Heart (Canta Sapa, 1855) was an Oglala Lakota veteran of the 1887 visit to London. He remained with Buffalo Bill's Wild West until 1905 or later. Long Wolf died in 1892 while performing with the Wild West in London. He was buried in Brompton Cemetery. A century later, in 1997, his remains were repatriated. Arnold Short Bull (Tatanka Ptecela, ca. 1845–1923) was a medicine man and member of the Sicangu (Brulé) Sioux. Along with his brother-in-law Kicking Bear, he became a principal leader of the Ghost Dance religion among the Sioux at Pine Ridge and Standing Rock Agencies. After being jailed to quell the unrest, he was released under contract with Buffalo Bill's Wild West to perform in Europe for the 1891–92 season.

5. Theodore Wharton (1875–1931), under commission of the U.S. government, directed the motion picture *The Late Indian Wars* in 1912.

6. Joseph Horn Cloud (1873–1920) lost both parents and two brothers at the Wounded Knee Massacre. As a surviving witness of the massacre, he spoke

out against prejudice and advocated for compensation. He helped found the Wounded Knee Survivors Association in 1901.

7. Red Cloud (1822–1909). An Oglala Lakota leader from 1868–1909, including during "Red Cloud's War" (1866–1868).

8. American Horse, Wasechun-Tashunka, literally translated "White Man's Horse" (1840–1908), was a member of the Oglala Sioux Nation. American Horse joined Buffalo Bill's Wild West in 1886, replacing Sitting Bull as a leading American Indian performer. Fast Thunder (ca. 1840–?). A Lakota Chief.

9. Two Strike, Numpkahapa, literally translated "Knocks Two Off" (1831–1915). A Brule Lakota Chief.

Chapter 15

1. Glenwood Springs, Colorado

Appendix 3

1. In 1950 Franklin D. Roosevelt's son-in-law also committed suicide at the same hotel by jumping from a high-story window.

INDEX

Page numbers in italics signify photos.

abolitionist, 11
Alexis, Grand Duke, 123–24
Arkansas River, 86
Armes, George Augustus, 29, 38–39, 41–42, 56

Baker, Johnny, 163–64, 181, 184, 292–93
Battle of Warbonnet, 153
Battle of Wounded Knee, 172, 174–75, 180
Big Horn WY, 246, 256, 285
Boyer, Mr., 213, 216, 229
Boyer, Mrs., 212, 215–19, 226–27, 229, 243
Buffalo Bill: as buffalo hunter, 65, 70, 72–73, 76–77, 82–83, 87–90, 93; as judge, 117, 123–25; as actor, 131, 134, 138–42, 145, 147, 149, 160, 163–64, 167, 174; death of, 184
Buntline, Ned, 123, 131–37, 139, 141. *See also* Judson, Elmo
Burke, John M., 138, 144–45, 164, 166–68, 181

Camp Santanta, 85, 87
Carr, Eugene Asa, 87, 94, 123, 127, 151, 239
Chandler's gang, 15
Cheyenne (tribe), 152. *See also* Indians
Cheyenne WY, 91–92, 111–12, 114–15, 127, 215
Chicago IL, 132, 139, 142, 160, 164, 166, 171, 212, 223, 253
Chicago World's Fair, 182, 204, 216, 219
christening, 127, 131
Civil War, 2
Cody, Arta Lucille: as baby, 30, 33–34, 36–40, 42, 47–48, 53, 64, 69–72, 76–80, 82, 85; in childhood, 111–16, 128, 132, 141–42, 149, 152, 155, 159; death of, 184; divorce questions involving, 198, 200–201, 211, 219, 221–22, 224, 267, 294; photos of, *188–89, 191*; as toddler, 92, 93, 100–102, 105
Cody, Charles, 9, 20
Cody, Irma, 161, 184, *191*, 208, 211, 224, 227, 289
Cody, Kit Carson, 127–28, 132, 145, 149–52, 161, 201, 209, 267
Cody, Mary (May), 9, 205
Cody, Nellie, 9, 199, 205, 233–34, 238
Cody, Orra Maude, 131–32, 149, 152, 161, *189*, 267
Cody WY, 183–84, 201
Colorado, 85, 184, 200
Colorado State House, 184
Comstock, Billy, 70–74, 76
Custer, 152, 155–56

Deadwood stagecoach, 161–63, 165
Denver CO, 29, 173, 181–84, 224, 245, 261, 281, 285
Dismal River, 159–60
divorce, 119–20; proceedings transcript in, 197–298
Dodge City, 86
Dog Soldiers, 87, 152–55
Dunraven, Lady, 102–3
Dunraven, Lord, 102–3

Enabling Act for Kansas Territory, 11

Family Fireside, 2, 13

the Fifth Cavalry, 87, 151–53, 155
Finn, Lord, 102–3
Flatiron, 176
Fort Dodge, 86
Fort Hays, 29, 37, 39, 41, 45, 47, 49, 53, 65, 85–87, 199–200, 205, 235–38, 264. *See also* Hays City
Fort Kearny, 12–13
Fort Larned, 29, 85–87
Fort Leavenworth, 10, 13, 15, 20–21, 26–27, 34, 48; in the Cody's divorce depositions, 198–99, 214, 230, 232–34, 237–38, 246–47, 251–52, 262, 265–66
Fort McPherson, 89, 91, 99, 127, 132, 152, 160–61; in the Cody's divorce depositions, 200–202, 204–6, 237, 239, 241, 251, 253, 266–67
Fort Sheridan, 69, 71, 76
Free State men, 11

Garlow, Frederick, Jr., *193*
Garlow, Jane, *193*
Garlow, William Joseph "Bill Cody," *193*
Glenwood Springs CO, 182
Goddard Brothers, 63
Golden Rule House, 232–33, 246
Goodman, Al, 203, 209, 213, 227
Goodman, Mrs., 209, 225, 227, 230–31
Grasshopper Falls KS, 11

Hays City, 45, 47, 55–56, 62–63, 181. *See also* Fort Hays
Hickok, "Wild Bill," 14, 29, 50–52, 55, 145–46
Horn Cloud, 176–77

Indians: William Cody killing of, 8–9, 12–14, 20; on the frontier, 22, 26–27; conflicts with, 29, 31, 34–35, 37, 48, 55–56, 59–62, 64, 66–69, 85, 86–87, 89–90, 93–94; Louisa's relationship with, 99, 100–109, 113, 123–24, 126, 128; as stage and Wild West performers, 135, 139, 140–42, 146–47, 152–57, 159, 161–62, 165, 167, 170–75, 177–78. *See also specific Indian tribes*

Injuns. *See* Indians

J. Murphy wagons, 33
Judson, Elmo, 123, 126–27. *See also* Buntline, Ned

Kansas, 26, 71, 85, 87, 184
Kansas City KS, 9, 62, 198–99
Kansas Pacific, 28–29, 31–33, 63, 69, 70, 72, 82, 85, 198, 235–37, 248
Kickapoo, 10. *See also* Indians

Little Bat, 154
Louis Reiber, 1, 3–5
"Lucretia Borgia" (gun), 72–73, 83, 120

MacDonald, William, 99; wife of, 99–101, 103–4, 111, 115, 129
marriage, 21, 117–8
McDonald, William, 1–3
Merritt, Wesley, 151, 153
Meyers, Eliza, 21, 198–99, 230
Miles, General, 171–73, 175
Missouri River, 21–22, 26, 138, 144
Mormons, 12; emigrant train of, 10
Mount Lookout CO, 184
Multnomah, 166–67

Nebraska, 120, 184, 259–60
New York, 126, 131, 160, 201, 209, 226, 278, 282
No Neck, 109, 173–74, 176
North Platte NE, 91, 159, 161–62, 165, 168, *195*; in the Cody's divorce depositions, 202–4, 207–8, 210–11, 214, 216, 243, 255–59, 265–67, 269, 271, 275–76, 279–82, 284, 289, 294–95

Old Horse, 105
Old Frenchtown, 1, 17, 19, 69. *See also* St. Louis MO
Omaha NE, 91, 164, 166, 239, 293
Omohundro. *See* Texas Jack

Pahaska, 99, 105–7, 154, 165, 168, 172, 174, 176

Pawnee, 101–2, 104–5, 106–8, 160, 299. *See also* Indians
Perry Hotel, 41, 43, 45, 49, 86, 200, 264
Pine Ridge Indian agency, 163, 177, 179
pony express, 14–15
Prince of Wales, 169
Princess of Wales, 169
pro-slavery, 11
Pyramid Lake NV, 177–78

Quakers, 242, 268

Red Cloud, 109, 156, 159, 177, 179
Red Wolf, *194*
Reed, William, 91–2
Rochester NY, 146, 149, 159, 161, 202, 206–8, 223, 228, 254, 261, 268–69, 282, 292, 297
Rome KS, 31–32, 36, 45, 200, 205, 234–35, 237, 249, 250, 263
Rose, William, 31–34, 36–37, 235, 249, 263
Rosebud Agency, 177, 179
Russell, Majors and Waddell, 12–13

Salina KS, 29, 199
Scott County IA, 9
Scout's Rest Ranch, *195*, 203, 209, 257, 259
Sheridan, General, 85–87, 124, 151, 239, 252
Short Bull, 173, 174, 176–79

Shoshone, 173. *See also* Indians
Sioux, 87, 94, 100–101, 105–8, 151–52, 171, 173, 176. *See also* Indians
Sitting Bull, 109, 152, 171
St. Louis MO, 18, 19–22, 24, 26, 42, 48, 51, 62, 69, 70–71, 74, 82, 85, 87–88, 90, 143; in the Cody's divorce depositions, 197–201, 230, 233, 234, 237–38, 241, 246, 250–52, 264–67, 296

Tall Bull, 88–90
Ta-ta-la Slotsla, 173, 176–78, 180
Three Wells, 35–36
Texas Jack, 50, 105, 107–8, 132–41, 144–46, 148–49
Two Strikes, 179

Under the Big Top, 299–300
United States Army, 8, 19, 251, 264, 268

Victoria, Queen, 169, 229
Vroman, Mrs., 226–27

Walnut Grove Farm, 9. *See also* Scott County IA
Westchester PA, 202, 241, 254, 268
Woman's Dress, 109, 174, 176
Wyoming, 173, 184, 296

Yellowhand, 153, 155–56, 159

In the Papers of William F. "Buffalo Bill" Cody series

Four Years in Europe with Buffalo Bill
Charles Eldridge Griffin
Edited and with an introduction by Chris Dixon

The Life of Hon. William F. Cody, Known as Buffalo Bill
William F. Cody
Edited and with an introduction by Frank Christianson

Buffalo Bill from Prairie to Palace
John M. Burke
Edited and with an introduction by Chris Dixon

The Wild West in England
William F. Cody
Edited and with an introduction by Frank Christianson

Beckoning Frontiers: The Memoir of a Wyoming Entrepreneur
George W. T. Beck
Edited and with an introduction by Lynn J. Houze
and Jeremy M. Johnston
Foreword by Alan K. Simpson and Peter K. Simpson
Afterword by Betty Jane Gerber

A Horse's Tale
Mark Twain
Edited and with an introduction by Charles C. Bradshaw
Afterword by Shelley Fisher Fishkin

Memories of Buffalo Bill
Louisa Frederici Cody in collaboration with Courtney Ryley Cooper
With an introduction by Sherry L. Smith

To order or obtain more information on these or other
University of Nebraska Press titles, visit nebraskapress.unl.edu.

www.ingramcontent.com/pod-product-compliance
Lightning Source LLC
Chambersburg PA
CBHW020934180426
43192CB00036B/1147